We Remember WWII

Edited By

Ralph Riffenburgh

RoseDog🐾Books

PITTSBURGH, PENNSYLVANIA 15222

ISBN # 0-8059-9045-8

Printed in the United States of America

First Printing

For information or to order additional books, please write:
RoseDog Books
701 Smithfield St.
Third Floor
Pittsburgh, PA 15222
U.S.A.
1-800-834-1803
Or visit our web site and on-line bookstore at *www.rosedogbookstore.com*

DEDICATION

This book is dedicated to those of the participants
who have died since its inception:

Fred Arndt, Sam Atkins, Fred Blair, Burdette Boileau,
Dean Bowman, Peg Calhoun, Dorothy Christiansen, Emily daSilveira,
Leonard Dart, Bill Dunseth, Bob Feeney, French Fogle,
Jim Giles, John Gius, Homer Henrie, Hal Johnson,
Jean Lemm, Willis Lemm, Henry Meyer, Robert Pay,
Ivan Schreiber, Don Stoll, Wilbur Thomas

TABLE OF CONTENTS

INTRODUCTION

Mt. San Antonio Gardens is a life care retirement community with the majority of its residents, known as Gardeners, in the 70 to 90 age group. For many of this generation, World War II was the defining time of our lives. About 10,000,000 Americans served in various uniforms during the war. But everyone was involved. At the present time it can be hard for people to visualize the total dedication of our country to the war. Our land had been attacked and our way of life was in danger. There was almost complete involvement of the citizens in the efforts of the war. If you didn't have friends or relatives in harm's way, you had involvement in war production or other activities. And you were certainly touched by rationing: meat, butter, tobacco, gasoline, liquor, sugar, coffee.

The attitude of the country was one of cooperation. The degree of trust in others was unusual. Most people going somewhere would pick up servicemen without a thought. (However, there weren't always rides. One Friday night in December at 11 PM, I went to the Union Station in Washington and found several hundred people waiting for the few places on the train from New York to Richmond. I needed to get the 25 miles to Quantico, Virginia, where I was a corpsman at the Naval Hospital. A marine and I rode the street car to the end of the line and started hitch-hiking. We had a couple short rides but walked over half the way with a temperature of 28 degrees and a wind. I arrived just in time for reveille and report for duty at 5:45 AM.)

The wartime remembrances of the residents of Mt. San Antonio Gardens present a diversified view of this historic time in the United States. I have spent many months asking residents to write their memories and have done oral histories on a number whom haven't felt able to do the writing. The volume includes memories of a large number of persons, not only military stories but those of all aspects of the wartime life. For convenience, the stories are grouped, somewhat by chronological time and partly by area of involvement and by the type of involvement. This diversified group of stories presents what life was like during the war, as evidenced by a group of people who lived it, selected only by their residence at Mt. San Antonio Gardens.

CHAPTER 1

BEGINNINGS OF THE WAR

World War II started in Europe in 1939, though the United States was not directly involved at that time. As it increased in scope and the territorial ambitions of the Axis powers became obvious, it was increasingly likely that the US would become involved. The Army was expanded with a draft and the production of materials necessary for a large military operation increased rapidly. Some of this, of course, went to the British, who were holding the line.

There were major arguments among the people and also in Congress as to how supportive the US should be to the British. There was a significant group of isolationists, the "America First" group. One of the big problems for Britain was getting supplies safely across the Atlantic and President Roosevelt gave the Royal Navy forty overage destroyers. To make this palatable to Congress and others, he arranged this as a trade for the use of bases in areas of the British Empire.

The great change in American opinion came with the Japanese attack on Pearl Harbor. The burning ships and dead seaman made everyone realize the danger and give support to the administration. Production of vehicles changed in an amazingly short time from cars to tanks, with similar changes in many, many fields. A few of Mount San Antonio Gardens residents were involved in the war even before Pearl Harbor. The book starts with the experiences of the beginning of the war in Europe by Ginette Shultes who witnessed the German conquest of Belgium as a young girl.

Homer Henrie was commissioned as a captain before Pearl Harbor and was involved in the development of procurement of materiel for the Army Air Corps.

Louise Powers, a Dutch citizen at that time, was in Chile from 1937 and worked for British Information Service prior to the US entry into the war.

Herb Smith volunteered in 1941 for one year service expecting to continue his schooling after that. After Pearl Harbor, it became apparent that he was in for the duration, so he went to officer candidate school. He remained in service until 1946 with duty in Paris.

Ralph Riffenburgh needed a job in the summer of 1941 and went to work in a gunpowder factory in Western Virginia. He was working there the morning of December 7. He left the plant in July 1942 to return to college prior to service in the Navy.

Mt. San Antonio Gardens has two residents who were actually in Honolulu on the morning of Pearl Harbor. Wilbur Thomas was working in Honolulu and saw the destruction at Pearl as well as being close to an exploding bomb with his wife and young child. He stayed on there, working in industry throughout the war.

Barbara Worchester was visiting an uncle in the Navy when the attack occurred. Her uncle was a high ranking naval officer and from his quarters at Pearl Harbor she was able to look directly into the approaching Japanese planes and down onto the ships in the harbor.

WARTIME BELGIUM
Ginette Shultes

May 10, 1940. I will never forget that date. In the early morning I heard loud rumblings and my first thought was that some military trucks were driving down the road. Belgium was neutral, as was the Netherlands, but still they had mobilized the army, just in case.

France and England had been at war with Germany since September 1939. It was "une drole de guerre". French soldiers were ensconced in the Maginot Line and the Germans were ensconced in the Siegfried Line, peering at each other and once in a while there was a skirmish. Songs were written about it; jokes were told about it. Famous Petain WWI words cropped up, "Ils ne passeront pas". (They will not pass) Everyone was convinced that the Maginot line was invincible. Well, the Germans circumvented it and attacked, coming from Belgium and the Netherlands. It was the blitzkrieg.

I finally jumped out of bed and heard the horrible sounds of the Stukas, letting their bombs fall on us. Now we too were involved. My father had died in January 1939. My two oldest brothers had been called back in the French Army. One into his Moroccan regiment and the other, who had been working for the French government in French Equatorial Africa, joined a regiment at Lake Chad, in Chad. My older brother had given us instructions that should Belgium be invaded we were to rejoin his wife and her two children in the North of France.

Mother was undecided on what to do. Finally, when there were no longer trains or any other mode of transportation, she decided we too should leave. So we packed our bikes and off we went. Everyone in Belgium and Northern France had the same thought; escaping the Germans. The roads were clogged with refugees on foot, bikes, horse drawn carts, and cars that ran out of gasoline and were left on the side of the road. Soldiers, just as bewildered as we were, also were among the column of refugees.

Here we were, the three of us, trying to join my sister-in-law and the children. We slept wherever we could, in barns or on the side of the road. Whatever food we had taken with us soon was gone and then began the foraging for food. Not easy with everyone else trying to do the same thing. Our greatest fear was being overtaken by the Germans.

One of the most horrifying moments of my life was when we were strafed by Messerschmitt fighter planes. Here we were on a country road and all of a sudden the planes appeared out of nowhere and began strafing. Everyone jumped into the ditches and I found myself all alone on my bike, unable to move, frozen. Lucky for me, a British soldier jumped out of the ditch, pushed my bike aside, grabbed me and dumped me into the ditch! Thank God for this kind man. After the planes were gone and I found my Mother and brother, we continued on our trek trying to get to Ecaillon, the village where my sister-in-law was staying.

It was a frustrating experience as we were going round and round, directed here and there but never making any progress. Finally we reached a small town and to our horror, here was the German army. Already as well organized as if they had always lived there, their signs directing their soldiers were all in the right directions. What a let down!

Still my mother did not give up. She remembered WWI when the front line was always moving; one day a village was in French hands, the next day it might be in German. So she decided to try to find a place where we could stay for a few days and see what would happen. We found a farm where the farmers were willing to let us stay in the barn and also invited us to share their meals. After a few days we felt we were imposing, as no food came to the village and supplies were low for the villagers. We set out to return to Brussels.

With heavy hearts we took our bikes and rode back to Brussels. Brussels had not suffered much as it had been declared an open city. We resumed our lives under strained circumstances. There were curfews and always some sort of edict; you could not do this, that was verboten, etc. I went back to school. Now our most important worries were about finding enough food. We were under rationing. In the beginning of the war, the rations were always available but as the war went on, many of our supplies went to Germany and we were left with little. There were long queues at the stores and not enough for everyone.

It was a dark period of our lives, always hoping that soon the allies would return and that the Germans be pushed back. It seemed that everything was against us. The winters during the war were extremely severe, not our usual mild winters. Coal was hard to obtain. Electricity and gas were limited to a couple of hours each day. We were fortunate to have relatives in the country where we could go and buy food on the black market. Of course that was against the law and if caught, we would be punished. Lucky for us we never got caught. You could get anything on the black market and we had to resort to it, even though we didn't think it was honest. That was also true of heating fuel.

The highlight of our days was listening to the BBC and getting good news (hopefully) but then there was always the dread of being picked up by one of the German listening vehicles that roamed the streets. As far as being bombed,

Brussels was not injured that much. Finally in September 1944, we were liberated by the British army. Not that it alleviated the food shortages and other problems but at least we knew the war was nearly over.

Another threat was the German flying bombs, the V1 and V2 rockets. Some were destined for England but many were aimed at Antwerp, the large port where the allies received their supplies. The terrifying part was that one could hear them overhead. That was true of the V1, but no one could predict where they would come down. When the noise stopped, you held your breath, waiting to see where they would land. The V2 was even more terrifying as they were silent. They just fell. There was no way one could take shelter, but just hope you were not in their path.

Finally May 1945 came and the war in Europe was over. What JOY! It is not easy to put this into words; it is so far away. We are thankful that we all survived and our family was reunited in August 1945.

ARMY PROCUREMENT
Homer Henrie

I was a small town judge in Xenia, Ohio in 1941. Xenia is near Dayton and Wright Field and I knew a Colonel Jones at Wright. It looked as though we were going to be in a war so in October they lowered the required age for Captain to 32. I was 32 and the Colonel said he could get me commissioned as a Captain. I said I didn't want to do court-martials for drunks, etc and he told me he wanted me for the legal aspects of procurement. I went into the Army Air Corps as a Captain and was stationed at Wright Field, working in procurement of airplanes and supporting equipment.

A few months after Pearl Harbor I became a major and the first of January 1943 I was sent to Washington to the Pentagon. I made Lt. Colonel in a few more months and Colonel Jones from Wright Field was now moved to the Pentagon as a Brigadier General in charge of procurement. I was then assigned to work with him again. We made a number of trips to Los Angeles as it was the home of much of the aviation industry. We flew out in a DC-3 that flew at about 160 MPH and stopped overnight along the way. There was also a Major General Willie Jones who was inspector general and whose visits were dreaded. About an hour from our overnight stop, I would radio ahead and say we needed overnight for General Jones and party of three. When we arrived, I would meet the base colonel and he would ask how General Jones was. Fine, and then he would say "which one?" When I said "It isn't Willie." he would be so relieved he would invite us to the officers club for drinks and dinner.

We negotiated with Hughes, Lockheed, North American, and Douglas. Hughes was really interested in airplanes and personally held the California-New York speed record. On one trip he took us on a personally conducted tour of the Spruce Goose. Hughes wanted to make a photo plane for the government to check the bombing results of the B-29's. We felt that the B-29 could take pictures as well as drop bombs and we didn't need another. However, orders came from General

Arnold, chief of Air Corps, to order it. I don't know but I think that Hughes talked to Elliot Roosevelt, a Brigadier General pilot and the president's son and Roosevelt told the Secretary of War who ordered Arnold to buy it. They shut three of us in a room with Hughes and said not to come out until we had a contract. I ordered lunch, burger and shake, for all and figured millionaire Hughes might pay for it but he never carried money and I ended up paying. We finally agreed on a contract. Hughes wanted $700,000 per plane for a hundred, which was OK, but he wanted $2,000,000 for the first three in order to recoup his engineering costs if we cancelled the contract before many were delivered. We finally agreed to this. Hughes personally test flew the first prototype. It crashed and he had a spinal fracture. None of the planes were ever delivered and the contract was cancelled. I think the spinal injury in that plane was the beginning of Hughes drug use.

On a procurement trip to Witchita, I dealt with Walter Beech, the founder of Beech Aircraft Co. He loved airplanes and flying and was a pleasure to work with. He died during the war and his place in the company was taken by his wife. I didn't know Kansas was dry and one couldn't buy liquor there. A friend from Syracuse Law School was there on business and he was less naïve; he brought a bottle of Scotch.

As the war began to get toward the end, the military began to think about terminating contracts. A group representing all services met to provide a manual and what must be considered and covered. It was very secret as the war was still on and we didn't want the companies to cut production yet. On one trip to Los Angeles, General Jones met a Marine aviator who was just out of the hospital from combat in the Pacific. He offered to drop him in Atlanta and we flew back the southern route. The marine got the royal treatment when he was landed in Atlanta in a general's private airplane.

The unions were pushing for more power and were threatening to strike Hughes Tool, which made drilling bits to keep oil flowing. The Army decided to take over the company and we had another meeting with Judge Patterson on a Sunday. He felt the Air Corps was the most involved in oil use and with Hughes so he asked us to do this. General Jones' group were the trouble shooters, so we got the problem. Jones ordered me to take over Hughes Tool. I called a Colonel in Wichita and asked if he had the proper manual. He thought it was somewhere and I told him to find it, get a team and fly to Houston and take over Hughes that afternoon. I won't say what he told me but he did it. We signed a contract with the Hughes management to operate it for the Air Corps and things went on as before except that the unions couldn't shut down a government plant.

I had made full colonel in early 1945. On one trip to Los Angeles, a Jewish colonel went with us who was a friend of Howard Hughes. He called me just before we were to return to Washington and asked if the General would mind if he didn't go. Hughes had offered to fly him back in his own plane. While in LA, we went to dinner at Romanovs. The colonel and Hughes had provided the financing for the restaurant. We had the best table - quite impressive for a small town Ohio boy. Later this colonel asked if I would like to go to Germany as a colonel with the occupation. They wanted a lawyer but turned him down - he made a motion to his large nose and said they didn't want to have Jews dealing with the Germans. I had been in five years and was ready to go home and refused this.

THE ROUTE TO PARIS
Herb Smith

During the peaceful year of 1941, I volunteered under the Selective Service Act (Draft) to serve one year in basic training, after which one supposedly could return to civilian life and get on with normal endeavor. And then came December 7, 1941!

With a war then underway, I decided I had best seek a commission, the only route to which was Officer Candidate School (OCS)-and the only quota offered my camp was three places for the Chemical Warfare School at Edgewood Arsenal, Maryland.

Never having had an hour of Chemistry in my life, I nonetheless took out three old field manuals on chemical warfare from the library, read them, and then bravely appeared before the board. Imagine my surprise when I realized that I had read three more field manuals than any member of the board-and was sent off to earn a commission in the Chemical Warfare Service.

The result after graduation from OCS was assignment as Post Chemical Officer for Camp Butner, North Carolina. In addition to presenting countless drills against chemical attack for all units stationed at the camp, I had one memorable evening. I was post officer of the day (which involved the inspection of all of the out-lying guard posts) when Gypsy Rose Lee, the then well-known stripper, came to camp. When she learned of my evening's activity, she enthusiastically suggested that she would like to accompany me in the squad car on my appointed rounds. Thus it was that I spent an evening in the back seat of a car with Gypsy Rose Lee.

Early in the fall of 1944, by some miracle, my guardian angels seemed to realize that the Information and Education branch of the Army was where I really belonged. I was, therefore, assigned to a "quickie" Information and Education course at Washington and Lee University (enabling me to salute the tomb of Robert E. Lee on a daily basis!).

Upon completion of yet another army course I was quickly placed aboard the last of the grand old four-stack ocean liners, the Aquitania, for transport to the European theater of wartime operations.

The gods were constantly with me, for I was assigned to the Information and Education headquarters in Paris. The purpose of the Education Branch, to which I was assigned, was to plan a post-hostilities education program for the G I's awaiting shipment home. Thus complete universities, staffed by outstanding faculty from the U.S., were established at Shrivingham, England and at Biarritz, France. Additional training facilities were developed through arrangements with jewelers, etc. for on-the-job training, and through the regular correspondence courses offered by the Army. In total, the program offered the foundation for the later wonderfully helpful and successful G.I. Bill.

Extra-curricularly, Paris offered totally atypical and often bizarre opportunities because of the wartime situation. My afternoon with Gertrude Stein and Alice B.

Toklas is largely memorable because of the wonderful attention Toklas paid to me (serving schnapps and cookies - no famous brownies!). Stein clearly treated me somewhat disdainfully because I was commissioned, not enlisted, and because I was neither a writer nor an artist. Another time, a party where I spent some of the evening with Marlene Dietrich was celebratory because the actress had just learned she was a grandmother.

When army buddies from combat units were on R&R in Paris, they always wanted to visit the Folies-Bergeres. Thus, I almost qualify for the Guinness Book of Records for attendance there in a single year!

The Information and Education Headquarters was shifted to Germany early in 1946, and I was shipped home in the spring of that year.

WAR YEARS IN CHILE
Louise Powers

In April of 1937 my brother and I left Holland to go to Santiago, Chile. My brother went to work there for the Royal Dutch Shell Co. and I "to have a good time" after having been a Montessori teacher for two years in a city near Rotterdam, called Dordrecht. My aunt and uncle were stationed in Santiago, representing the Netherlands in Chile, and they had invited us to stay with them. To me, having lived in Holland with its London-like climate, it seemed as if the heavens opened up when I arrived! Sun every day, no worry about leaving the garden furniture sitting outside during nights, clear blue skies, and parties all the time. My aunt and uncle were in the diplomatic service, hence all these social activities.

It wasn't long after our arrival that my brother found quarters to live in the apartment of a young medical doctor. He, my brother, was going to remain in Chile, while I had been invited to stay with my relatives for one year. However, after the first year (1937) I somehow remained and, when 1939 came around, the Second World War started. Holland was overrun by Hitler's armies in five days and that was when we realized that I wouldn't be able to return to Holland. The result was that I remained in Chile for nine years!

After one year of just "having a good time " I started working at a Montessori School in Santiago. By that time my Spanish had made great progress. However, my pupils who were of kindergarten age, were heard to speak Spanish with a Dutch accent!

In 1939 I took shorthand and typing lessons in the British Institute and went to work for the Information Service of the British Embassy. One year later the American Information Service of their Embassy asked me to come and work for their Radio Section, which I did. Nelson Rockefeller was the Coordinator of Inter-American Affairs at that time. All programs were aimed at propaganda for the Allies. "The Hit Parade", "Frente al Conflicto", the "Quatro Huasos" and so on. There lived, and still live, many Germans in the South of Chile.

We, the Dutch, were working with the British and American colonies in Santiago, doing all we could for the war effort; fund raising in all sorts of forms, on the golf field, on the stage. I must have knit hundreds of bivouac caps and scarves for soldiers and sailors! Our talents were also put to use for numerous fund raising parties. My brother played the piano by ear and I was a crooner. Other friends put on shows like square dancing on the stage, etc.

The same feeling which we have today, after the terrorists bombings of New York on September 11 (my birthday!!) 2001 obsessed us then in Chile during 1939 -1945, namely, "we are in this together, we will get out of this together, we see the way before us, we shall be victorious". Lots of British and American friends in Chile joined the armed forces of their countries.

The most important thing that happened to me in Chile, was that I met my husband there. He had come down from the U. S. with a friend to work in the U.S. Embassy where his job was, among other things, the "Black List". Not having been accepted by the Army because of brittle bones, he went to work as an economist.

And, since he was a Californian, that is how I live here in Mount San Antonio Gardens!

MAKING GUNPOWDER
Ralph S. Riffenburgh

In the spring of 1941 my mother was injured in a car accident and was in the hospital for four months. For financial reasons, I was unable to return to Caltech. I was looking for a summer job in Blacksburg, Virginia, my hometown. Finally I went to the new gunpowder factory in Radford, 14 miles away and applied for a laboratory job. The head of labs interviewed me and when I told him I had been at Caltech, he told me he was a Caltech PhD. He informed me that there were no summer jobs but said, "If you will work for a year I will see that you are rotated through all the aspects of the lab and get you a good background in industrial chemistry"

I took the job and started work on day shift. We worked shifts that rotated each week. My first job was measuring powder grains. Most gunpowder is made from nitrocellulose and is extruded in small cylinders. These varied from pencil lead size, an eighth of an inch long, for rifle powder to half inch diameter, inch long grains for 8 inch cannon. All had one or more holes to control burning speed, the larger types having 7 holes. There were limits on the sizing and we had to measure the distance from the edge to the hole, hole size, etc. under a measuring microscope and calculate the averages for 20 grains, for each batch of powder.

Soon I was doing solvent analysis. The plant received two tank car loads of ether and of alcohol each day and each batch had to be analyzed for purity, and other factors. The lab received a gallon of each batch and used only a quart or so unless the tests had to be redone. Most antifreeze for automobiles at that time was alcohol so I decided to take some that was thrown away for my car in winter. Our lunch boxes were checked on entry and exit each day but I had a thermos for milk and I took it home filled with alcohol. The thermos was never checked and I ended up with enough for antifreeze for the winter. The alcohol had been denatured and was dangerous to drink although one of the men tried redistilling it several times to get rid of the denaturing impurity and drank it without apparent damage.

Security was tight and they had unexpected searches for matches. A safety match gave a week lay-off and a strike-anywhere match meant immediate firing. Some of the smokers had a hard time with this.

Later I was one of two techs assigned to the solvent recovery job. This was the only lab job done out of the lab. The nitrocellulose was placed in a mixture of ether and alcohol to make it extrudable. After extrusion and cutting, it was taken to solvent recovery. There were 27 solvent recovery houses each with five tanks holding 5000 pounds of powder. The houses were widely placed with large earth mounds around them so that if one exploded it would not take the rest. The powder was placed in the tanks and warm nitrogen run through it for several hours to dry the powder. We had to check every tank each shift to make sure oxygen wasn't leaking into the tank. We carried a gas analysis machine from house to house and each of us did half the houses. We had to have special shoes, made without metal, to work in solvent recovery and couldn't carry such things as keys, which might spark. I was faster than my partner and on midnight shift I would lie down on the cement floor in the warm solvent recovery house under a tank of gunpowder and take an hour nap with my jacket for a pillow.

Certain types of powder are double base - they use nitroglycerine (NG) mixed with the nitrocellulose. This comes out in sheets and about 10 are sewed together and then cut into one inch squares with a one third inch hole in the center. These are used for high angle mortar shells. Like everything else, the NG had to be tested. The lab had a car that went around and picked up samples of gunpowder, solvents, etc. The tech on NG rode up to the NG line and then walked back with a special wood carrier for two small rubber bottles of nitroglycerine. It wasn't allowed in the car. We had a special strengthened room and wore heavy plastic facemasks working with it. As most heart patients who use NG have discovered, too much gives terrible headaches. The first few days are miserable as one's skin absorbs enough to produce headaches but they pass within a week. One tech was chewing tobacco and forgot he had the facemask on, filling the inside of his mask with tobacco juice. One of the others had annoyed me for some time. He stuck his head into the NG room and made a smart remark. I had just emptied one of the rubber bottles and threw it to him, asking, "Are you quick minded?" By the time the bottle reached the door, he was far up the hall. I'm sure he set a speed record.

One Sunday I was working day shift and Pearl Harbor was announced over the loud speaker. They told us we would be working six days rather than five now. At that time, Radford was making about 80% of all our country's gunpowder. Later Sunflower Ordnance in Kansas was using six powder lines to our three.

In March, I decided I needed more schooling before the draft took me and I volunteered to work 4 to 12 shift all the time and went to Virginia Tech during the day. At this time, I was placed on ether extraction. Another test for each batch of powder was to soak it with ether, then pour off the ether. The ether was boiled off on a copper water bath as no fire could be near it. The amount of material extracted by the ether was then weighed with a chemical scale. My smell of ether was so strong that my mother could tell from two rooms away when I came home.

When my year was up, I left the powder plant and returned to school full time. I was majoring in chemistry and found most of the college labs a waste of time as I had learned most of the techniques at the powder plant.

DECEMBER 7, 1941
Wilbur Thomas

December 7, 1941 completely changed my family and my life all starting at 7:55 on a Sunday morning. I had graduated from UC Berkeley in June 1938 with a degree in Food Technology. This was still depression times but I had managed to get a job in the laboratory of a major canned food company in Hawaii that had a factory in Honolulu. I was married in October and by December of 1941 our son was ten months old.

Sunday morning seemed quite normal. With a young son we were up early. There had been a number of practice alerts in recent months but the enormous noise made us decide we should find out what was happening. We lived in a valley not far from a hill that gave a good view of Pearl Harbor so we drove there. The smoke and noise suggested this was not a normal alert. I turned on the car radio. It was 9:00 AM and Webb Edwards was about start his program when he added to his formal announcement , "this is the real McCoy, take cover." By then we had seen what were obviously Japanese planes bombing Pearl. It was common knowledge that a number of B-17 bombers were to arrive that day from California and we saw them flying around trying to land. Most of them landed and were destroyed on the ground.

After we came back from the hill where we viewed the carnage, we were walking to a neighbor's house a block away. A shell came down across the street. Fortunately there was a stone wall just in front of where it landed and there was no damage.

The early local newspaper accounts were wildly inaccurate. We, of course, heard the explosions that were then attributed to Japanese bombs. Just a few days later it was quite apparent that it was our own anti aircraft shells that caused almost all of the damage in Honolulu. The batteries were manned with inexperienced soldiers using World War I ammunition. The fuses on the antiaircraft shells weren't set properly and they only went off on hitting the ground. Our shell was one of these. Only one of the forty such incidents was due to a Japanese bomb.

There was only one road around Oahu and it passed just above Hickam Air Base and Pearl Harbor. Soon it became common knowledge that the navy had lost two battle ships sunk and six badly damaged. Two carriers with supporting cruisers had gone to sea just a few days prior or we would have had no major fleet left. Over 2000 people were killed. The top army general, Short, was so paranoid about possible sabotage that he had all of the ammunition locked up and the airplanes out in the open. Of course they were almost all destroyed.

The reaction of the general public was much the same as after September II 2001. Everyone wanted to help. Most of us had worked with the local Japanese who were primarily second generation and we knew them as American friends. After a few days the military realized that most of the small businesses and the general laborers were Japanese and common sense prevailed rather than what happened in the mainland US. The only spying was carried out by Japanese nationals at the consulate in Honolulu.

Military government was soon established and price controls set. Everyone had to have an ID and had to have a work permit to be out of doors after sundown. The air was so clear in Honolulu that there was no twilight. Car headlights were painted over so you could barely see where the road was. One major problem was that other than pineapple and sugar there was little food produced in the islands. Life for most of us was fairly normal. If you wanted to visit friends at night you stayed till the next morning. The Quartermaster Corps Corps did a remarkable job of keeping necessities available most of the time.

One night we were bombed. It turned out to be one of our pilots who became lost and planned to dump his bombs at sea. He was actually over a populated area but fortunately the bombs landed in an empty field rather than on nearby houses.

In March, 1942, the army with the help of a lieutenant who was no longer on active duty, created what was known as the BMTC (Business Mens' Training Corps). I signed up because I had been in the ROTC for two years at Berkeley. We were completely fitted out with uniforms, pistols, rifles, and gas masks. We had training missions, designed to give us experience in coping with an invasion. It was years later that I realized that with the use of code breaking it was known the Japanese were planning an invasion somewhere in the Northern Pacific and Hawaii could be one of their possibilities.

On December 10, 1941 Guam fell to the Japanese and on December 23 they took Wake Island. By mid March 1942 the Japanese had conquered almost all of the Pacific. The British had lost Singapore and we were almost defeated in the Philippines. Doolittle's raid on Japan on April 7 must have been a shock to the Japanese. Then we were starting to have some success in the Solomon Islands. The Japanese must have known that Midway had to be taken.

By mid May those of us in the BMTC were practically on active duty every night. We knew it must be that the Japanese were going to try to take Midway. We now know that the breaking of the Japanese Naval code gave us minute detail of the Japanese plans. Their failure to invade Hawaii on December 7, 1941 dictated the attack. On June 3 we were ready for them. At a cost of 307 casualties, 1 carrier, and 147 airplanes we defeated the Japanese with 2500 casualties and the loss of 4 carriers and 332 airplanes. Life was more relaxed now. We could stay out till 10:00 PM and go to movies in the evening.

I will never know why all women who were not working and their children were ordered to leave Hawaii. I can only assume that the fact that the war was to take on a new phase that would mean a tremendous influx of service men and civilians associated with the war effort made it necessary. My wife and our son, now 18 months old, left on a troop ship. She stayed with her parents in San Diego. We stayed in touch with letters. I was quite fortunate in having a friend in the Navy and got permission for my wife and son who was now two and a half years old to come on the first ship for returning families in mid-April 1943. The next two years were much different. We were still under military rule but the fact that there had been no attempts at sabotage meant the military was much more relaxed. Only those of us living in Hawaii knew the ordeals that our service men went through on all those island landings. Many of them who came back for R and R showed from their manner what it had been like.

PEARL HARBOR

Barbara Worcester

My father, a lawyer, had moved the family from Washington, DC to California after working there on a case and deciding that was where he wanted to live. My uncle, Navy Captain J. B. Earle, was stationed in Hawaii and had invited me to visit. He and his wife had three children, grown and gone, and they wanted me to live with them a time. Ruth Billheimer, society editor for the LA Times, had put together a group of girls to make a prolonged visit to Hawaii. An aunt was a friend of hers and added me to the group, making twelve. Most of the girls were going to find a man. When we arrived, there was a picture of all of us in the paper and we were besieged with requests for dates. There were thousands of unattached men in the military in Hawaii and many of them wanted to get married before an overseas assignment. The girls would get a call, go on a date, and the man would propose the first date. Nine of them became engaged while in Hawaii. I was able to go to four Hawaiian weddings. Others went home to be married.

I went to Hawaii for a month in June of 1941 and didn't return until April 1942. The first six months were the best time of my life. The peacetime Navy had a continual round of parties, dances, and other social events and thousands of men to choose from. Living with my uncle, I had more Navy contacts. My uncle lived in one of seven senior officers' quarters on a hill just back of the oil tanks of Pearl Harbor, overlooking the entire Naval Base. We were in one of the upper two, next door to Admiral Kimmel, commander of the Pacific Fleet. My uncle was chief of staff to Admiral Bloch, the commandant of the fourteenth Naval District.

My uncle was known as a stern disciplinarian and the young officers were afraid of him. However, he was a wonderful person to be with at home. He had a good sense of humor and was fun to be around. One of his favorite tricks was at the end of a dinner to grasp the tablecloth and jerk it off the table without spilling a cup or dish. Young officer guests were horrified when they saw this start and he enjoyed shocking them.

We saw a lot of Admiral Kimmel. He was a friendly, easy-going man. His wife had not come to Hawaii, so he frequently was in my uncle's house for cocktails. He was there the night of December 6. My aunt was looking out over Pearl Harbor and said, "I've never seen so many battleships in harbor at one time."

Kimmel replied, "Those are my orders."

Once Lord Louis Mountbatten visited at Pearl Harbor and Admiral Kimmel gave a big party for him. I wasn't invited but I invited all the other girls of the group to our house where we could see Mountbatten and the other dignitaries arrive.

In the early morning of December 7th, my uncle was called to the base when the destroyer USS Ward spotted a miniature submarine. My aunt woke and was on the porch when she saw Japanese airplanes. She came in and woke me. The planes were coming in low beside our hill, on a slow bombing run to bomb the ships. They were just about our level and the nearest only 50 feet away. One pilot looked directly at me and seemed to slow down. I could see his face quite clearly.

One plane dropped a bomb in a crater in our back yard and covered the house with mud. None of the bombs was dropped on the tanks; that would have created a holocaust as most of the oil and gasoline for the fleet was stored there. If it had exploded it certainly would have engulfed our house. All the men had gone to the base and the other wives came over to our house and we watched together. The Americans had considerable antiaircraft fire going. They were shooting toward us as that was the way the planes were coming in. Our roof was severely marked by antiaircraft shells but fortunately none came in the windows to endanger the occupants.

My uncle had a high power telescope and I was able to see the details as the Arizona sunk. I knew several young men stationed on the Arizona. I could see the sailors jumping off into the oil-covered sea. Small boats from the harbor came and picked many of them up. The smoke from the bombs and burning ships would drift over, obscuring my vision and then drift away. It didn't seem real but seemed like a movie. The oil on the water caught fire and many of the sailors were badly burned.

There was a pause and then the second wave of Japanese planes came. I was able to see the Oklahoma turn over with the bombing. The fires went on most of the day and none of the battleships escaped, only one cruiser, the St. Louis. That night we were evacuated to Honolulu. There was no protection left and we fully expected the Japanese to land troops and take over Hawaii. When this didn't happen, the next day we were allowed to return to the quarters.

The day after the attack, I went to see one of the Japanese planes that had been downed. The pilot's body had been removed but his parachute was still in place. I had a piece of silk from the parachute for a number of years.

For days the family could not contact us and find out if we were safe. My father had a cousin who was an Army general in San Francisco and he was finally able to get a message through and report that all was well with us.

My uncle got me a job in the Navy offices. I was a confidential secretary. I typed confidential messages for various ships and officers and then delivered or made arrangements for delivery to the correct location. My aunt worked in the hospital in the burn ward.

Admiral Kimmel was relieved of command and Admiral Nimitz was sent out as Commander of the Pacific Fleet. He moved into the house next door and I did meet him, though everyone was so busy that we didn't have social opportunities. All was chaos in Hawaii at that time and it took some time to settle down. I was able to see several of the battleships have temporary repairs and be sent off to the mainland for complete repair.

In March all dependents were sent back to the mainland. My uncle was in charge of this and my aunt asked to stay. He said he couldn't allow this but we were the last group to leave. We went back on a sister ship of the Lurline that had been taken over by the Navy. It took us 12 days because of zig-zagging to avoid submarines and we sailed through a storm that was very close to a hurricane. The ship rolled terribly. The hold had cars and prisoners' berths. One could hear the cars crashing together during the storm. Finally we were back in California.

CHAPTER 2

THE WAR IN EUROPE

The United States was essentially fighting two wars. The war in the European theatre was primarily the Army's war, with the Navy heavily involved in moving troops and materiel to North Africa and Europe and in the protection of the sea-lanes. In the Pacific theatre, however, the Navy was the primary mover but there were also many Army units represented.

It took a long time to spool up the American military, both building and producing all the things it takes to fight a war and in recruiting and training the people involved. The first American involvement in the European theatre was the invasion of North Africa in 1942. The conclusion of this campaign was followed by the invasion of Sicily and Italy. While the Italian campaign was progressing, the US Army was also building up huge forces in England for the Normandy invasion.

The invasion of southern France and the much larger one at Normandy put the war on a new footing. From the first difficult landings, a momentum developed, freeing France. When it seemed that Germany was on the run, the last great German offensive caught the Allies by surprise. This tremendous fight was the "Battle of the Bulge."

The air war continued in Europe from before the North African invasion, to the final surrender of Germany. Though parts of it were flown in direct support of Allied armies, much of the air war, particularly the heavy bombing, was strategic and relatively detached from the battles on the ground.

Following the final German collapse and surrender, Europe was in a shambles and American troops stayed in many control and governmental capacities for years.

Residents of Mt. San Antonio Gardens were involved in many aspects of the war. Some were active from the earliest American activities in Europe, while others became involved later.

This section starts with a vignette of a superior officer who Jack Harloe met several times over a number of years.

Rob Johns describes his Army time with the stages of training, his assignments, with last minute changes, and finally his year at the front in France. His job was going ahead of the artillery and planning the proper placement of the guns before they arrived, resulting in a Bronze Star award.

Dex Barrett went on active duty with the horse cavalry immediately after Pearl Harbor. He spent three years in various capacities, taking training and then giving training to others. He finally arrived in France in January 1945 and was wounded three weeks before the end of the war in Europe. He spent two years in military hospitals before being retired from the service.

Jack Harloe went in the Army from ROTC prior to Pearl Harbor. He was in England in the fall of 1942 and became the aide of a general. He spent three years with the general, including North Africa, the Italian campaign, and finally Paris.

Alton Sanford served in the invasion of the Aleutians where he was given a transportation job involving the planning and loading of ships for invasion. He was involved in the Philippine and Okinawa invasions, primarily in administrative and transport duties.

Jim Giles story, written by one of his companion officers, primarily is of the Italian campaign and then goes on to the invasion of Southern France. Jim was an artillery officer who started as a second lieutenant and ended the war a lieutenant colonel as division staff officer for artillery.

Fred Weinrich was an anti-tank soldier who was transferred to the military police. He spent most of his time in Southern France, coordinating transportation and handling the problems of too many soldiers in a foreign country.

Dale Pittinger was drafted before the war, in spite of being married with a child. He was trained in artillery but then transferred to the infantry and became a sergeant. When he went to Europe he was then assigned to tanks. Dale was injured on Easter, 1945 when his tank was fired on and his elbow was broken. He was in a hospital in England at the end of the war.

Walter Lehman left Germany in 1939 after his parents' restaurant was destroyed. After a time in Columbia, he came to the United States, New York. In 1942 he volunteered for the US Army. Trained as a radioman, his unit was moved and changed and didn't go to Europe until some months after the invasion of France. He was a sergeant radioman with an engineering unit of Patton's army, moving rapidly across Germany. Near the end of the war Walter was able to visit his old home in Augsburg. He found that his grandparents had been taken to the concentration camps.

Tom Burdick applied for the Air Corps but was sent to a military police unit. They arrived in North Africa just at the end of hostilities there and were used in escorting and controlling POW's. He continued in this work in Sicily and Italy. His unit was being sent to the United States for eventual transfer to the Japanese front when the war ended.

Bob Nairne started ASTP but ended up as a replacement BAR rifleman in an infantry company in Europe. He was sent to various hospitals after having his hand injured in combat.

Bill Arce was first assigned to ASTP but instead sent to an infantry unit to train for the invasion of France. He was a heavy machine gunner from the Normandy campaign to the battle of the bulge, where he was frost bitten and sent to a series of hospitals. His unit received a unit citation for their heroism in the battle of the bulge.

LT. COLONEL FLEMING
Jack Harloe
August, 1942, Staten Island N.Y.

The British vessel H.M.S. Glenstrae backed out of its Staten Island berth and headed across the New York harbor, bound for the East River, Long Island Sound, Cape Cod Canal, Boston Harbor and Halifax, Canada. The Glenstrae, a cargo vessel equipped to carry 150 passengers, would be joining "UGS 18", (the "S" standing for slow). Aboard was my detachment of 40 Transportation Corps enlisted men and a small (3 officers and 8 enlisted men) Ordnance headquarters, commanded by Lt. Col. Fleming, a reserve officer with long service, called back to active duty. As the senior officer aboard, Fleming was also the "Troop Commander" for the voyage, responsible for all military personnel.

Once in Halifax, the Glenstrae was scheduled to take aboard 100 British women and children, evacuated from London at the height of the German blitz, now being repatriated to their homes. It would be impossible to prevent fraternization between enlisted men and the British civilians once they were aboard. I told my own detachment that segregation would be enforced only during hours of darkness, with a curfew half hour before sunset. Above all else, no military or civilian persons were to be allowed on deck after dark; nor was anyone allowed in the deck-loaded trucks.

Duty rosters for an "Officer of the Deck" patrol would be maintained for the duration of the 24 day voyage from Halifax to Liverpool. It was now 8 days since leaving New York. During this time, 35 ships had been collected to make up the convoy. We sailed at dawn and immediately found ourselves enshrouded in dense fog. Speed of the convoy slowed from 6 to less than four knots. The convoy's commodore, appraising the Glenstrae's relatively luxurious accommodations, had chosen the ship for his flagship. He had no qualms about expressing his low opinion of the seamanship demonstrated by the other skippers. A radio silence kept him from conveying his opinions as ship after ship misinterpreted his whistle signals, turning to port when, for example, the Commodore had signaled for a turn to starboard.

Three days out of Halifax, the fog lifted; but tensions grew as we noted that not a ship was in sight. The Commodore announced that we would return to port unless we could rejoin the convoy within six hours. Slightly before the deadline a

Canadian destroyer escort came alongside and hailed us. We were ordered to reverse course and rejoin the convoy 25 miles astern.

Then the inevitable happened. During my after dark deck patrol I spotted a glowing cigarette in one of the deck mounted 2 and 1/2 ton trucks. Opening the door, I discovered Col. Fleming and one of the British women seated in the cab.

"Sorry, Sir. Your standing orders: No one on deck after dark."

Fleming made no effort to leave. "Dammit, Lieutenant, I make the rules here and I'll break them when I want to!"

"Sorry, Sir, you must extinguish your cigarette and leave the open deck," I countered.

"Lieutenant, you are confined to your cabin for the duration of the voyage and I intend to file charges of insubordination against you when we dock," he said.

I complied with his orders, taking meals in my cabin for 20 days.

While disembarking in Liverpool, Col. Fleming came up to me and said "I am rescinding the confinement order, your conduct was superior."

He and his detachment boarded a train for East Anglia, my unit journeyed south to Cheltenham. Nothing more was ever heard from Fleming. Until ...

May, 1943, Oran, Algeria.

One morning, nine months later, after sailing to North Africa in the second wave of reinforcements, I was serving as an aide to a general. The morning's mail on my desk included a bulky file - a transcript of a general court-martial held in Oran. A name caught my eye: Lt. Col. Fleming had been tried for conduct unbecoming an officer, relieved of his command and sentenced to return to the States for a "less than honorable" discharge. His offense: throwing rocks at Arab civilians.

June, 1947, Pershing Square, Los Angeles.

Returning to my office from lunch, I cut through Pershing Square. As I walked along, a familiar face appeared - none other than Lt. Col. Fleming, seated on a bench in tattered clothing. There was a flicker of recognition as he started to rise, but I kept on walking, passing him without acknowledgment.

THE SUMMER OF 1944
Robert Johns

I graduated from High School in the summer of 1942, at the age of 17. By the time I got established in my dorm room "On the Hill" at Cornell, the war going on in the outside world had heated up and everyone was talking of what the consequences might be for people of our age. While I was continuing on with my studies and considering my options I received a letter from the President giving me "Greetings" and advising me that I was to report for duty to the Grand Central Terminal Building in New York City. I passed the physical, and was sent to Camp Yaphank on Long Island to receive my uniform and to see some rather graphic movies of the really bad things that could happen to you if you managed to expose yourself to any venereal diseases. While there I also found out what KP is and what "fall in" and "fall out" mean.

After two weeks at Yaphank, I found myself on a train going south along with a lot of other green recruits from the New York area. We were sent to Camp Butner, North Carolina to train with the 78th "Lightning" Infantry Division that had just been activated. The "Cadre" was made up of mostly Southern officers and non-coms. The idea was to send the recruits as far away from home as possible to cut down on the number of deserters. The one luckiest thing that happened to me at that time was my assignment to the Field Artillery rather than the Infantry of the 78th Division. This was the result of some clerk having discovered that I had had a whole semester of Field Artillery ROTC at Cornell. Little did I know at that time how lucky this was.

After three months of basic training, a whole summer of field operations, weapons qualifications, and finally a nasty rainy-snowy winter of the dreaded "Tennessee Maneuvers" we were declared ready for action. After digging foxholes all over Tennessee for four months I later found that I only had to do this once under actual combat conditions. Thanks to the Infantry usually having been there first and done all the digging the Field Artillery didn't have to work so hard. By that time I had accumulated two stripes and was qualified to be what is known in the FA as a Scout Corporal. In Battery "B" 309 Field Artillery there was a certain shave tail 2nd lieutenant named Weber who thought a Scout Corporal was created to be his body guard and maid servant. I really didn't go along with that idea and I told the lieutenant so one rainy, muddy, snowy evening in Tennessee. He had lost his sleeping bag and his mess kit out of our jeep and he thought I should give him mine because he was cold and hungry. I would have loaned him my mess kit, after I had used it myself, but I wasn't going to give him my blankets so he could make a sleeping bag.

We were sent to Fort Lee Virginia to recover from our exposure to the elements in Tennessee. When we got to Fort Lee the lieutenant told the first sergeant to tell me to remove my corporal's stripes that I had so laboriously attached to my uniform. When the Colonel heard of this, I was told to put the stripes back on pronto. I'm not sure what he told Lieutenant Weber but I didn't see much of him afterward.

After a few weeks of rest and recuperation at Fort Lee I was told that I was going to be given a special furlough to go home for two weeks. Then I would go to Camp Miles Standish, Massachusetts where a large group of soldiers was being prepared to go overseas. At Miles Standish I learned all about how to conduct myself if ever I was to become a prisoner of war. The main point of this was to make plans for your escape as soon as the enemy was lax enough to allow for it, or even if they weren't lax enough. During the approximately three weeks that I was at Miles Standish my comrades and I were given several overnight passes into the great town of Boston. We found that the citizenry there was very supportive of us. It was impossible, in those days, for a soldier or a sailor to buy a drink in Boston. The reason being that there was always a Bostonian who would buy it for you. This made for quite a bit of drinking among soldiers and sailors but, of course, not to excess.

The third day of June dawned bright and clear and we all hustled aboard the great old Matson Cruise Liner "Mariposa", now converted to a troop carrier. When I say hustled it was, of course, the old Army hurry up and wait. We made it aboard, however, with all our gear, although we hadn't been issued any weapons as yet. The "Mariposa" had been converted from a comfortable luxury cruise liner, to a fairly uncomfortable Troop Ship. The officers got the inside cabins according to rank, with the higher-ranking officers in the upper deck cabins and the 2nd lieutenants inside near the engine room. The rest of the troops were billeted on the outside decks in eight high pipe berths. The berths in each stack were so close together that each stack was filled from the bottom up and emptied from the top down. The "Mariposa" was selected as a troop ship because the old girl could do about 28 knots flank speed which was considered to be too fast to allow the German submarines to get into firing position for their torpedoes, unless they were very lucky. She also zigged and zagged quite a bit in order to try to outguess any wily German U-boat skipper. Everything went pretty well until on the third day at sea we ran into a North Atlantic storm. Those poor guys that were caught in those eight high berths got pretty sick and there just wasn't much you could do about it except clean up after them. As a corporal, and as one of the few who wasn't sick, I was put in charge of a mop and bucket brigade to keep the starboard promenade deck clear. I started with about thirty men and finished at the other end of the deck with about six. I didn't feel much like getting back in my bunk at that point. It also turned out that was the same day that the loud speaker on the ship notified us of the great battle that was taking place called "D" Day. A great cheer went up from all hands that were still in condition to do so.

A few days later we began to see aircraft overhead and we were informed that they were friendly British planes that had come to escort us to a safe harbor. We had suddenly slowed down quite a bit and there seemed to be some air of indecision in the direction and movement of the ship. During the night we noticed that the ship had stopped and we heard the sound of shore movements and steam train engines. When dawn arrived we found ourselves in Gourock, Scotland, in the Firth of Forth. Later we were told that we were intended to be the first replacements for battle casualties in the "D" Day operation. We had been unable to land at the French port of Brest because it was still occupied by German troops who would not surrender even though they were surrounded. The Germans continued to occupy Brest for several months after "D" Day.

It turned out that the casualties of "D" Day, although very severe, were not as great as the High Command had expected. For this reason there was no great rush to ship all these replacement soldiers over to the beachhead. Some quick calculations were made and the next thing we knew our whole shipload of soldiers of all grades and classes was on its way by English train to the South of England. We traveled all night and were detrained at the town of Barnstaple in the county of Devon, located on the South shore of the Bristol Channel. This location had been picked because London, at that time, was undergoing nightly attacks by German bombers and the much feared buzz bomb rockets. About five thousand of us were lodged in a tent city comprised of GI pyramidal eight man tents. We all thought that our stay there would be short lived. However, time dragged on and on and we were still there hearing reports of the progress of the fighting but not being sent to join it. During our entire stay there we were on an eight-hour alert to be sent across the channel to France. Some of us did manage to stretch a few eight-hour passes into longer stays in the idyllic little town of Ilfracomb on the Bristol Channel. There were a number of British families staying there to escape the bombings in London and some of the daughters, of about my age, were quite charming indeed.

In August, a number of us with the more expendable MOS's (Military Occupation Specialty) were hustled onto a small British channel steamer and sent on our way to the Utah beachhead. We disembarked into a landing craft and were deposited on the floating pontoon dock that had been constructed by our Engineers. The Pontoons were covered by a network of perforated steel plates which rolled with the waves but were stable enough for us to march ashore at route step and on up the rather low bank above the beach and then on inland about two miles. By now we had our weapons and a full horseshoe pack of spare socks, boots, under garments, toiletries, first aid kit, extra ammunition, filled canteen, and mess kit. This was all wrapped up in two GI blankets and covered with a shelter half (half of a pup tent with one tent pole and six tent pegs) and topped off by the soldier's best friend, his steel helmet. This was a pretty good load to carry on a hot August afternoon. I often wondered why the High Command was so anxious to storm Omaha beach with its high cliffs and steel reinforced concrete fortifications when Utah beach seemed so much easier to overcome. Of course when we hit the beach there weren't any machine guns or artillery trying to blast us to pieces.

The next morning we were picked up by the Army's workhorse vehicles, the two and one half ton GMC truck, which became known as the Jimmy. The name has stuck to this day. From then on we were moved along by the Jimmies, just a few miles behind the front lines, as the fighting troops pushed on toward Le Mans and then Paris. Paris fell a few days later and we were then hauled to the Foret de Fontainebleau, about 24 kilometers from Paris. We were billeted in an old French Army Barracks in a walled compound that was designed to be a fortress. It was all constructed of fieldstone and appeared to be several hundred years old. We thought that then surely we would be assigned to fighting units, but we remained in Fontainebleau. It really was better than the tent city in England and certainly better than being trundled along from one field to another. The Foret was a beautiful wooded area with riding paths and footpaths crisscrossing among the trees. The barracks were clean and well kept despite their age and life settled into a bit of a routine for a while. I was assigned to be in charge of a sixty man squad as their Squad Leader under Staff Sergeant Bill Trinkle who had four squads under his command. We spent the days doing close order drill and hiking through the Foret to keep ourselves in good physical condition. Bill and I became pretty close friends during that time. He was an infantryman and a real down to earth, get it done and do it right sort of person. As September was drawing to a close Bill was shipped out and I never heard from him again. He didn't know where he was going and there was no way that he could find out where I eventually was assigned. That was the way it was in the war, people would come and go and you never knew what happened to them. This was probably truer of the replacement camps than the organized outfits, but it happened everywhere to some extent. The replacement camps became known as the Repple-Depples. (Replacement Depots) The one I was in was duplicated in many other places.

Toward the end of September, 1944, the weather changed quite rapidly. It became colder and it started to rain quite frequently. The Foret was no longer the inviting place it had been during the late summer. On the twenty first day of October I was told to pack my gear and be ready to ship out the next day. Some combat outfit finally needed me. October twenty second dawned cold and overcast with a slow drizzle. A hasty breakfast was soon followed by the appearance of three very muddy Jimmies. I was told to load up in one along with four other men whom I had never seen before. We started talking and wondering where we were going. It turned out that they were also Artillerymen so we guessed that we were going to be assigned to our specialties. I was the only non-com with my two stripes; they were all cannoneers. The Jimmy we were in, after slopping through mud up to the axles several times, finally pulled up at an old farm house with one end wall in ruins and several holes in the roof. A very dim light was coming from one of the cellar windows and the driver of our truck went inside to report our arrival and get the paperwork to take us to our new assignment. As he came out with the papers in hand I stuck my head out of the canvas that covered the bed of the truck and said, "Hey, sarge where are we and where are we going".

He replied, "This is Arracourt, France, the head quarters of the one hundred and first field artillery battalion, and you guys are going over to where I'm dug in. You'll get your assignments in the morning."

By this time the rain had become constant and quite a bit harder. It was now pitch black outside and the truck could only go ahead slowly with one slit of a blackout light to guide it down the muddy track ahead. The wheels spun several times in the mud but the Jimmy was in all wheel drive and we managed to pull on through. After what seemed like an eternity of slipping and sliding, but was probably about half an hour, we pulled off the road into an open field and slid to a stop. Since I was the only non-com among the four of us in the back of the truck I was sort of in charge. I again stuck my head out of the canvas cover as the driver dismounted into the muddy field where he had parked the truck. I asked him where we were supposed to go. He said, "I'm going over to my dug-out but there's only room for me. You guys better stay put where you are until the first sergeant comes to give you your assignments in the morning."

So saying he disappeared into the mud and rain and we tried to bed down on the cold steel floor of the truck with the two GI blankets each of us had in his pack. It was a bit difficult to get comfortable on that steel floor, but it sure looked a lot better than that cold wet muddy field we had seen in the dim light of the blackout lamp. We were tired and hungry, with nothing to eat since breakfast, and a bit scared too because it appeared that every one in this area was living in underground shelters and we were sitting out in the open field in a truck. Nevertheless, we all did drowse off until we were awakened by loud explosions so close to the truck that each one almost blew the canvas cover off the truck. This was our first exposure to the sounds of war and we didn't know whether this was incoming enemy shellfire or outgoing fire from our own guns. These explosions continued for about half an hour. But since nothing dire had happened to the truck after the first few salvos, we figured we were better off in the truck than lying on the ground outside in all that mud and rain. As it turned out, the thoughtful sergeant truck driver had parked us directly in front of a battery of 10 inch howitzers. Four of those big guns were banging away, laying down a barrage that was the jump off of the fall campaign for the green 26th Infantry Division.

I didn't know it at the time, but the 26th "Yankee" Division had first arrived at the beachhead about a month previously. The Division had immediately been assigned to drive trucks on the so-called "Red Ball Highway" to bring gasoline and supplies to Patton's Third Army. The Third had pushed ahead so rapidly, after the fall of Paris, that it had run low on fuel, ammunition and supplies. It had forced Patton to stop at the Seille River and wait for supplies to catch up. Now with several green divisions added to his force, and with plenty of the materials of war, he was ready to resume his campaign on the Western flank of the line of battle. The "Red Ball Highway" took its name from the many signs posted along the way, which contained nothing but a large red ball painted in the center to guide the unfamiliar truck drivers along the road to Patton. As soon as the 26th had completed this mission they were given a place in the line of battle and told to "dig in". This is precisely the time when I was assigned to Headquarters Battery, 101st Field Artillery Battalion, 26th Infantry Division.

The morning dawned gray and overcast but free of rain. Joe King, known affectionately as "The Old Clam Digger", greeted us. Joe was the First Sergeant of Headquarters Battery. He was truly unique and the only first sergeant that I ever met with a friendly, cajoling manner of asking you to do something that you really didn't want to do. Something like standing guard duty all night when you had just come in hungry and cold from a mission up front. It turned out that the 26th Infantry Division was the New England National Guard Division and the cadre was mostly composed of Down Easters. The Boston papers, during the whole time we were in action, were full of our exploits. Joe told me that I was now assigned to the Survey and Recon Section of Headquarters Battery. He took me over to a dugout that was roofed over but had about six inches of mud and water underfoot, looking like something out of World War One.

In the dugout were the fellows with whom I was going to spend the next year of my life. Our section leader was Paul Davis, Staff Sergeant, married and about 27 years old, also a member of the New England cadre. Paul was a good guy, but he would rather write poetry than fight the enemy. Everybody was suffering from eternally wet feet, there were socks hanging out to dry all throughout the dugout. I was given a warm greeting by all the men there and that was surprising because it was so crowded and nasty in there. Many of the men and officers were suffering from "Trench Foot" caused by loss of circulation in the foot due to cold wet conditions. To help combat this we were eventually issued galoshes to snap on over our combat boots. This continued to be a problem until the ground froze and it stopped raining and started to snow. Then woolen socks were a better solution.

I'm going to pause for a moment to explain the makeup of an Infantry Division, as it existed in WW II. A division consisted of three regiments of infantry, each regiment consisted of three battalions, each battalion consisted of three companies, and each company of three squads. The division artillery consisted of three battalions each one assigned to support one of the three regiments of infantry. Each artillery battalion had three firing batteries, each consisting of four light 105 mm howitzers. The supporting field artillery was always in firing position and was only out of position when moving ahead. In my entire year's experience in action with the 26th "Yankee" Division we never moved to the rear. This was not true of several US divisions in the Battle of the Ardennes, sometimes called the "Bulge". When the Germans jumped off in that fight the US 103rd Infantry was completely overrun and several other divisions were forced to retreat with severe losses of men and material.

The night of my arrival was followed by about a week of sporadic rain, continual gray skies and the firing of our own 105s, located about half a mile ahead of our position. Our infantry was experiencing very heavy action and casualties. The Germans were determined not to let us get moving like Patton had before the fall of Paris. The job of the Survey and Recon section was to accompany the battalion commander and the three battery commanders on the mission to locate and establish new gun positions farther forward as the infantry moved ahead and needed our close support. I was the instrument operator, under Sergeant Davis.

The battalion commander was a lieutenant colonel, and the battery commanders were all captains. The colonel had a ½ ton command car as his lead vehicle and the captains followed in line behind him in their jeeps. We had a ¾ ton open truck with all our survey gear and work crew. All of these vehicles, except ours, were equipped with radios. We in the truck used to joke about being the colonel's armed guard, because we were the only ones with rifles. All of the officers were armed only with Colt 45's, a big heavy pistol that wouldn't hit a barn door at 50 feet.

On about the tenth day after the jump-off our infantry finally made a break through and moved ahead a few miles. Our battalion commander was told at the staff meeting the night before that it was time to consider moving the guns up to better support the guys up front. We took off early the next morning for our first mission in the face of the enemy. The colonel was seated in the rear of his command car with his white hair streaming out from under his steel helmet. Able, Baker, and Charlie battery commanders followed along dutifully in their jeeps.

Proceeding on, our little column breasted the hill that our guns had been hiding behind and there before us lay a rather wide valley with the tree lined road we were on leading off toward another hill in the far distance. At a distance of about three miles down into the valley there was a nearly right angle cross road with an old building on the right hand side where the roads crossed. There were two columns of our infantry moving up along this road, one on either side of the road. The men in each column were spread out about fifty feet apart. This is the typical way infantry marches so that casualties would be reduced in case a shell was to explode on the moving column. You could pretty well tell where one squad ended and the next began by the location of the BAR men. Each squad had one and the BAR stuck up in the air over the top of the soldier's head. The BAR, or Browning Automatic Rifle, was the only automatic weapon given to our infantry soldiers in those days. It was full automatic, like a machine gun, but it fired very slowly. However, due to its long barrel, it was very accurate.

Our column slowed a bit as we caught up to the infantrymen and we started to pass between the two columns. By the time we had gotten down to the cross road the colonel decided to pull off into the courtyard around the old building we had seen on the right side of the road and wait until the infantry columns had moved on up. We left our vehicles and went into the lower part of the building. It was a two-story structure but most of the roof was gone and there was rubble all over the floor. The colonel and the battery commanders spent the time looking at the fields on the other side of the road and along the cross road that ran off in that direction. It seemed like a rather open unprotected location to us but who were we to object. As soon as the infantry cleared the cross road and moved on into the distance a bit we were told to mount up in our vehicle and that the battery commanders would put a stake down in the location that they would pick for their number one gun. Three batteries, four guns each. Our job would be to survey those stakes in and then connect the survey to the center of the cross-road, which could be located on the map. From this a fire chart could be made that could be used to control the aim of the guns at distant targets.

The captains got their job done in a hurry and were busy showing Paul Davis where they had placed the stakes. Meanwhile we had unloaded our truck from our survey equipment, the tape and stake pins, the aiming circles, and the little red and white survey poles. Suddenly a shell burst about 200 yards from where we stood then another about 200 yards behind us. The colonel let out a scream, "every man for himself", jumped into his command car and took off down the road leading back to our old gun positions. The captains didn't waste any time in following the colonel's orders. That left us with our truck unloaded, our gear all out on the ground, and the shells still coming in. We had already had a look around and found that the infantry hadn't been gone from this position long since there were a number of slit trenches right where we were standing. We each found one of these life-saving holes in the ground. The shelling continued sporadically for about fifteen or twenty minutes and then stopped.

We learned several things from that first day in combat. Never stop at a crossroad; the Germans have them zeroed in. Never put a gun battery in an open field without protection for you and the guns from observed fire by the enemy. Also when a German eighty eight gun fires you don't get any warning because the muzzle velocity of its projectile is faster than the speed of sound. Shells from our one oh fives go whine bang. Shells from an eighty-eight go bang screech. The bang is what gets you. You may not live to hear the screech.

When the shelling stopped, probably because in the beginning darkness the Krauts thought they had wiped us out, we popped out of our holes and surveyed the damage. Our truck had taken a near miss. It had one tire blown off and several shell fragments had made holes in the body. There didn't appear to be any serious damage and when Jake fired her up she ran just as good as ever. We threw all the equipment in and took off back up the hill like our colonel had about an hour or so before. We went as fast as she could go with only three wheels working.

The next day we heard that the colonel had been relieved of duty and re-assigned to a rear echelon job. Our new CO was a major who had been the battalion executive officer. His name was Wilbur E. Burton. He turned out to be almost as aggressive as General Patton himself but he was also pretty wily when it came to staying out of trouble. We went on many more forward missions and were fired on many times but we were rarely exposed to direct observed enemy fire as we had been in that first experience. Toward the end of the campaign we were moving the guns two or three times a day and we didn't stay long enough in some places to record the name of the town or village. Our new commanding officer was respected by his subordinates and soon promoted to light colonel. He awarded our Recon and Survey section the Bronze Star Medal for Valor in the Face of an Armed Enemy. It was not a unit award but a personal award for each one of us. I later was promoted to sergeant technician with three stripes.

THE HORSE CAVALRY IN WORLD WAR II
Dexter Barrett

In June of 1938, I graduated from the University of Illinois ROTC program with a Second Lieutenant's Reserve Commission in the United States Horse Cavalry. Shortly after Pearl Harbor on December 7, 1941, I received orders to report for active duty at Fort Riley, Kansas, and arrived there on February 25, 1942. I was assigned to "C" Troop in the Replacement Training Center, where inductees received their original military training. At that time, they were still training two horse squadrons (a squadron was composed of three troops), and we rode every day. In April I was assigned to a Basic Officer's Refresher Course at the Cavalry School, which was scheduled as a three-month review of what we had previously learned in ROTC.

Prior to that time, I had telephoned my wife every weekend to advise her what was going on. She insisted she wanted to come to Kansas, but I stated that I might receive orders to a different Cavalry post and might not be there when she arrived. She finally stated she was definitely coming, arrived on a weekend, and stayed three years. We were able to find a one bedroom apartment in Junction City, immediately west of the Fort.

At the end of the three-month course, I was assigned to the Cavalry School Weapons Department as in instructor in all weapons, from the .45 caliber pistol to a 155 mm. howitzer. We fired all weapons on various ranges, and also conducted training exercises with live ammunition. We taught not only other officers, but also the OCS (Officers Candidate School) "ninety day wonders". These enlisted men, mostly non-commissioned officers, received second lieutenants' commissions at the end of their three-month course. Sometime in 1943, I was sent to Camp Hood,

Texas, to attend a two week "Dirty Fighting Course", using a textbook written by an English army major, which stressed that warfare was NOT for gentlemen, and we should forget the idea of fair play against the enemy. It also included Instruction in village fighting, woods fighting, and various grenades.

Upon my return to the Weapons Department, I was advised I was their grenade "expert", and was also assigned to build and use a village for combat training. In early 1944, I was sent to an Advanced Officer's Training course, again for three months. At the end of that course, I was assigned to the "Battle Courses" Department of the Replacement Training Center, where I trained recruits in village and woods fighting. On some of these training exercises, I was exposed to more dangerous situations than I experienced after going overseas.

In December of 1944, upon my return home from the Fort, my wife advised me that I was being sent overseas. Some woman, who obviously had prior access to orders, called to see if they could rent our apartment, even BEFORE I knew I was leaving. Orders came through next day, and I was given ten days leave before reporting to Fort Meade, Maryland for overseas assignment. We arrived there on December 28, and I was ordered to entrain for New York, where we boarded the Queen Mary on December 31. I noticed one group of GI's who were brought to the gangplank by a cordon of MP's. Evidently they had cleaned out all the stockades and brought the recalcitrant men to the ship under guard. Before I boarded, as a senior First Lieutenant, I was given the funds that had been taken from these prisoners, and was told NOT to distribute the money until our third day at sea.

They blew the ship's horn at midnight, and we sailed from New York early on January 1, 1945. There were eight of us officers in a cabin meant for a couple, but we had two triple bunks and one double bunk. We had two meals a day, and went so far south during the voyage that we could walk on deck in shirtsleeves. As instructed, on the third day out I distributed the funds to the prisoners. I made up a list of names with each man's funds, and had them receipt for the money to protect myself. One man never did show up, evidently slid down the anchor chain while we were in harbor, and I eventually turned his money in to a military bank in London, where they didn't know what to do with it, but I was in the clear.

We arrived in Northern Scotland on January 10, and were trained to a replacement camp outside London, where we stayed for two days. I eventually arrived at a "repple depple" (replacement depot) near Strasbourg, France, from where I was assigned to "C" Troop, 94th Cavalry Reconnaissance Squadron (mecz), of the 14th Armored Division. They were garrisoned near Phaulsbourg at that time. A mechanized troop was made up of three platoons, plus a light tank company. I was given the Second Platoon, which consisted of about 26 men, six "Jeeps", and three armored cars. These were really mobile radio stations and had a small 37 millimeter cannon and one .30 caliber light machine gun with "armor" which wouldn't stop much more than a .30 inch bullet.

About a week later we started east, over the Rhine and into Germany. My platoon was assigned to perform reconnaissance in front of a tank battalion, which had at least three companies of heavy tanks plus auxiliary forces. Mechanized

Cavalry is not combat units, but is expected to locate the enemy, determine composition and size, and report back to the battalion commander. My problem was that the commander's Idea of reconnaissance was to "drive down the road until you're shot at, then come back and tell us about it". I had been trained to "sneak and peek"; not exposing yourself over a ridge until you had surveyed the ground ahead and determined it was safe to advance. The major was not always happy with my rate of advance, but I told my men to follow their training and I would handle the major.

As we approached the "Siegfried Line" we were sent out on a night patrol to measure the concrete tank traps and distance between, so our engineers could determine the amount of explosive that would be needed to blow them up and allow our tanks to come through. We were close enough to the enemy lines that we could hear them talking, but did our job without being detected. Two days later a massive assault started in our sector, with the infantry and armor advancing well, and we followed behind until needed.

At this point, we were mainly "chasing 'Jerry' back to Berlin" and never actually were near any active battles. As we progressed, I "captured" several groups of people, both men and women, who always turned out to be forced labor French or Belgians, who were happy to be free. They wanted to know how soon they could head back west, but that I couldn't tell them. We reached several small villages where the inhabitants told us the Germans had left before we got there and they wondered what took us so long to arrive.

On April 18, 1945 (the war ended May 8) at about 2:00 PM, we arrived in the small village of Berg, Germany, which was our assignment for that day, and my platoon took over a "gasthaus" or beer parlor, and spread out to get some sleep. I checked the distribution of my vehicles, looked for some eggs, and returned to the room where my men were sleeping. The only available space on three benches around the edge of the room was under a window, that is NOT recommended, but not much was going on. Just an occasional shell to let us know the enemy was still there. I stretched out and went to sleep, but was awakened by the sound of the window above me breaking. The other men were leaving the room in great haste, and I decided I'd better go, too, so I tried to stand up, only to have my right leg flop back and forth. I dropped to the floor and hollered for help, and some of the men came back. They cut my pant leg open and I could see flesh all the way down, so I knew I wasn't an amputee. I had some morphine syrettes in my pocket, so I had them give me a couple of shots. Fortunately, there was a military medical Jeep outside our building. They put me on a stretcher and across the hood of the Jeep with another wounded man across the back, and off we went to a field hospital.

I spent a couple of days there until they determined that my femur (large thigh bone) was broken about three inches below the hip, and they put me in a plaster cast for transport. One night in a hospital in Paris, on the floor of a large building, then flown across to an English hospital near Worcester. I was put into traction with a pin through my knee, and about 30 pounds of weight hanging to hold the bone in place for knitting.

In June, I was placed in a large plaster cast from both my ankles to my chest, with my legs spread apart to keep the fracture in the proper healing position. The doctor advised me that the spread of my legs was larger than allowed, and larger than the cabin doorways on the hospital ship, but he said "If I know you, Lieutenant, I don't think that will stop you". Sure enough, when we arrived at my hospital ship cabin, two men carrying me on a stretcher, I was too wide for the doorway. I said, "Fellows, Just turn me up on my side, the cast won't break". They did, got inside nicely, and I was put in a lower bunk of a triple decker. There I stayed for ten days and they would come in twice a day to roll me over so I wouldn't get bed sores.

We arrived at Newport News, Virginia, ten days later, and I was eventually entrained to Memphis, Tennessee, arriving the evening of July 3 to be placed in the officer's ward in Kennedy General Hospital. My wife had arrived In Memphis on the 3rd, phoned the hospital, but they had no record of me. After staying overnight, she called and found out I was there. She came out to Kennedy, where they were in the process of cutting me out of my cast. It was very hot, and my wound had obviously been draining, so when they upended me quite a bit of smelly liquid poured out. I wound up in traction again, but there had never been any pain because it turned out my sciatic nerve had also been severed and I was paralyzed below the knee.

Once my bone had knit enough, and they decided I could be ambulatory, they built a full leg brace for me, with ability to bend at the knee, and in which I was actually sitting on a round padded ring at the top. With the addition of crutches I was quite able to get around, so they would say "hold what you got and get some more", and send me off on 90-day leaves. By that time, we had our car in Memphis, so we would go off visiting and traveling. In May of 1946, my knee had loosened up from the time in traction enough that they operated on my severed sciatic nerve. The knee had to bend at a 90 degree angle so they could get some slack to tie the two ends together, and I came out of that with my leg In a 90 degree cast at the knee. After the surgery had healed and I came out of the cast, I had to work in physical therapy to get the leg to straighten out again. In June they turned Kennedy General into a VA hospital and transferred me to Fort Custer outside Battle Creek, Michigan. We found an apartment in Augusta, just west of Custer, and I would drive into the Fort daily for therapy. Again the 90-day leaves, and by then we had been able to buy a new Oldsmobile in 60 days, whereas other people were waiting six months. So off we went again in the new car, until I received a telegram to return for retirement from the service which became effective on June 20, 1947.

MY ARMY CAREER
Jack Harloe
After finishing college in June 1941, I was commissioned a second lieutenant of Infantry in the Reserve. In September, 1941, I received orders to report to Ft. Myer for physical and then report to the third Armored Division at Camp Polk,

Louisiana. Camp Polk was a year old and already had 15,000 troops. I was assigned to "I" company of the 32nd Armored Regiment, the maintenance company.

One month after arriving, our Regiment was sent to McDill Field in Florida for duty and training in Air Base defense. All "I" company equipment was moved on a train of mostly flat cars, along with two battalions of tanks and reconnaissance half-tracks. Field training was hot, with alligators, snakes, and mosquitoes. There was an active social life and on a Sunday morning another lieutenant and our dates were playing tennis. Following this we went to a drive-in where we heard about Pearl Harbor on the radio of the car parked next to us. We raced back to the field but it was on alert and our ID's were in the BOQ. We had to call another officer to bring them down before we could get back to duty.

Six days later we were back at Camp Polk, which was just starting an epidemic of hepatitis that eventually involved almost 10,000 cases. No useful activity was going on, so I asked for three weeks leave and went to Washington, where my father, a West Point graduate, was a Colonel of Engineers. Marion and I decided to get married at this time and we managed to get all arranged for a New Year's Day wedding in Webster Groves Missouri. We then went back to Camp Polk to try to find housing.

The 3rd Armored was now training hard and I was scheduled to go to Ft. Knox for 6 weeks in May to Advanced Tank Gunnery School. I had previously applied for the new Army Transportation Corps because my degree had been in Transportation in the School of Foreign Service. (and because my father was a friend of the Chief of Transportation.) The 3rd Armored was ordered to report to the desert training center in California July 15 and at the same time I was ordered to report to the Transportation office in London. About this time I developed hepatitis.

Marion and I packed up what few belongings we had and drove to Shreveport, LA, having one flat tire along the way. By then I was so nauseated by the jaundice, all I could do was lean against the car and watch as Marion and a passing motorist changed the tire. At the Shreveport Airport there was an American Airlines "starlight express" plane leaving soon for Atlanta and Washington. My orders bumped a civilian off the flight and I went on in the passenger's place. I was so sick that the stewardess made up an in-flight bunk for me; I climbed in and lay there watching the stars go by and wondering if I would live long enough to see England.

My father met me at the Washington Airport and thought it best if he took me direct to Walter Reed Army Hospital. After 6 weeks in Walter Reed I was well enough to be placed on 30 day convalescent leave. For leave, Marion and I went to a resort in the Poconos, Eaglesmere, PA and enjoyed ourselves thoroughly.

Marion and I went to New York together, staying at a very comfortable upper east side hotel. Each day, I would pick up my musette bag and take the subway to Brooklyn Army Base. And, each day, I was told to come back tomorrow. Until a certain evening, after we had gone to bed, I told her "tomorrow I won't be coming back."

"Loose lips sink ships" was the motto pasted up in the subway overhead advertising placard. Some idea of the seriousness with which this was viewed can be gained by our routing. The British Commodore commanding the 60 ship convoy routed us through N.Y. Harbor, the East River, Long Island Sound, Cape Cod Canal, Boston Harbor and on to Halifax, Canada. In Halifax we embarked 100 British women and children returning to London after the "Blitz" or heavy German air raids in 1940, lasting until the summer of 1942. In total, it meant that we would be at sea for 28 days, landing at Liverpool. Submarine activity was noticeable along the way. As a passenger ship, we were located in the protected center of all the vessels in the convoy.

I was ordered to Cheltenham, England for processing then sent on down to Wilton for duty in the British Southern Command Rail Transportation office. This office reported to a London office; but it also had responsibilities for administering to American personnel assigned wherever the British had Rail Transit Office at each of the major stations in southern England. I found my self out on the road most of the time, trying to find our American units, pay them, medicate them and transfer them when needed. With my Corporal Driver, my .45 caliber automatic, a jeep, and the organization payroll, we became the invisible main supply line for the American Units.

Having left Polk one year ago as a 2nd Lieutenant, I received a promotion to 1st Lieutenant on reaching London. The orders for the promotion were published in due course and noticed by Col. Ed Leavey, a West Point Classmate of my Father's. He called me to his office and asked me if I would like to be assigned as Aide to Brig. Gen. Tom Larkin, and he warned me that the latter would be moving almost immediately. For the next three years I served as aide to General Larkin. Every time he was promoted, I was too. He ended the war as a Lieutenant General, I as a major.

Although the General couldn't say anything about the secret mission we were about to undertake, I found myself boarding a British P & O passenger vessel on a snowy 1942 Christmas Eve in Glasgow. Within a week, I learned, we will be in a California-like clime. Once the ship sailed, the word was out that we were destined for passage through the Straits of Gibralter to Algiers in N. Africa, arriving in January 1943. It was the N. African invasion!

While in Africa, I acquired several liaison aircraft for staff use: a Piper L-4, an Aeronca L-3, and a Stinson L-5. In July of 1943, I obtained a C-47 (DC-3) converted for long over-water trips. This I assigned to General Larkin who used it extensively. It was modified with a plush interior and was named "Skylarkin"

I was able to obtain flight instruction in the liaison aircraft from our command pilots and was able to use them myself.

I made one trip home while in Oran. The General assigned me as an armed courier carrying requisitions for important supplies. The trip was not without its humorous aspects: Unfavorable weather grounded our northbound flight at Raleigh -Durham, N.C. Passengers from the flight were placed on a northbound train to Washington and on to New York City. Here Marion eagerly awaited me, languishing in a Times Square fleabag, the Hotel Martinique, the only accommodations available in wartime New York.

Returning to Oran was routine, with one exception. While stopping overnight, I encountered actor Jimmy Stewart, also staying overnight. He was flying, with his squadron of B-24s, on his way to England. Remembering that I had had a cousin who graduated from Princeton about the same time Stewart did, we talked about that. Since he had just been briefed on weather, we discussed it. I was relieved to know it was a go to Dakar.

After twelve months in North Africa, we moved our headquarters to Caserta in Italy, about 40 miles east of the port of Naples. My existence was taking on almost a family tinge: my Uncle Jim (Rankin), commanding a Field Artillery Battalion was located about 40 miles north of us. I got him on the phone and arranged a date for me to go up and visit him. My Uncle's battery of 155mm. howitzers was located at the mouth of the Garigliano River, which empties into the Bay of Gatea about 30 miles south of Rome. In other words Jim's guns were the "anchors" so to speak for the left flank of the American Division. They had recently replaced a British Division. So recently, in fact, that they were still wearing British helmets in an effort to delay German recognition of a change in troop disposition. When I came up from Caserta I had carefully followed Jim's instructions as to time of arrival and location.

"Whatever you do, don't fly over or in front of the river." I landed on a section of road about a mile behind the guns. We covered the plane with camouflage netting to make the plane more difficult to spot.

My Uncle and I shared one of the small tents with a dug out interior. The guns would be firing intermittently throughout the night. There would be no sleep this night. Jim took me and his corporal driver on an extended after-dark tour of all of the Infantry front line company level command posts (CP's). There were six of them and we didn't finish until shortly after midnight. At each stop we would go into the CP (usually a house or a barn}, get out the maps and ask for the coordinates of their units and then ask them to indicate where the infantry people could identify targets they wanted fired on. One they particularly wished to hit was a German unit that formed a chow line at daybreak each day. Our company officers coming in for the briefing looked particularly haggard; one of them saying "these bastards are trying to kill us."

All during one stop at a CP we could hear a tank engine, apparently moving around in the darkness. Since we knew our division had no tanks operating in the area we had to assume they were German. The noise did not sound louder after a time so we ignored it. The Germans were probably indulging in psychological warfare.

I took off the next morning and flew back to Caserta. Ten days later, the General got a telephone call from 5th Army Headquarters saying that my Uncle had been seriously wounded and would be moved to a hospital attached to our headquarters here in Caserta. Jim was wounded when he joined other officers, standing on a road studying a map. The shell came in right at their feet. They were standing in a road looking at a map. German Artillery saw them too and fired two well placed rounds that did a lot of damage. He arrived by ground ambulance an hour later, and, after an examination, he was scheduled to be air lifted from Naples back to Washington, D.C. Although my uncle was eventually able to resume his career as a civil engineer, it was several years before the VA doctors approved full time work.

The invasion of southern France eventually led to our headquarters moving from Caserta, Italy to Dijon, France. The winter there was a cold, wet, miserable one, particularly for troops fighting battles. Our situation was much easier than that. At least we got a warm meal to eat, and a dry bed to lay my head.

This was the time of the Battle of the Bulge. For the first time it was possible that our own headquarters might be overrun. Once that possibility was removed, the war began winding down.

Yet everyone in our headquarters had one more move to make; this time to, of all things, PARIS. We moved there in February, 1945. And, as if by a common unspoken consensus, there began to appear request for leave from our staff for air trips to Italy, England, Holland, yes even Germany!

Suddenly our flying staff was busy. Our C-47 took a load of officers on leave to Milan, Italy with a stop on the way back at much extolled Biarritz. The final days of war were arriving. Many in our headquarters had long months of overseas service. The General and I were eligible to go right away, but the General held out for June of 1946.

As though the impending separation of our adored "Skylarkin" had become known to it, 4166 took off from the steel mat runway at Frankfurt, Germany, struck sharp metal on the take off run, veered sharply to the right, ground looped and caught fire. Nobody was hurt but gone was the plush interior, but even more significant or tragic, gone were all the many happy hours. Maybe just as well. Maybe better to have it happen while we were still flying it.

It was June 15, 1945 when we left for Washington. Our immediate staff lifted off from Orly Field in a C-54 bound for the Azores, a refueling stop, thence on to Gander in Newfoundland then down to Washington and a long anticipated reunion with our families. For me, my wife Marion and a three year old son, born while I was overseas. Following the war, I served seven more years in the reserve, as a Lieutenant Colonel.

LOADING FOR INVASION
Alton Sanford

I took ROTC at the University of Maryland and had a reserve commission as a 2nd lieutenant of infantry. I was called to active duty just a couple weeks after Pearl Harbor. I was first sent to a mini Ft. Benning course for newly activated reserves at Griffith Park in Los Angeles and then assigned to the 40th division, a California National Guard Division just being activated. The division was being used for guarding the California Coast, tunnels, roads, etc. I was first at Del Mar racetrack where we lived in the jockeys' quarters. Later we were sent to San Francisco and had quarters in buildings at the San Francisco Zoo.

The 40th division had four regiments and divisions were being made triangular (three regiments) so my regiment, the 184th, was transferred to the seventh division. We were sent to Ft. Lewis, Washington during an "Alert" and then to Ft. Ord,

California for combat training. From there, we were shipped to the Aleutians, going to the island of Adak. Our unit did the Kiska invasion, which had no opposition, but I was now personnel officer and stayed in Adak. Following this we were loaded to return to San Francisco but at the last minute they took us to Schofield Barracks in Hawaii. Here I became transport quartermaster for our regiment. Our group took the logistics plan and was responsible for loading invasion ships so that the material came off in the order the planners felt it would be needed.

The regiment took part in the Kwajalein invasion but the planning group stayed in Hawaii, making plans for the next operation. We were planned for an invasion of Yap but later this was changed to the Philippines. By this time I was a Captain. Our ships left and then stopped briefly at Manus, off New Guinea, for loading some materials. Then we went on to Leyte.

On Leyte my job was to see that the ships were properly unloaded and materials available in the right order when needed. The first night ashore, the bullets were flying ahead but I was back of the lines of contact. After the unloading was completed, the transport personnel were available for the commander's needs. We sat on the beach and watched the kamikaze attacks on our ships. I was placed in command of the headquarters company that was made up of service personnel: truck drivers, cooks, bakers, clerks.

The regiment moved south but then found the opposition was in the other direction. They moved, but left all their baggage and equipment and we were given the job of bringing it up to them. The roads had been badly torn up by heavy equipment and we had trouble getting trucks through. We took the tracks from weasels and placed them on the big 6 x 6 trucks so we could get through the mess. We also paid natives a dollar a bag to bring the personal bags over on water buffalo. It was amazing how many could be loaded and tied to a buffalo at that price.

After the Japanese were defeated, we had to reload the ships for the Okinawa invasion. We used landing craft to reload the ships, which was difficult due to choppy water. I rode to Okinawa on an AKA, a combat transport, with the cargo. There was a typhoon while we were approaching Okinawa and we had to float around, waiting for the ocean to calm down. We watched the landing from the ships and after the first troops cleared the beach, went ashore. The opposition was rather mild on this beach. There were some casualties, but low in comparison with other areas.

The headquarters company had a camp 300 yards from a main road. One evening there was machine gun fire on the road. We thought it was a Japanese attempt at a breakthrough. I thought I was in for my first taste of "combat" with a fighting force made up of cooks, clerks, and mechanics. We set up our defense line and sweat out the night. When dawn came I could see people walking around casually so I took a sergeant and walked down to the road. There were Philippine guerillas and when I asked what the shooting was about during the night, they said they were celebrating New Year's Eve.

The transport quartermaster team had its own little area and were assigned special duties. I was to set up a camp for soldiers with "battle fatigue", a form of psychological break from pressure. This was set up in an protected area. We could still hear shells whistling over our heads but they landed beyond. There were psychologists to help the soldiers. Some were returned to duty while others couldn't make it. They found that those with an acute onset could often go back to duty while those in which it came on gradually over days were less likely to recover promptly.

I was originally with E company before my transport assignments and kept up with the people in it. It was in heavy fighting and two sets of officers were killed or wounded before Okinawa was taken. When the island was secure, our group was still in place, planning the logistics of reloading the division for invasion of Japan.

I developed a hand infection (jungle rot) and was in a field hospital for a time. During this time another typhoon struck. The structures were temporary and were all being blown apart. We patients were loaded on amphibious vehicles and taken up to another hospital on higher ground.

Once I went to a movie in a natural bowl in the ground. During the movie there was a sudden roar of antiaircraft guns. We shut the movie down so as not to make a target and I went to the rim of the bowl. I saw all the guns on the island firing and was told they had just heard that the war was over!

Everyone was anxious to get home and troops were placed on every conveyance going back. Some lucky ones were flown but most went by ship. The number of points for time overseas was calculated and we went back in sequence, those with the most points going first. Eventually my turn came up and I went back on a troop transport, taking three weeks. When we came in the Golden Gate to San Francisco they had bands on boats, fireworks, and flags for a fine reception. At last I was home after 2 ½ years overseas. My six month old daughter was now three.

JIM GILES AND THE ARTILLERY
Jim Skinner
Jim Giles has been a resident of the Gardens since 1991. He is unable to tell us about his Army time so his wife, Joan, asked a friend and fellow officer to recall his memories of Jim during the war. "We" may indicate the two of them or the entire unit.

Jim Giles was in the ROTC Field Artillery at Texas A & M. His major was Chemical Engineering and he had a very high standing in his class. In his senior year he received orders to report to active duty on completion of his degree. Except for 16 who couldn't pass the physical, the entire class went in as Second Lieutenants. Jim was sent to the Battery Officer's School at Ft. Sill, Oklahoma.

We had very primitive equipment. We were actually practicing with French 75s brought over after World War I. The American army was very deficient in artillery pieces. The first 105 Howitzer was shown to us at Ft. Sill with all the officers on the post in a big auditorium late in December of 1941. It was the only 105 Howitzer and it had been hand-made. We didn't get those Howitzers until after we got into North Africa in 1943. In early December, five of the Battery School officers, all Aggies, were assigned to the 36th Infantry Division in Brownwood,

Texas, a National Guard outfit. None of us wanted to go to a Guard division, but to a regular division. We requested change, but no one received it.

Jim and I were both assigned to the 133rd Field Artillery Battalion. We soon found out that the reason we were sent to the 36th was to bring it up to full strength, trained to go into North Africa in the coming November invasion. We didn't get to because of the shortage of transport to take us over there.

In March, the Division moved to Camp Blanding, Florida, to go into intensive training again. We had to take three 25 mile hikes per week in terrible heat in June and July until we left for the Carolina maneuvers. In Carolina we decided to do them at night, which meant we marched all night and worked the next day but at least we weren't as hot.

Then in August, all of a sudden, the whole Division was ordered to Camp Edwards, Massachusetts, to prepare for invasion training. We were supposed to leave November 1 for North Africa, but were cancelled out. So we stayed at Camp Edwards all winter with the snow, strange to us from the South, until April 1st, 1943 when we left New York harbor. We landed at Mers el Kabir, the harbor of Oran and Algiers on April 13th.

As soon as we landed in Oran we were moved to the Rabat area, just north of Casablanca, close to Port Lyautey. We set up in a beautiful cork forest. Our mission was twofold; prepare for landing in Italy and prepare to stop any German advance coming down through Gibraltar and into North Africa. This latter mission was no problem at all.

We trained hard during this period, but mixed in a few trips to Casablanca, Fez, Memphis, and Marrakech. They were unusual cities for us to see at that time in our life. It was during this period that Jim was placed in command of B Battery.

In August we were moved to a new training area near Oran to continue our invasion training on the Mediterranean and to get ready to go to Italy. It was here that Jim was made Assistant Battalion S-3. It was a nice promotion for Jim because it was a Major's spot and he had just made Captain. After a lot of work and lots of errors we got our Battalion aboard an attack personnel carrier called the Funston, and left September 8, 1943, to land at Salerno on the 9th of that same month. It was an uneventful trip until that early morning when we were told that Italy had surrendered. Many thought that would make the landing easier, but the Germans had not quit, so the war still went on.

In early darkness, we had to climb down rope ladders to the small boats that were to take us ashore about four miles away. We circled for about two hours and then went in about an hour before we were supposed to. The landing was very confusing, it was mass confusion really, and the battle on the beach wasn't anywhere near over. Our trucks and guns had not been put ashore so we just dug in around the old Paestum ruins and waited until our equipment came in about three o'clock. Our Battalion was giving fire support to the Infantry about six o'clock that night.

We were strafed a couple of times by German planes, but no casualties. We also received some artillery fire but again no casualties of any importance. The 10th was spent establishing the beachhead and preparing the attack to begin, to reach out and go north to Naples. Easier said than done.

The next day the attack began and we began to suffer heavy casualties, mostly infantry. Jim received the Italian Military Valor Cross for pulling wounded to safety under fire. We had about 30 men and officers up front as Forward Observers so we suffered casualties also. By nightfall we had made progress in capturing the "outside" town, Altavilla, but lost four of our officers and about ten enlisted men. The Germans counter-attacked about 9 o'clock, but we took the town and recaptured most of our people that were there.

But we've had a crisis. Colonel Gaylor, the Battalion Commander, called all the officers together in the staff area and explained the situation: we had no communication with Infantry. So he sent two officers out of our Headquarters to contact the Infantry and get back to us with some radio so we would know what was going on and support them. We never heard from them again until the war was over and then they were in the hospital.

So we had to send more officers out. He picked Jim and one other to do that job, and told me to stand by to take over if either of them was lost. Jim put on his gear, borrowed a rifle (all we had were pistols), and with one enlisted man, went forward to find our Infantry. We heard from him by radio in about 20 minutes. He reported that he was under heavy fire and couldn't find any of our officers, but had brought the Infantry Battalion Commander into his dugout. He was sending us fire instructions to support the attack starting in an hour.

On the third day, our Battalion and the 143rd were sent over to the eastern extreme left flank of the Division to fill a gap in the front lines between us and the British troops on the left. This was pretty breathtaking but was successful by good planning, which Jim had a lot to do with.

That night one Battalion of the 143rd, the 2nd, of 860 men was cut off, and almost all were captured, killed or wounded. In fact all of us were almost pushed off the beach that night, but a Regiment of the 82nd Airborne dropped just behind us and helped stop the Germans. We were only about 300 yards from the beach. That was our last battle in the Salerno campaign. We moved into Naples without much resistance and then to the rest area to be refitted with new men and materiel.

In October '43 Jim left the Battalion to serve as Assistant Division Artillery G-3. He was selected from lots of other guys because of his excellent planning ability. Most of the Regimental Commanders in the Division then were relieved of command and were replaced by younger officers. We didn't go back into combat again until the middle of November.

The battle of Cassino had begun, so we stayed in and around Cassino from December until May of 1944. During this time, the first TOT (meaning Time-On-Target) artillery barrage was planned, and fired on one spot, one mountain. Jim and his crew carefully calculated the time, etc. needed for each gun to open for all of the guns under the command - 140 guns. This was quite an undertaking. It had never been done before, but Jim and his crew did it, firing on Mount Lungo. It was something to see. It was then called the "Million Dollar Mountain" because that was the amount of money somebody calculated as the cost of the shoot - of the number of shells that were fired that night. Probably Jim did that calculation as he liked to do that sort of thing. We took the mountain but didn't take Cassino.

In January, the battle of Rapido River was underway, probably the most costly battle we were ever in, we lost so many Infantrymen. Then all the Infantry and three Battalion Regiments were sent back to rest and refit, but all the Artillery stayed in place and supported the other American Divisions as well as the Canadian Division, the Indian Corps, the British and the French.

It was during this time, a couple of things happened that should be noted. We watched the planes bomb and destroy the Abbey of Monte Cassino. It's a great question since then as to whether it should have been done. As far as we were concerned, it was the right thing because we felt that the Germans were up there, looking down our throats, observing everything we did, and shooting lots of artillery at us.

In April about 30 officers, including Jim and me, were sent on a job back to Naples. We were all sequestered for three weeks in an old castle on the Bay of Naples. Our job: plan the invasion of Southern France for August of 1944. It was our super secret, of course, and we couldn't even leave the castle. In fact, we were not told where or when; just do it as a new assignment. We couldn't leave, though Naples was just up the hill. But we were busy long hours and didn't have anything else to do, so it was all right. Jim received the Legion of Merit for this work.

We shortly returned to our outfit to get ready to go to Anzio. We broke out of the line at Anzio and our Division helped break the stalemate by opening up the German lines at Velletri, and on June 5th we marched into Rome with General Mark Clark, the 36th being the only division given the honor of accompanying him. The Italian Campaign has often been labeled the "Forgotten War" as it was overshadowed by the Normandy invasion, which started the day after the capture of Rome. We didn't stay at all, kept right on going, all the way north to Pisa, where our entire Division was then withdrawn and sent back to Naples to prepare for the Southern France Invasion, which Jim and I and other officers had planned earlier in the year. We got a few days of leave in Rome.

The Invasion was well planned and we had very few casualties. We landed at San Raphael, which is very close to Cannes. On the second day a special task force was formed called Task Force Butler, commanded by General Butler, who was our Assistant Division Commander. His mission was to proceed up the Route Napoleon through Cannes, then left on Montelimar to halt the retreating German 10th Army that was coming up the Rhone Valley from the beachhead. Our Artillery Battalion was part of this Task Force, and Jim went with General Butler as his Artillery Officer until the rest of the Division could join us. This was quite an adventure, with a big battle at Montelimar.

After that battle we took Lyon, then moved into the Moselle Valley, then the Vosges Mountains. We spent Christmas night in Strasbourg. The Battle of the Bulge wasn't going very well (that started on the 16th of December) so we were sent up there to help. We came up the southern route to help finish the Battle of the Bulge. Then we started getting ready to go through the Siegfried Line.

Jim and another friend, Dick, received seven days' leave to go to the Division's rest camp at Bains-les-Bains. This was "dullsville" so they had no intentions of going there, and told me they were going to Paris instead. Of course they had no passes, which were required to get into Paris, and couldn't get a room at the Crillon or the Ritz hotel where officers were supposed to stay but that didn't bother them. They came to me to get a list of places to go and things to do, and they left.

As luck would have it, about two days later, Dick's father had a heart attack, and Dick was given 30 days leave to go home to Pecos. He couldn't be found at the rest camp and when he finally returned, had missed his plane. The colonel cancelled his leave and reassigned him as a liaison officer to the infantry. Jim was with him, but because he was at Headquarters, he escaped the Colonel's wrath.

After passing through the Siegfried Line, we crossed the Rhine River at Mannheim. We went south immediately to Heidelberg, where we relieved the 63rd division and attacked Stuttgart. Then on to Munich with not too much resistance; it had been pretty well leveled by the Air Corps. Then we turned due south, straight through Bavaria, and on about April 15th our division was made a part of the First French Army under General d'Tassigny, a very stubborn and proud man. At this time, Jim was made Division Artillery G-3 and could have made Colonel very shortly if the war had not ended.

The night before the war was over we had a big snowstorm. Everything stopped since we were in the Bavarian Alps at the time. That night we received word that the war was to end at midnight. When Hermann Goering surrendered at the close of the war, it was to the 36th division. Jim was in the room with General Walter Hess, CO of the Division and took snapshots, which we still have. The 36th Division had been in actual combat for 132 consecutive days, setting a modern record for the U. S. Army.

We were to inform General d'Tassigny of the order ending the war. Jim sent a driver, a Sergeant, and me to find him. It took about three hours, since nobody knew where the French Headquarters was. We finally found him and informed the General that the war was ending. He informed me, very politely, that it would take a General Officer to tell him that the war was over; otherwise, his war would continue. After many futile attempts to contact General Hess, our Commanding General, we finally got him, and he and Jim read the order and instructions on the radio. Thank goodness, d'Tassigny accepted them.

We had our last Headquarters of the war at Kitzbuhl, Austria, which was the Hollywood of Bavaria and Austria at the time, full of beautiful young ladies. The next week or so, we rounded up a lot of prisoners and the next thirty days or so was spent sending our soldiers home, but few officers. After receiving replacements, our Division was designated to train to be in the first wave to invade Japan, planned then for September 1st. But August 15, the bomb was dropped that ended the war. We were all greatly relieved, and learned it had certainly saved many of our lives. After that, we spent our time doing occupation duty, having parades and not doing much else. They broke up the Division and Jim came home to be mustered out as a Lieutenant Colonel after almost five years of service.

A MILITARY POLICEMAN IN FRANCE
Fred Weinrich

After finishing college, I went to work for Douglas Aircraft in Santa Monica in 1939. I was in the GFE (government furnished equipment) division. The company was responsible for building the planes but much of the equipment, such as radios, was then furnished by the government to meet their requirements. I was then sent to The Long Beach factory, where I worked for a time on the C-47, the military version of the DC-3 and then on the B-17. When the war came I tried to get out of Douglas and into the army but they wouldn't release me. However, I was then drafted and Douglas had no choice. I thought with my aircraft experience that I would go to the Air Corps but at that time they needed soldiers so I was assigned to the Army.

I was sent to Camp Roberts for basic and was then assigned to anti-tank training there. Our unit was then sent to Camp Meade, near New York, in the middle of the winter. After some training, we were sent to England. We went on the liner Isle de France, in company with the Queen Mary and the Queen Elizabeth, all of these being used as troop transports. We landed in Scotland but were then sent to Southern England for a time. Then we went to Yorkshire for more training. We were the first large replacement unit to be assigned for troop replacements after D-day.

We went into France out of Southampton on D-day plus three, into Omaha Beach. We were on a large transport, then changed to landing craft. Due to problems on the beach, we were dropped off in fairly deep water. It was over the heads of the smaller men. We were wearing specially impregnated uniforms and carrying a lot of equipment: helmet and liner, gas mask, rifle, extra ammunition, mess kit and rations, and other gear, totaling 75 pounds. In spite of this we made it through the waves to the beach. The beach was still littered with bodies and wreckage from the first assaults. We moved up in rain and mud to join the Second Division.

It was said that one could almost walk across the channel on the continuous boats on D-day. This condition actually continued for 3 to 4 months. A tremendous amount of equipment and supplies was sent to France and the beaches were stacked with equipment for over 10 miles. We not only could supply our Army and the English but we also fed the French.

The British under Montgomery were held up at Caen. A major roadblock was the German defense of St. Lo, the key to breaking out into the heart of France. Here we launched one of the great bombing attacks of the war. Heavy bombers were flying back and forth between there and England. Cherbourg had been taken and Patton started from there along the coast. Our unit moved inland in parallel with Patton. There wasn't need for an anti-tank unit there so I was assigned a time as a quartermaster. Our column and Patton's were moving so fast that the infantry couldn't keep up. We hitched rides on tanks and fuel or supply trucks to try to stay with the progress.

As we captured French towns and cities from the Germans, there was a major problem with traffic. A group of us were then assigned to the military police. We took over the control of transportation and also essentially began the administration of French towns. We ran the city of Dieppe when the troops were being landed there and controlled the traffic to get them to the front. I also was in LaHavre. Here the Germans had abandoned the city but due to miscommunication we launched a major air attack and destroyed half the city. Our unit was the first into LaHavre. The railroad was wiped out and the mud kept the trucks to a minimum and the military buildup was huge. Finally the things they needed began to flow to the combat troops.

As the war progressed, units would be pulled from the line and sent to Southern France for a week of R and R. Our MP group was sent South to help control this area. Troops would be coming down and fresh troops going forward. In addition, there were huge amounts of supplies and fuel going to the lines. Injured and bodies were being transported back. We had to plan and manage all this traffic. In addition, many of the troops on R and R were difficult to control and we had this responsibility.

The older German soldiers were mostly happy to surrender to the Americans. They would plan to be in an American area as they were treated better there than by the British or French. And the last place any of them wanted was with the Russians. Some young German soldiers that were active Nazis would not surrender easily and were a problem as POW's. However most of the POW's were happy to be out of the war and were no problems. Many were shipped to Britain and often on to the United States. We had some POW's working in our area.

The rapidly moving American forces often by-passed towns and areas with German troops. When these troops found there was no communication and no supply, they would surrender to the nearest American unit and increased the number of POW's. Headquarters didn't approve of the by-pass and slowed down to assure that Germans weren't in the rear. It turned out that the famed Siegfried Line was largely unmanned and our armored columns could have gone straight on to Berlin. In the battle area, our Air Corps had complete control and shot anything that moved. This necessitated the Germans moving at night. They had insufficient fuel and had difficulty retreating as fast as the Americans came forward.

We had more problems with our own troops in my area than with the Germans. The combat troops on R and R were often problems but there were also hijackings of trucks by our troops. The standard of exchange in Europe at that time was tobacco and C-rations. These would be stolen from the trucks and put on the black market. We even found some of the military police involved in taking bribes not to report thefts or black market activities.

We had built a fuel pipeline in France and one of the MP jobs was to see that people didn't tap into the line and remove fuel. Another problem was the French North African troops who the French brought over to Southern France. There was mutual dislike between the French and these troops. We had no problems working with them but had to watch their relationship with the French. We were unable to control everything and used the French police widely for local problems.

American black troops were used as drivers for many of the truck transport routes. There was some racial problem and ill feeling that we had to control. There were frequent murders and we had only a small jail. We would hold the criminals overnight and then send them on to a major holding area.

Most of my work was in the office. We were controlling transport which also meant finding places to put the thousands of troops we arranged to move. There were huge numbers of military police involved - 40 to 50,000 in the Southern part of France. Those of us stationed in offices were put up in luxury hotels. The MP's were into everything as no one else had authority over the areas. I also had to work in the courts at times. Here we had gendarmes used for security in the court.

When the war was over, we received over a million troops in Marseille to send back to the US. At first it was announced that they would all be flown back but this idea proved impossible within a month. Troops were placed on anything that went back; cargo ships, aircraft carriers, as well as troop ships. The Marseilles area was a mad house. We set up shows, ice cream parlors, a brewery, all controlled by the MP's. Ninety percent of the MP's were combat troops who had rotated out and weren't trained as MP's. By the time they learned what they were doing, they were sent home.

I went home in early 1946 on an old cargo ship. There were a lot of the men that gambled the whole trip. One of the big surprises when we reached Boston was to find that the cooks for the Army station were all German POW's and they had all grown fat as cooks.

MY WAR

Dale Pittinger

I didn't volunteer for duty; I was drafted when I was 31 years old, married, and the father of a six months old son. I had my first good job, making $300 a month, a good salary in the depression days of 1939 -40. I signed up for the draft in Glendale, California. Six months later, after I had moved to Oregon, the Glendale draft board advised me that a group of my peers wanted me to report for induction into the military.

I reported to Ft. Lewis, Washington in June 1941, six months after the German invasion of France. After physicals, my group of about 250 men was sent for basic training to Camp Callan near La Jolla, California, now the Torrey Pines Golf Club. It couldn't have been a better location, near the ocean it was warm in the daytime in July, August, and September, with an ocean breeze and cool nights. To add to my good fortune, my wife and baby son moved to Ontario California, about 100 miles from Camp Callan, to live with my brother and his wife. We had other family in Ontario to provide support. I had almost every Saturday afternoon and Sunday off so I went to see them often.

When our 13 weeks of basic training was finished, I, with my company, was sent to Ft. Bliss in El Paso, Texas for advanced training in artillery, for another thirteen weeks. El Paso is the worst climate I have ever experienced; hot and humid day and night in the summer and cold and windy in the autumn and winter. There wasn't much snow but the wind and cold temperature left no doubt that it was winter.

We trained in anti-aircraft artillery, firing 90 millimeter guns, learning to track with radar. I was assigned to a master gunner course, mostly surveying. We were responsible for establishing the positions of the four guns of the battery so they could all fire to the same point up to three miles away. The guns might be located as much as a quarter mile apart in a circle, diamond, or square.

The data from the height finder and the radar had to be fed to the guns location and it varied to each gun, depending on the relation of the guns to the director. I understood it then but after 60 years I wonder how I learned it all.

The cadre who trained my company were mostly regular army personnel who had spent some time in Panama. They were mostly Southerners of limited formal education. Their accent was deep south - Georgia, Florida, Louisiana and we had trouble understanding them. After the 13 weeks learning artillery, I spent another 13 weeks as cadre, the training staff for the next influx of soldiers.

After the training of the new recruits, we expected to be assigned to a coastal station as defenders of a port from enemy aircraft. However, the complexion of the war had changed to the offensive and danger to our ports seemed minimal so it was decided to switch us to infantry. We had a choice but to keep my rank, I was now a sergeant, I had to go to infantry training at Paris, Texas, near the Arkansas border. The weather was miserable with snow and much colder than El Paso. Paris had about 5000 people before the war but with over 5000 army personnel it was ill equipped with facilities. There was only one theatre and no good restaurants, though there were plenty of bars and beer joints. Very boring when we had leisure.

We arrived in Paris three days before Christmas and had just settled into our new quarters when some sadistic planner scheduled a week's training bivouac. This meant sleeping in pup tents in the field with no trees to break the wind, no fires after dark, and no mess hall. We ate rations where we could find shelter, usually lying in sleeping bags in our tent. I was cold all the time for eight days. I was one of the lucky ones who didn't catch cold. About 25% of the troops went directly to the hospital on returning. I never had an experience like that in combat.

After the thirteen weeks of training, we were sent to Fort Meade, Virginia on a troop train made up of the oldest passenger cars the railroad owned. We slept in our seats, covered with our overcoats on a four day, five night trip. We had mostly cold rations but hot coffee and occasionally soup. We were happy to get to a regular camp. We were there about a week and were issued new uniforms, boots, and overcoats for overseas. We had some orientation classes on ship procedures and debarkation drills in case we were torpedoed.

We were then sent to a camp near West Point in upstate New York. This was really cold with deep snow. The drill field had been swept but the surface was ice.

We sailed to Europe on the Queen Mary the first week in January. It had been converted to a troop ship and had almost 6000 troops. The staterooms intended for three had 23 men. The bunks were hinged to the wall four high with the first bunk one foot off the deck and the top bunk one foot below the ceiling. It was quite an acrobatic feat to get in the top bunk. They served two meals a day, eight and three thirty. They were British cooking and war time rations; soup, overcooked vegetables, bread, and very little meat. There was a PX aboard but it was out of everything but candy bars two days out. There wasn't even beer.

By luck, our company was assigned the job of military police on the ship. My job was to keep curious GI's away from the engine room. We worked eight hour shifts and mine was 2PM to 10 PM. On my first day I was on guard near the crew dining room. As they came out after eating, one crewman asked where I was from as he had been in the US for a time. I told him "California" and he was really interested. He started questions and then stopped, saying, "Say, Yank, you look hungry." I agreed as we had only a light lunch because we were on duty before the 3:30 dinner hour. He said, "I'll be right back." He went into the dining room and reappeared with a pork chop sandwich and a cup of coffee with milk. The sandwich was great but the coffee horrible. I had the evening meal of crew rations the next four days, a lot better than my fellow soldiers.

The voyage from England to France arrived at Le Havre, a disaster of a bombed out city. We then bused to the train station and boarded a 40 x 8 train, designed by the French for 40 men and 8 horses. We slept on the straw covered floor. There were no toilet facilities and we stopped every four hours at a train station or a nearby hotel. The food was "C" rations again. When the train stopped the mess crew set up their big kettles and warmed the cans from the rations. Once we stopped near a restaurant serving horse meat steaks. Most of the soldiers went there and ignored the train whistle to get aboard. We were threatened with court martial and the train no longer stopped at towns of any size. The horsemeat steaks were worth it.

After two days travel we arrived at the replacement center. I expected to be assigned to an infantry division. Late the second day I was summoned to headquarters and ordered to get my gear and weapon and be ready to go in half an hour. When I was ready, a sergeant in a jeep picked me up and we were off. I asked him what outfit I was assigned to and he told me 777th Armored division in tanks. I couldn't believe it; I hadn't been within 100 feet of any tank.

A tank destroyer, a Sherman tank without the turret, had been fitted with a 90 mm gun and a few days after I arrived, the colonel, two majors, and other brass took me out of the town in Belgium to a valley. Up on the hill was a German Army lookout, now abandoned, made up of a railroad passenger car overlooking the valley road. This was to be our target.

I explained to one of the majors that the destroyer didn't weigh enough to stand the recoil of the 90 mm gun and we would have to re-aim after each shot. We needed to be able to fire several rounds a minute in combat and this wouldn't work.

"Let's see", said the colonel, so I fired. The first round was low and probably hit just under the foundation of the target. Before I had time to make a correction, the colonel said, "Fire again." That shot was much too high, over the target and halfway up the hill. More graphically, the tank destroyer was lifted off the ground. I didn't hear anymore about 90 mm rifles until I was out of the service, when I heard they had adapted a 90 mm to the much larger Pershing tank, about twice the size of a Sherman. So much for my value as a gunner.

The lowest job in the five man tank crew is the loader, the one who places ammunition into the breach of the gun, preparatory to firing. You need a strong back and quick reflexes; the more shells you can fire per minute, the better chance you have of staying alive.

We couldn't afford to give the Germans a second shot if they missed the first. The Tigers had a much more powerful gun and our side and rear armor was no match for this. We did have power traverse of our turret, allowing us to aim much faster than their manually operated turret. We could get three rounds off to their one and the Sherman was a faster tank. Our strategy was to fire and move, then fire from a different position. We avoided direct exchanges of fire.

Our outfit had five Sherman tanks, each with a five man crew, a 75mm gun and a 35 mm machine gun, and five smaller tanks with three man crews and one 35mm gun. These smaller tanks were much faster than a Sherman and were used as scouting vehicles to explore territory ahead of the much slower Shermans.

Our crew consisted of the tank commander, who was in charge and directed maneuvering and firing, the gunner, the driver, the assistant driver who manned the 35mm gun, and the loader. Since I had no tank training, I was the loader, the lowest job on the tank. I loaded the shell into the breach of the gun. We fired armor piercing shells, anti-personnel shells, and high explosive at the command of the tank commander.

My first action was in Germany, near Munster. We saw a German Panther tank on a hilltop. We were in a valley and in a bad position if they saw us. Our driver sought cover in a small grove of trees.

To add protection to the thin armor on the sides, Sherman crews placed two railway ties along the side and tied them to the tank with wire cables. This protection added 16 inches to the width of the tank. Our driver didn't consider that and in the grove got stuck between trees. When he applied power, the tracks dug holes and we were stuck. The solution was to cut the ties loose. As the newest, least valuable member of the crew, I was selected to take the axe and cut the cables.

I crawled out on the side away from possible German rifle or machine gun fire and cut the cable. Then I crawled around to the exposed side, expecting fire at any time, but was able to cut the cables and get back into the tank unharmed. We left in a hurry. Later in the day we exchanged fire with German tanks but they weren't Panthers.

We operated in the western part of Germany from which the German Army had withdrawn but they left their armored vehicles behind to command the roads. Their tanks were out of fuel but they could and did stop traffic as long as their ammunition held out. We captured several crews who had run out of food and ammunition. Mostly they were happy to be prisoners. I remember one German captive who said, "For me the war is over." I think most of them felt this way. This was after the battle of the bulge when the back of the German offense had been broken.

Usually at night we would find a farm house or barn to sleep in. We circled the tanks and left one man on watch at the machine gun. The rest of the crew found the warmest place we could, usually a pile of hay or straw in the barn. We had very warm overcoats that we couldn't wear in the tanks as they were so heavy they restricted our movement.

One of our crew members was called English because of his accent. He liked to stay in the tank so he frequently got his wish. He was pessimistic, often telling us that, "today is a bad day. We are going to catch a shell today. I've been through North Africa and my number is up." Or, "I hate to take you young guys with me but today is the day."

We would respond, "Shut up, English. Thank your lucky stars that we are here to protect you." He often got spooked, thinking he saw German soldiers near the tank, and started firing the machine gun. That would wake everybody up and irritated some sleepy tankers. He always insisted he had saved our livers by scaring the Germans away.

One night, after stopping in a little village, we were meeting the gasoline tanker for fuel in the town square the next morning. As we were pouring gasoline, we saw mortar fire coming in. Mortar fire is silent; you see it before you hear it. When it exploded near our tank we ran for cover in a nearby building. As we ran, I felt something hit my right arm just above the hand. I didn't stop to look until we were inside the building and then found a piece of mortar shrapnel had pierced my jacket and was lodged in my arm. The jagged piece was about five inches long and was still hot when I pulled it out. It bled profusely but luckily there was a medic with our unit and he stopped the bleeding and bandaged the wound. It pained a few days but then was OK but I received a Purple Heart for being wounded in combat.

Some soldiers said the medics carried Purple Hearts in their medical bags. That wasn't true: I didn't get mine until later in a hospital in England but they did have it on the records. Fortunately we didn't have to fire much in the next few days so the wound didn't interfere with my loading.

Each day we were given strip maps of the territory we were to cover, an area about 20 by 5 miles. One day we went too fast and went off the map, running into a German roadblock where one of their out-of-fuel tanks was waiting. The German tank blew the side off our lead tank, disabling it. Two members of the crew were injured and the Germans offered to release them to our medics if the medics would come for them.

One of our medics was a Jewish boy from Long Island named Ginsburg. He told me many times that if they captured him the Germans would kill him. He realized it was his duty to go after the wounded. He came to tell me good-by and asked me to pray for him. I told him the Germans didn't know he was Jewish and it would be OK. He spoke a little German and got along fine. The two wounded men were brought back but the Germans kept the other three and the disabled tank. We got a replacement tank in a couple days.

It had been snowy and rainy since our arrival in Germany in January. It was now late March and the snow was gone and the rain less, so we could move a little faster. We seldom moved after dark as a tank with headlights would be an attractive target. We advanced slowly to the area of Munster. This was a steel producing area that was still producing steel for the army, though it had taken a lot of bombing. Our mission was to stop traffic in and out of Munster and we were in this position for about two weeks.

We then were given a week R and R. This came about every six months for tankers. I hadn't been with them that long but I was included. We went to a small town on the Rhone River. Our squad was assigned a large, very modern house as quarters for our stay. We moved all their furniture into one bedroom and put sleeping bags on the floor of the other bedroom, the living room, and the dining room. We housed 25 men, the crews of five tanks. We were warm and dry and had a shower but we still had army "C" rations.

Our crew found a Volkswagen bus that was out of fuel. It was revived with high test tank fuel and was our transportation for a week. We got some gray paint from our motor pool and painted the bus gray with a white star, just like our tank. When we left, we towed the bus behind tank with a chain. About a mile out of town, the major commanding our battalion came on the radio, "Will the smart asses towing a Volkswagon behind their tank disconnect it immediately. That is an order. So much for our bus.

Our next assignment was to Hanover, several days away. We had to cross the Lahn River but all the bridges had been destroyed as the Germans retreated. The corps of Engineers with supporting infantry had located an area where they planned a pontoon bridge. The infantry came in on three gliders full of soldiers and cleared the area on both sides of the river. They worked during the day and had no German planes bomb them. Each night we would parade the tanks to the embarkation point with headlights on and then turn off the lights and go into the woods. One night some planes dropped bombs in the river where they assumed the bridge was. After three nights, we skipped a night then the next night crossed the completed pontoon bridge with lights off. Our tank was one of the first to cross. The Germans dropped a few bombs before all twenty tanks had crossed but no one was hit.

The next day was Easter Sunday. In the afternoon we were lead tank for five Shermans when we saw shells exploding ahead. The first was half a mile off, the second a quarter mile and our driver immediately went off the road into an apple orchard. We had no warning to secure the gun that extended 10 feet ahead. The turret where I was sitting was whipped around, throwing me out of my seat against the gun, breaking my left elbow. I was incapacitated so they put me in the assistant driver's seat where I could fire the machine gun. I couldn't load it so they stopped occasionally to reload the gun.

That night we found a medic but they didn't do much unless you were bleeding. My arm was very swollen and the jacket sleeve too tight. The medic cut the seam of the sleeve and gave me two pain pills.

The next morning we were traveling a country road when we started to get rifle fire. That meant a bazooka could reach us that would pierce our side armor. Our gunner said the fire was coming from hay stacks we were passing so I turned my machine gun on them at waist high level. Germans came flying out of the hay stacks, running in all directions. It was hilarious. We didn't try to hit them but just laughed.

That evening we caught up to a medical unit with a doctor. He took one look at my arm, badly swollen and turning green, and said, "Sergeant, for you the war is over. You have a million dollar wound."

I was sent to a field hospital in the auditorium of a high school. Cots had replace the seats and the stage was the operating room. The lights burned all night as they were receiving wounded from the battlefields. The third day I was sent to England to a military hospital outside Oxford, where therapy started. I had my arm in a sling but could get around OK. After morning therapy I was free for the rest of the day. Supply trucks made two or more trips to Oxford for supplies. I was able to get the 10AM truck into town and return on the last run, about 3 PM.

Oxford was a beautiful town and I was interested in the colleges, which served as a model for Pomona College. Easter break came while I was there and many students stayed on campus. The dining halls were open and I was invited to lunch on several occasions. The students were too young for military service and were interested in America. I was 33 and almost a father figure to them. When classes returned after Easter, the invitations ceased but I visited there and the town of Oxford many times. There was one older hotel that served good food and I went there with other soldiers for lunch.

Years later my wife and I visited Oxford and I was looking for the hotel and couldn't find it. I asked a young policeman the location of the Stag Hotel. He didn't know it and asked when I had been there. I told him 1945 and he replied, "I hadn't been born then. Could you mean the Anglers?" It was the Anglers and the food was still good.

While I was in England, VE day, the end of the war in Europe, occurred. Shortly thereafter I was sent home on a hospital ship, a Converted Kaiser ship, far from the elegance of the Queen Mary. We avoided the shipping lanes as there were still a few German subs that hadn't surrendered. It took 14 days from Southhampton to Charleston, South Carolina. I had asked to be sent to a hospital in Vancouver, Washington, near my wife and son. The Army seemed never to grant a first choice but sent me to Spokane, only 40 miles from Spirit Lake, Idaho where my mother in law lived.

Therapy continued and my strength improved. I found a public golf course in Spokane that made no charge to invalids during the week. This was good therapy also and in about two months I was given 30 days sick leave. My wife still had our car so we drove to California to visit my family. While there, the war with Japan ended. I returned to the hospital and was medically discharged in November 1945 with four years and four months service. The officer presenting me with my discharge asked if I would like to reenlist. I declined.

RETURN TO GERMANY

Walter Lehman

I grew up in Augsburg, a city that was founded by Roman legions in 15 BC. Early in 1938 the family moved to Munich where my parents took over a restaurant. In spring of 1939 I was called for a physical by the Wehrmacht. I had been through all the examinations and got to the last stop where the physician said: "This must be a mistake. It says you are Jewish."

"No, it's true." I replied.

"In that case we can't use you but thanks for coming in."

Later encounters with the Wehrmacht proved much less cordial; of course by then I was working for General Patton.

Later in 1938 there was a historic unpleasantness that became known as Kristallnacht because the streets were covered with broken glass. My parents' restaurant and home was totally destroyed. We left the neighborhood and went to a park along the river Isar where we spent the night walking. The next day the Gestapo came to make arrests but fortunately could not find us. We spent over a week at the home of friends, going for that walk every night. By the time we returned home, the arrests were over but the place was no longer livable.

We decided we must leave Germany ASAP and made arrangements to obtain immigration visas to Colombia with the help of relatives who already lived there. We made reservations on a German cruise ship that was to sail from Hamburg on August 31. On September 1 the war in Poland started and the sailing was cancelled. No other passages were available from Hamburg.

Eventually, with the help of 3 pounds of black market coffee my father obtained fake reservations from Genoa to Buenventura on the Pacific coast of Colombia. Even though fake those reservations enabled us to obtain transit visas for Italy and Panama.

Once in (still neutral) Italy my father contacted a cousin in London who bought the tickets. We now had valid reservations and in October we finally departed from Europe on the Italian liner Conte Grande.

The voyage across the Atlantic and through the Panama Canal was uneventful. The 24-hour trip from the Pacific coast across the Andes Mountains on a narrow gage train to Cali was interrupted by two landslides. The following year we stayed in Cali where I worked for an electrician. The call from the U.S. consul informing us that the visa were available was most welcome.

Back we went on the little train to the Pacific where we boarded a Swedish vessel to Panama City and on to New York.

We settled in an area near the north end of Manhattan called Washington Heights. There were so many refugees from Germany that it was also called the fourth Reich. I started learning English and found a job as an electrician. In 1942, unhappy with my job, I decided to enlist in the Army. The recruiting office informed that as non-citizen I couldn't enlist but could be drafted. The local draft board was very obliging and a few weeks later I received my draft notice.

I reported to Ft. Dix, New Jersey, where tests and vaccinations were administered and uniforms were issued. A troop train took us to Fort McClellan, Alabama for basic infantry training. That was a miserable place to train. In the morning the ground was be frozen and we were shivering. By noon the frozen mud melted and we were perspiring and anticipating another evening of cleaning uniforms and shining shoes. There was little time off and not much chance at leave.

In May, basic training completed, I was sent to Fort Meade, Maryland where the 76th Infantry had recently been organized. Because of my relatively high IQ test scores and my electricians experience, I was sent to the 301st Engineer Combat Battalion, a unit of the 76th Infantry Division. Training with the engineers, we learned to build bridges and roads, make maps, set up the water supplies, plant and remove land mines (sheer misery) and to dynamite structures (clean fun). We did frequent hikes with full field packs and rifles: 5 miles in one hour or 10 miles in two hours.

One day I saw an announcement on a bulletin board of a radio course with the Armed Forces Institute "ask your commanding officer" it said. I went to see the CO and asked and he said, "We just received orders to send three men to radio school. You are one of them." I went to radio school for several months and returned to find there were no radios in the battalion. Back I went to roads and bridges until the radios began to arrive. More radio operators were assigned to the battalion and I was put in charge of the section. We were also expected to establish and maintain telephone communications.

The division was now brought to full strength with recent draftees. We built roads, bridges and minefields in Maryland and at camp AP Hill, Virginia for much of 1943. In Virginia we slept in pyramidal tents and ate "al fresco". The country was swampy, densely overgrown and populated by rattlesnakes, copperheads and of course mosquitoes. The training was to prepare us to fight in the jungle. In October we received orders to pack and report to the railroad siding. Our destination was classified. A friendly bartender claimed to know that it was Wisconsin. After two days on the train we unloaded at Camp McCoy in Wisconsin. The fall of 1943 was filled with more roads and bridges, fortunately in cooler, drier climate. About one half of the officers received orders to report to replacement depots in various oversee locations. Officers fresh out of OCS and new recruits soon filled the vacancies. In early January the entire division was packed in trucks and convoyed through northern Wisconsin to the upper peninsula of Michigan. We started arctic training. We were issued down sleeping bags, mountain packs and tents, and tracked vehicles for use in deep snow. Conventional vehicles were winterized.

Fortunately it wasn't a very severe winter and we were able to use our trucks and didn't have to hike in snowshoes. A base camp consisting of log shelters was constructed by the engineer battalion, initially for its own use and later used by other units after we returned to Wisconsin. The major excitement was a fire that burned one of the shelters. It started when gasoline was used to light a wood stove. In the spring I was assigned to simulate artillery. This meant throwing firecrackers at practicing troops. One caught in my overcoat and went off two inches from my ear. The ringing lasted over a week. At this time once again half of the division was sent oversees as replacements. The division was brought up to strength with draftees and men who had been assigned to ASTP college training. Some of these had had engineering training or other technical courses and were very useful in communications.

In the summer, D-day came and went and we were still in Wisconsin. Almost monthly we were placed on alert for shipping out but the alerts were always cancelled. Finally with another alert pending, our favorite bartender said, "This one is for real. You are going to Boston."

Sure enough, we spent several days on the train and found ourselves at Camp Miles Standish near Boston. This was an embarkation camp, largely manned by German prisoners of war. They were very helpful and dispensed lots of good food. They would say, "Go on over and finish it so we can go home."

On the last day in camp we were given a sack supper and marched to the train. The train rolled about two hours and went to a pier where the troop ship USS General Richardson was docked. This was a brand new army transport operated by the US Coast Guard. Just before we went up the gangplank Red Cross ladies handed everyone coffee and donuts. Into the belly of the beast we went. I went down and down to a berthing compartment. Then I went up and up to the topmost of five bunks. Above my head was an I-beam that supported the deck above. I sat up quickly only once. The resulting collision with several tons of steel trained me to move more slowly.

After we went to bed, the loud speaker announced, "Chow down in the galley." We all went and ate hot dogs. Someone said that there would be a sick bunch but I didn't think the ship would sail for hours. I awoke at midnight and we were at sea. I remained seasick for several days unable to eat or drink. The liberation of France was completed while we were at sea and we thought the war would be over before we could join in.

Meanwhile in Plymouth a V-2 rocket had destroyed our destination dock and the ship was rerouted to Southampton. The fog kept us from docking for two days. At this time we heard about a big battle on the Belgian border. On landing we went to Christchurch Barracks in Bournemouth. These were very ancient barracks with all the class distinctions of the old British Army (special latrines for officers, sergeants, corporals etc.) I had one pass to London where I was able to visit the cousin who had helped finance our escape to South America.

In England we built a Bailey bridge for practice. Bailey bridges were built from prefabricated materials like huge erector sets. They had Mr. Bailey, the inventor, come and check our bridge. He liked what he saw. We had been trained to do it rapidly and well, even blindfolded so we could build at night.

A 4-wheel drive Dodge weapons carriers served as company command car. The radios were mounted in the back of the vehicle and my place was with the radios. When the driver was tired it was my turn to drive. By then I was a sergeant. The Captain wanted me in his vehicle as I spoke German. We drove the trucks onto an LST (landing ship, tank) named Normandy. The trucks were chained down on deck and the troops sent down to a squad room. LSTs are flat-bottomed vessels and pitch terribly in heavy seas. Soon most of the troops were seasick and the smell was terrible so I went on deck to sleep in the truck. Two crewmen came around to check the vehicles. They looked at mine and said, "This one is too loose. I wouldn't be surprised if it went over the side." After they left I tightened the tie-downs with a wrench until the tires were nearly flattened.

We spent the night on the English Channel and landed at Le Havre midday. We drove the trucks off the ship and never stopped until evening. I was assigned to find wine and women. With my high school French I was lucky to find wine. We kept rolling each day and part of the night, by-passing Paris and on into Belgium where we began to hear artillery. We stopped at a small town called Biwer in Luxembourg. Here we were billeted in a basement that had been a wine cellar. Germans had shot holes in all the barrels before leaving and the wine was all gone. Although it was never tried in Nuremberg this must qualify as a major war crime.

Next we proceeded to Echternach on the river Sauer that is the German-Luxembourg border. Radio silence was ordered to not disclose how many units were approaching. The division was assigned to Patton's Third Army to guard the border. There were many pillboxes on both sides of the river. We had taken many of them but snipers infiltrated during the night and to hide in the pillboxes and make life dangerous when day came. The Navy sent armor plate that was used to bullet-proof a bull dozer and to seal the pillboxes by welding plates over the openings. This worked well and our patrols started going across the river into Germany and sealing pillboxes all over our sector of the Siegfried Line.

Once across the river we received orders to proceed east. There was continuous movement and flux. Contact with headquarters was frequently lost and re-established. The Germans dynamited the roads and we built bridges across the craters. Our bridging equipment traveled near the front of the advancing columns. The Germans kept theirs at the rear. If we blew a bridge, their tanks would back up in a traffic jam and the bridging groups couldn't reach the site. This was a factor in the outcome of the battle of the bulge.

We were sufficiently far ahead of the air bases that our planes had to return about one hour before dark. Around dinnertime, when our planes were gone, Luftwaffe planes from nearby airports would strafe our locations. We shot one of them down with a truck-mounted 50-caliber machine gun.

I was kept busy on the radio, reporting roadblocks and calling bridge platoons to the road craters. At one time the first platoon had a mission to build a footbridge across a river. The far side was reported cleared of enemy forces. When the bridge detail arrived there was an unfriendly reception by SS troops. A vigorous dose of US artillery persuaded them to withdraw farther into their fatherland and the bridge was soon completed.

Toward the end of March the Wehrmacht began to lose control of its units. This resulted in thousands of POW's, many searching for food and shelter. There was no need to guard them. We collected their weapons and sent them to the rear.

During the last few days of the war the battalion executive officer and our company commander, while pursuing a reconnaissance mission in their jeeps, were stopped by a small SS unit. The exec asked: "don't they know the war is over?" and walked toward them to persuade them to surrender. They shot and killed him. His driver, an outstanding marksman, returned fire and killed a number of them. Out of ammunition, the survivors attempted to surrender. He waited until they came closer and then mowed them all down. None survived.

We continued into East Germany and stayed in a small town called Krimmitschau for weeks. The war wasn't officially over but the fighting had ended. We were told to see about SS formations between our lines and the Russians. I later heard there really weren't any SS but our function was to make sure the Russians didn't surprise us. We were ordered to stop at the river Elbe. That is the river that after crossing Germany flows into the North Sea at Hamburg. Several of us crossed the river on the maintenance pathway on top of a pipeline and tried to converse with Russian soldiers on the far side. Conversation was difficult and mostly in German. Hershey bars were immediately recognized and most welcome.

One morning in May at 2 AM we were ordered to pack up and leave town no later than six A.M. as the Russians would take over. This seriously distressed the Germans living in the area.

We then moved south and west and crossed from what was to become East Germany into Bavaria at the village of Hof. The company was housed in an old castle and the communications section was assigned a room on the top floor of the tower in order to get better radio contact. It was too good to last and on we went to Weiden, a small city where there was a good Wehrmacht barracks large enough for the entire regiment. Across the street was a camp that held 10,000 SS POW's. I went in with our commanding officer and found the cooks and instruct them to cook all the pork to prevent infections. In Germany all pork was inspected for trichinosis at the slaughter house and only meat which passed could enter commercial channels. Communications were important as we had only two battalions and the headquarters to control some 10,000 SS prisoners. The concerns proved unfounded as interrogators had already removed potentially dangerous elements. Soon we hired the SS as valets; uniforms and barracks soon looked better than ever. The pay: one Hershey bar a day. They did an excellent job as they were eating better than they had in years.

The battalion exec had found some Luftwaffe recreational radios but they needed tubes. I was assigned a jeep and driver and went south to Augsburg and Munich searching for tubes. I didn't find any but was able to find some old friends. I went to my grandparents' home and was told that they had been taken to the camps. I had a haircut in a barbershop across the street from my old family home. They still knew how I wanted it cut. On we drove to Munich for the tubes. We stayed in a lovely hotel with the best lodging and food I'd had since joining the Army. Tubes were not to be had for cigarettes, Hershey bars, or even money. I inherited one of the radios, shipped it home and modified it for American tubes after returning home.

After the war's official end I was able to go on a recreational tour to the mountains. In Garmisch I saw a Broadway show, Rosalinda, (Die Fledermaus) that my parents had taken me to in New York on my last leave before going overseas. We went on to Berchtesgaden and Hitler's Eagle's Nest. Here I was able to see Goering's double sized bathtub.

Soon the 76th infantry division was disbanding and I was sent to an engineer unit at Regensburg. The mission was to repair the 1000 years old masonry arch bridge over the Danube. The SS had dynamited one of the arches during their last night in town. We constructed a Bailey bridge across the gap, high enough above the original bridge to enable the local stonemasons to restore the bridge while traffic crossed over the Bailey span. The rest of 1945 passed and I returned to New York about Christmas. The trip wasn't as rough as the trip over. I was soon sent to Ft. Dix and discharged.

WITH PRISONERS OF WAR
Thomas Burdick

I took the Pacific Electric "red car" from Pasadena to the Induction Center in Los Angeles on January 7,1943 as a 19 year old draftee in World War II. A short time later, I drew my olive drab private's uniform from Fort MacArthur, San Pedro, and thought, "This Army is a cinch. You are issued your clothing and then get a liberty pass the same day." Little did I realize that I would not get home again until I was honorably discharged at the same place two and three-quarter years later after serving in North Africa, Sicily, and Italy. Surprisingly, the same could almost have been said two years earlier when I was an enrollee at the Civilian Conservation Corps camp in Cucamonga. Never could I have dreamed that I might have a connection with Italian prisoners who were fortunate enough to be shipped to the same physical facility for confinement. Incidentally, the camp and barracks have long since disappeared, the ultimate victims of that great Southern California scourge, houses, houses, and more houses.

I completed my basic training at Florence Internment Camp, Florence, Arizona and immediately requested a transfer to the Army Air Corps after having had visions of becoming a tail gunner on a bomber. I was transferred all right but to the 379th Military Police Escort Guard Company, understaffed but rumored to be going overseas. We landed in Oran, Algeria, two days before the Africa campaign was officially over, marched seven miles to a staging area, and awaited further orders. Nobody had ever heard of us! We later learned we should have gone to Casablanca.

The next day we marched back to the port and boarded a ship completely ringed with barbed wire. "We're going to 'escort' Italian prisoners of war back to the States" was the joyful hue and cry. Wrong! The next day it was back to the staging area and to Chanzy, 76 miles inland on the slowest train I have ever encountered. From this base or returning to it, we crammed prisoners from various points of North Africa into "40 and 8" freight cars of World War I vintage. We rode on top and surrounded the cars when the train stopped. Nobody ever tried to escape; not even members of the proud German Afrika Korps who, although captured, proclaimed Germany would still win the war. This was our major activity throughout our stay in Sicily and Italy although the mode of transportation varied from foot to truck. We were to be deployed to the Pacific after receiving a furlough in the States-all, of course, obliterated by the A-bomb.

The episode just recorded wasn't my first experience with that most famous military cliche, "Snafu." That actually occurred at Fort MacArthur when I tried to volunteer for what we were led to believe would be a "cushy" job. It happened at 5:30 a.m. I was in the middle of three rows of at least 100 men each when the "officer in charge," a young private first class, commanded, "All those who can type, step forward." I nearly died in the crush of bodies. Obviously, I wasn't picked. But we met the seven who made the grade a short time later on KP duty, ladling out breakfast to those of us in the chow line. I did, however, learn well my first lesson in the Army: never volunteer.

I'll always remember those stirring words, "Be ruthless, be violent." of the commanding general, Lucian K . Truscott, of the reinforced Third Infantry Division on the eve of our invasion of Sicily from our staging area in Bizerte. We landed on D-day, H-5 hours on "Blue Beach". Several days later our "second" barrack's bag was delivered first; the essential one (containing my future Pulitzer prize-winning diary) never made it, lost forever in the shuffle. The front moved rapidly; so fast that the 379th occasionally got ahead of the infantry and tanks from whom we were supposed to accept prisoners.

I had a miss and a hit with 7th Army Commanding General George S. Patton. The miss was arriving at the field hospital where earlier he had slapped a battle-fatigued GI and the hit when Patton's jeep driver, on this occasion a colonel, came to a cross-road, stopped, got out, seeking directions for a certain outfit. Unbeknownst to either of them, the area was under shell fire and a buddy of mine and I were taking cover in a ditch where we could oversee the situation in semi-protection. I jumped up, told the colonel what he needed to know, and saw the jeep with the general's stars and Patton some yards behind. My uniform was in total disarray-pants out of their leggings, etc. The colonel "on the double" got into the vehicle, whirled around, and went back from whence he had come. I thanked the Creator profusely that Patton, a notorious stickler for proper dress, had not had the opportunity at close range to chew me out for my sloppy appearance.

The Italian campaign for me was punctuated by three occasions: first, viewing from the badly demolished village, the U.S. bombing of the abbey on Monte Cassino. Second, being in the packed Piazza Venezia in Rome on June 5, 1944 and third, passing by the gas station in Milan where Mussolini and his mistress Clara Petace were strung up by Italian partisans after being captured from the Germans. Only the second is worthy of elaboration. Rome fell to Mark Clark's 5th Army on June 4. Some of the 379th were in the piazza the next day when an American colonel of Italian descent came out on Mussolini's famed balcony to give the huge throng a news brief. All I could detect was the word "Invazione," (of France) when a youthful signorina gave me resounding hugs and kisses which other GI's likewise received. Vicariously, we were all heroes. It capped my military career-even more important than the one promotion I received.

That was my advancement to the rank of private first class by an Act of Congress. If one hadn't earned the honor by his own skill and daring after so many months, the government automatically gave him the raise.

Whenever there was something that needed to be done and there weren't assigned personnel around to do it, the MPs got the job; such as picking up the dead after a skirmish, directing traffic, or unloading arms and ammunition from landing craft, some times under enemy fire. Which reminds me of a final quip - MP unloading ammo (to a commissioned officer):

"What do we do if a bomb hits?"

Officer: "Stick your hand up your rear like the rest of us do."

Being a youthful MP wasn't all fun and games as one might think despite our First Sergeant, Charles Daugherty telling us, "You young punks don't realize it but you're having the adventure of your lives."

"Baloney," we replied to the guy we called the "old man". He was 30. But it had to be a whole lot better than the life endured by MP's in Iraq 59 years later. Most of the Italians, the French, even the Germans wanted to be liberated. Many of the Iraqis obviously didn't.

A RIFLE SQUAD REPLACEMENT
Bob Nairne

I was one of many future ASTP (Army Specialized Training Program) students attending Cal Berkeley who, upon the closure of that program, were called to active duty and sent to serve elsewhere, usually in the Infantry. I reported to the Presidio of Monterey and along with four other rookies was sent to Fort McClelland in Alabama. Why only five of us were dispatched to Alabama remains a mystery. Upon arrival we all went through Basic Training.

Following a short furlough, orders took me to Fort Meade, Maryland with the understanding that from there I would attend a cadre school. Approximately four confusing weeks later, while boarding an ocean going vessel, the Marine Devil, the realization came that cadre school was no longer in my future.

The convoy split somewhere in the Atlantic Ocean and my section entered the Mediterranean Sea and docked at Marseilles, France. That rainy night was spent in pup tents on a hill near an airfield. The next morning we were flown, (C-47's) to a metallic airstrip outside Nancy, France. At dusk trucks pick us up for a night long, stop and go, trip to what turned out to be Dickweiler, Luxembourgh. Dickweiler is a small town near Echternach and the Sure (Sauer) River.

I was joining the 2nd Platoon of E. Company, 2nd Battalion, 22nd Infantry Regiment of the 4th Infantry Division. The 4th had a proud WW2 history from being the first division to land on Utah Beach on D-Day, the St. Lo breakthrough and so forth. The 4th was suppose to be in a semi-safe area after being chewed up in the Hurtgen Forest. The word was that E Company was down to 63 men and badly needed replacements. I was interviewed in a dugout, assigned to the 1st squad and given a BAR (Browning Automatic Rifle). BAR's were familiar to me but I couldn't remember if I had ever fired one or just witnessed a demonstration. On the job learning.

It was mid December and the Bulge was beginning. We were on the southern flank of the main German thrust. My first stint in a fox hole occurred that night. I was escorted out to a hole on a snow covered hill overlooking Dickweiler and told "If they come, they'll come from that direction". It was very cold and I was scared and trying to come to grips with the situation. How did I get here?

The next day or two an order came down, "There will be no retrograde action in this sector". As soon as we learned what "retrograde" meant we realized we were committed to our present positions. German tanks and infantry attacked our area. The tanks got through; we stopped the infantry and the tanks never returned. The remainder of December was spent in defensive positions with almost daily combat-reconnaissance patrols; once across the Sure (Sauer) River in canvas boats.

In January new objectives were assigned and the long, dirty, dangerous job of pushing back the Bulge began. We'd go on patrols to probe the German positions. When fire was received a plan would be devised and a solution to the problem attempted; not always successfully. Casualties were common. In the infantry of the day there was no rotation; you were there until you were killed, wounded or became sick. Once mended or cured, you returned.

In late January orders were received to begin an advance through the Eifel-Ardennes area with the taking of Prum, Germany the primary objective. We were trucked around, Wiltz, Bastogne, Houffalize, Trois Verges and St Vith; all towns that received the bulk of the German December offensive. It was raining, some snow was melting and bodies of earlier combatants, both sides, were being discovered everywhere. Dead animal parts, especially horses, began to smell but then so did we.

In early February we attacked and took Sellerich, Brandescheid, Obermehlein, Neidermehlein and Prum. These were all fortified towns of the Siegfried Line.

A NOTE-Over a number of years, in the 1970's, I obtained copies of documents, daily reports, maps, overlays, etc. on my area and time of the war. My primary source was the Military Field Branch of the Military Narrative Division in Maryland. These documents have enabled me to put names to places and objectives I otherwise wouldn't have known. They were of great value in helping me remember my daily position. During the war much of my time was spent in a hole with my head down.

Below, in Italics, is an example of a 22nd Infantry Regiment (Combat Team 22) daily report.

Feb. 7, 1945-Combat Team 22 continued the attack toward PRUM on 7 February with the 1st and 2nd Battalions abreast. (2nd Battalion on the left.) A platoon-size combat patrol of Company E moved out at 0400 hours to take Objective 11. The remainder of the Company followed and the hill was secured at 0830 hours. Company G bypassed Objective 11 to the north and after eliminating machinegun and small arms resistance, captured OBERMEHLEN at 1400 hours. Enemy counterattacks prevented further 2nd Battalion progress. Company E, on Objective 11, was hit by a tank-infantry counterattack from the direction of NEIDERMEHLEN at 1430 hours and the company withdrew from the hill.

Below, an example of a battle summation.

February 4 thru 12, 1945-In the nine days of offensive action---4 through 12 February---Combat Team 22 had advanced approximately 10,000 yards through the SCHNEE-EIFEL (Ardennes). This offensive action includes cracking the SIEGFRIED LINE, taking BRANDSCHEID, and moving over extremely rugged terrain to seize the EIFEL strong point of PRUM. Adverse weather conditions prevailed throughout the period; there was either snow or rain and sometimes both each day and roads, either icy or muddy were heavily mined. Initial enemy resistance was from the 326th and 340th Volksgrenadier Division and the 108 2nd Security Battalion. However, after the SIEGFRIED LINE had been breached the 2nd Panzer Division was rushed to this sector on February 7th and 8th. In the hard fight for NIEDERMEHLEN on February 9th, our 2nd and 3rd Battalions destroyed their 1st Battalion, 304 Panzer Grenadier Regiment of the 2nd Panzer Division. The Combat Team took 1,273 prisoners during these operations and approximately 150 Siegfried Pillboxes and Bunkers were reduced.

After Prum was secured we rested for ten days, refitted and received replacements. A soldier named Borachas was assigned as my ammo bearer, a 3rd such replacement. In addition to his own arms he also carried additional clips for the BAR. Not a popular position.

On the morning of March 1 we attacked across the Prum River; the river was little more than a trickle that was spanned by 2X8 wooden planks. We went up the ridge and cleared the woods that faced a farm field containing a fortified House/Barn on a knoll. A lieutenant led in this action. This was only the second time in my approximately 75 on line days that we were led in action by a commissioned officer. Early on that day he was shot in the elbow and retired to an aid station but while he was with us he led from the front.

The plan to take the fortified position on the knoll was as follows. The 1st Platoon would go around to the woods on the right and give covering fire and the 2nd Platoon, using marching fire, would head directly at the objective. When we reach a small rise in the field the 1st Platoon would cease firing and we would rush forward. This was not an uncommon maneuver but usually the defenders would retreat to another preordained position. This time the enemy was not in the fortified House/Barn but dug in approximately 25 yards to its right.

Anyway, we reached the small rise and the next thing I knew I was on my back. I'd been shot through my left hand which had held the stock of the BAR, and either that bullet or another hit the BAR's clip, which exploded doing damage to my right hand. There was blood and bones were exposed in my right hand up to the wrist but I could still move my fingers. Barochas (sp), my ammo bearer on my right, had been hit in the head and was dead. On my left, a rifleman named Hartman, was calmly returning fire. My BAR was a mess so I wrapped up my right hand in a triangular bandage, stayed low, and began to realize that if I could make it through the remainder of the day and that night my chances of an adult life were greatly improved. We spent an alert, watchful night in the house/barn.

Another 22nd Infantry report that pertains to the above action.

March 1, 1945--Combat Team 22 had forced the crossing of the Prum River; seized a bridgehead that includes the high ground at coordinates (082805 and

(084814) and had partially seized the high ground east of PRUM. The enemy, elements of the crack German 5th Parachute Division had been stubborn to the point of fanaticism; and enemy pockets still remained in the woods southeast of PRUM. The Combat Team sustained moderate casualties.

Ours was only a small part of the above action but of the 16 to 18 men who started across that field, 3 were killed and 6 wounded. More than moderate casualties to us.

The following day I went back, walking wounded, to an aid station and then an evacuation hospital where the first operation took place. A month was spent in a hospital near Orly and Paris and I was then flown to a hospital in England for another month. That hospital was located quite close to Torquay, an interesting area.

While in the latter hospital I received the Purple Heart as did most of the people in the ward. For the presentation ceremony those of us who could stand were told to come to attention, in our pajamas, and salute. Those who couldn't achieve an upright stance were told to assume a prone position of attention; I don't remember if they saluted. Those with busted up bodies that didn't allow them much of anything had their awkward angles hidden with sheets. I was embarrassed by this, still am, and wonder whose feelings were being protected. YA GOTTA LUV THE ARMY !

I was on my way back to my outfit and in LaHarve, France when the war in Europe ended. I rejoined my Company in Dinkelbuhl, Germany, a thousand year old walled town now on Germany's Romantic Road. Nearby was a huge DP (displaced persons) camp. We were not to remain in Dinkelbuhl long.

The 4th Infantry Division, an assault division, was among the first half dozen divisions to be returned to the States. It didn't take a military genius to realize that we were slated for the invasion of mainland Japan so when the atomic bombs were dropped I, for one, was thankful.

My military career ended when I was discharged at Beale Air Force Base near Sacramento.

Observations

Over the years I've read many accounts of the war that contained uncomplimentary comments about replacements. During my time, mid December 1944 to March 1, 1945, and in the 4th Division replacements were the only ones doing all the actual fighting. I never met anyone who knew anyone who knew anyone, in a line rifle company, who had landed on D-Day. They were all gone; dead, wounded, sick or promoted out. Experienced divisions, at the rifle company level, were entirely manned by replacements and we still won the war. Combat survival, in my experience and at my level, was much more dependent on dumb luck than on training or skill.

AN INFANTRYMAN IN EUROPE
Bill Arce

The attack on Pearl Harbor was tough on our family. My father was born and raised in Honolulu near Hickham Field and had not returned to Hawaii since going to sea at age 16. Every Sunday night we listened to "Hawaii Calls" on the radio. It was broadcast from the back of the Ala Moana Hotel and you could hear the waves crashing on Waikiki Beach. December 7, 1941 changed all that. "Hawaii Calls" came on for only a few minutes and then signed off "for the duration." I'll never forget the tears in my Dad's eyes as he thought of family and boyhood friends, not knowing if they were OK.

As a junior in Oakland High School in Oakland, California my buddies and I tried to enlist in the marines to fight the people who had attacked us, only to be told to come back after graduating. We did but I didn't pass the physical. I found out for the first time that I was color blind and had a heart murmur. My attempt to enlist in the Air Corps failed for the same reasons. I was also told that a hammer toe operation I had undergone when I was 14 also caused my rejection. I had been a starter in baseball for three years, played football and had not been rejected by the marines for this condition but the Air Corps couldn't accept the foot problem. That was my first realization that the military could act in strange ways.

I decided to ask the draft board to call up my number so that I could find out if I could pass the army physical. I did pass it so I asked if I could volunteer to join the paratroops. I was told yes and within a few weeks I was sent to jump school at Ft. Benning, Georgia. The first day there, during the physical exam, the doctor took one look at my foot and washed me out. I was told that I was transferred to the Army special training command which sounded to me like some specialist combat unit. When I joined the unit that was starting training in another area of Ft. Benning, I discovered that on completion of basic training we would be sent to colleges to become engineers, doctors or other specialized duty. Although this was not what I wanted, it seemed to be what the Army wanted. About three weeks before our training was to end, we were notified to which college we would be assigned. I was to be shipped to Pomona College but I never got there.

Heavy infantry casualties resulted in non-coms, machine gunners, BAR teams, and mortar men being pulled out of the 94th infantry division and sent as replacements to Europe. The remaining privates, some of whom had not finished high school became non-coms and the college bound ASTP students became low men on the totem pole. We soon learned that "Please pass the butter" didn't mean a thing. It had to be "Pass the bleeping butter". I was assigned to Company D, 1st Battalion of the 376th Infantry Regiment of the 94th Division, training at Camp McCain, Mississippi. This was a heavy weapons company in which I became the #1 gunner in a water cooled machine gun squad. I got to carry the 51 pound tripod over my shoulders while the #2 gunner carried the gun. The other three squad members carried ammunition. After an abbreviated period of heavy training, we entrained to Camp Shanks, New York for shipment to Europe.

I anticipated sailing in a convoy protected by many Navy vessels as shown in newsreels at the movies but such was not the case. Our entire division plus a hospital unit took about 20 hours to board the biggest cruise ship in the world, the Queen Elizabeth. We were told there were about 19000 of us on board and there was no convoy! The ship was so fast that by changing direction every few minutes no sub could get a sight on it fast enough to torpedo it. We disembarked onto barges in Loch Ness, Scotland and went by train to the south of England. About two weeks later we crossed the channel, landing on Utah Beach almost 3 months after D-day but not too late to do battle.

To this day, I thank God I didn't have to land on Utah Beach on D-day. How anyone survived that hellish ordeal is hard to understand. By the time we landed, Patton's third Army, which we were joining, had broken through at St. Lo and liberated most of Normandy and Brittany plus Paris. We assumed combat positions on the Brittany peninsula near Nantes and were to proceed west to capture the submarine bases at St. Nazaire and L'Orient. This combat involved what was referred to as hedgerow fighting. These old hedges had dirt bases from centuries of wind blowing the dirt onto them and they lined the fields. We put our gun behind the hedge mound or if it was real high, we dug a tunnel through to fire it. In both cases we were protected from small arms fire, unlike the riflemen who were exposed as they left one hedgerow to attack the next one. We gave them covering fire but many of them didn't make it. I remember how sorry we felt for them while they felt sorry for us because we drew heavy artillery and mortar fire. Maybe we kept sane by feeling sorry for the other guy. Hedgerow fighting was very tough combat, taking a high toll of infantry, especially riflemen.

As we advanced out of the Brittany Peninsula, the Germans became more and more condensed. They began using anti-aircraft machine guns as flat trajectory weapons. These weapons were four machine guns fired by a single trigger and they had devastating results on us. Some high-ranking officer made the wise decision to stop our advance and dig into very strong defensive positions. By doing so, we penned about 400,000 Germans against the ocean. It didn't make sense for them to attack to break out because by now the main German forces had been pushed back almost to their border. As a result, combat action was reduced considerably and the casualty rate went way down from where it had been. I've been told that newspapers referred to this as "the phoney war". It wasn't phoney to those men who were killed or wounded during the shelling or combat patrols that still took place. One of our ammo bearers is buried at the Brittany cemetery not far from where he was hit.

Unfortunately we didn't get to stay in this "phoney" war. We were replaced by the 66th division and traveled by jeeps and trucks to catch up with Patton's army near the Saar and Moselle Rivers triangle. This happened to be the deepest part of the Seigfried line. We resumed combat action just across the Moselle River. Our machine gun was used to give riflemen cover fire as they attacked across fields and orchards, approached towns, advanced down streets, worked their way through rows of "tiger teeth" and attacked pillboxes. Firing into the aperture of a pillbox got us plenty of return fire from their machine guns. It was important for us to keep firing until one or more riflemen could get close enough to throw hand grenades through the aperture to eliminate firing from the pillbox. Needless to say, we attracted lots of small arms fire as well as mortar and artillery fire. I only recall two occasions when German infantry were close enough to lob hand grenades at us. Thank goodness they used concussion grenades instead of shrapnel grenades as we did. This combat action continued until the battle of the bulge. Here that action is described in the unit citation we received.

HEADQUARTERS 94TH INFANTRY DIVISION, U. S. ARMY
26 September, 1945
UNIT CITATION
Under the provisions of Section IV, Circular 333, War Department, 22 December 1943, the 1st Battalion, 376th Infantry Regiment is cited for extraordinary heroism and outstanding performance of duty in action in Germany, during the period 14 January 1945 to 18 January 1945. The 1st Battalion, 376th Infantry Regiment was ordered to capture the towns of Tettingen and Butzdorf and thereby breach the Siegfried Line of fortifications protecting the Saar-Moselle Triangle. Employing lightning like tactics and surprise, the objectives were captured with light casualties and strong defenses were set up. At approximately 0300 on 15 January, the enemy launched the first of a series of counterattacks when 400 enemy infantrymen swarmed down the hills and surrounded the towns in a desperate effort to regain the vital ground. The Germans were driven back after sustaining staggering casualties. Seven more determined attacks by numerically superior forces were repulsed in a like manner. Carrying parties braved intense artillery, mortar and sniper fire to bring up ammunition and medical supplies. To deceive the enemy as to the true strength of our forces, the gallant defenders maneuvered rapidly from house to house through holes blasted in the sides of buildings with satchel charges and bazookas all the time directing heavy fire upon the Germans. At one time, 35 enemy tanks were counted in the streets of the two towns, but the men of the 1st Battalion, disregarding point blank fire from the tanks and despite these overwhelming odds, courageously resisted and repelled every attack. In spite of heavy casualties and the fact that the men occupied front line positions for five days without sleep, they bitterly contested every foot of ground, tenaciously held the positions, killed approximately 850 Germans, captured 150, destroyed 8 tanks and 11 half tracks. The unconquerable spirit displayed by those men in the face of superior odds, and their self-sacrificing devotion to duty are worthy of the highest emulation.
BY COMMAND OF MAJOR GENERAL BARNETT
My most nightmarish memory of combat took place on the fourth day of our being surrounded during that action. One tank got so close before spotting our gun it could not depress its gun low enough to hit us. The tank fired but hit the base of the house behind us. My closest buddy crawled out around the corner of the farmhouse and fired a bazooka at the tank. The tank gunner turned his attention to machine gunning my buddy and the #2 gunner and I were able to scramble into the farm house. My buddy won the Silver Star for his heroic action but was also badly wounded.
Once we were no longer surrounded, I got my buddy back to an aid station by dragging and half carrying him through the knee-deep snow. While there, I bent

over to brush snow from my boots, felt dizzy and fell down. An aid man said I probably had a concussion and sent me back to a field hospital for observation. About 10 days later, I rejoined my unit, now pulled off the line to regroup and get replacements. I was the only man in our squad left from the original squad members.

We returned to combat in time to recapture Butzdorf which the Germans took in a counter-attack after we were relieved. We continued to advance and in a few days were almost through the Siegfried Line when during a heavy German bombardment two shells landed almost simultaneously on each side of our foxhole gun emplacement. I was so dizzy I could hardly stand and was sent back to another aid station. Waiting to be checked, I brushed snow from my boots and cut my finger. I found a small piece of spent shrapnel stuck in my foot but I couldn't even feel it. An aid man stuck a needle into my leg but I didn't feel that until he got about four inches below my knee. I was told that I had a severe case of frostbite and was sent back to an evacuation hospital. From there I was flown to a general hospital in Wales. Subsequently I went to a rehabilitation hospital. I was given one-week furlough after which I reported to a replacement depot. I didn't realize it then but my combat days were over. Instead of returning to my unit, I was shipped to a construction battalion to guard prisoners clearing debris from the Rhine River. The war ended in Europe and later in the Pacific after which I returned home to be discharged in early January, 1946.

Footnotes: On January 17, 1995 I drove into Tettingen exactly 50 years after the combat involved in the presidential unit citation. To my surprise, hundreds of "tiger teeth" were still standing and a small house had been built on the foundation of one of the pillboxes.

On the 60th anniversary of the invasion of Europe, I visited the graves of a few buddies in the cemeteries at Normandy, Brittany, and Luxembourg. When I arose from the grave of our ammo bearer in Brittany cemetery, a young French family was standing there. As I wiped away some tears, the man said in English that they brought their children to give thanks to these men who had given their lives to give France freedom. There were quite a few French people visiting the museum, chapel, and gravesites. It gave me a warm feeling to know they appreciated our involvement.

CHAPTER 3

THE HOME FRONT

The war came home to everyone in the United States. Not only were friends and relatives serving in the military but a multitude of support industries required workers. Those who weren't thus involved couldn't get away from the use of ration books for many needs: butter, sugar, alcoholic drinks, tobacco, gasoline, tires. High schools and colleges were different as many of the young men disappeared. At other schools the V-12 and ASTP programs brought in many military students for accelerated programs and intensive training in those things needed by the military.

Many think first of the combat troops when considering the military but only a relatively small percentage of the military actually were in combat. The planning required for the overseas operations is tremendous. For an island invasion, someone had to figure the amount of ammunition and food needed. The potential number of casualties was estimated and the different types, so that treatment necessities were available. Communications equipment, cannon and machine guns with spare parts, extra uniforms, mosquito nets and a myriad of other things were required. All this had to be calculated ahead, procured, and then loaded on ships so that it might be unloaded in the right order to prevent running out of essentials.

Cooks, accountants, medical personnel, paymasters, secretaries, equipment repairmen, and hundreds of other specialties are required to support a combat unit.

Similar support was needed in the civilian community to supply, transport, and train the military. This section presents the effects of the war on those who were at home.

Betsy Grindle gives us a brief picture of what the war meant to a 12 year old girl.

Ruth Henzie tells the story of being in college during this time and then the problems with planning a war time wedding, just before the war ended.

Gina Dunseth also was in college and found the life very different with almost no men in the college. She found summer jobs and volunteered in war effort projects.

Nancy Ringle was a young married woman when the war started. Her husband worked in the aircraft industry and then in industrial relations at Caltech. They did a lot of traveling early in the war, using the overloaded railway system. Later she did hospital work. She recalls the differences in social life in war time.

Ted Woodson was a conscientious objector and an engineer with General Electric. GE was planning for post war products as well as for their war efforts, so he was assigned to develop an automatic washing machine for GE to produce when the war ended.

Masago Armstrong was a Japanese American who had just completed her masters at Stanford but was sent to a relocation center in Wyoming with her family. They were finally able to leave and work in the East until the war was over.

Fran Drake was newly married to a man working at the Douglas aircraft plant. She became heavily in involved in war work, finally having a responsible position with the Red Cross.

Angelyn Riffenburgh was in college but moved back and forth from her hometown of Charleston, West Virginia to Houston, Texas where her father was sent by the Air Corps.

Claire MacDonald spent the war in Pomona College. During summers she worked as a riveter in one of the Los Angeles aircraft plants.

Dorothy Campbell lived in Berkeley where her husband taught at the University of California and also worked on atom bomb research. They were in contact with many former friends and students going or coming back from the Pacific.

WAR IN PASADENA
Betsy Grindle
The Junior Red Cross had a project in Pasadena. Each Saturday morning a group went to the Green Hotel and made "Cartoon" scrap books for military hospitals.

In our breakfast room on one wall was a large map of the world where we marked the areas in which our troops fought. We marked the sites in Europe and the various Pacific Islands that were invaded.

Each of the family had our own sugar bowl, because of rationing. I don't remember whether other members would let us borrow from their bowls if we ran out.

We had blackout curtains on the windows at our Lido Island house.

One summer night several of us, 10 to 12 years old, went skinny-dipping in the ocean. A Coast Guard vessel came by with search lights, spotting along the docks on the coast. We dove under the dock and hid there, very scared, until the Coast Guard was gone.

ON THE HOME FRONT
Ruth Henzie

My high school sweetheart and I both had new experiences ahead as he reported to the Army the same week that I began my first year at Pomona College. While he trained in Texas and went on to England, I finished my freshman year. With two friends I tried to find "war jobs" in Claremont, of all places, and ended up just going to school for the summer quarters so that we all graduated in three years. We stayed pretty much on campus but made occasional trips to Los Angeles to see plays. I remember seeing Paul Robeson in "Othello" and Helen Hayes in "Harriet". Of course there were few boys at Pomona, so our extra-curricular activities centered on stage crew and lights, with great cast parties (and crew) after each production.

My boyfriend's furloughs were the big events, of course. After my second year I took one summer session off and we were married. My family was in Berkeley with my best friend who was to have attended classes there with me. But when I heard that he was coming home I stayed in my room, thanks to generous renters, and ate at the old Claremont Inn where I worked. I made all the wedding plans, and remember I had to take my ration book with sugar stamps for the wedding cake. Thanks to help from the Church for the service and the Inn for the reception and friends who spread the word by phone we had a fine wedding, I in a borrowed wedding dress. My family came but my father had to return to Berkeley for the last week of school and to pick up my friend who had stayed for finals. My sister in the WAVES in Atlanta could not come. All these very inconvenient arrangements were readily accepted because "a soldier was coming home."

V-J Day occurred while we were on honeymoon so Pacific duty was cancelled. I finished my last year of school while he completed his duty and then helped my father make over an apartment for us. The next year he began school in the first four-year class at CMC and I taught school. I was 20 years old and had 42 second graders. I worked on an emergency credential at the beginning salary of $1950 annually. But due to his GI Bill we saved most of it and when he graduated four years later spent almost all of it on a brand new Ford car.

We were lucky to come through the war years so easily. We worried about conditions in the war zones but they usually seemed far away. I loved war movies and was thrilled to see P-38's or a B-17 fly overhead. My husband always spoke fondly of his experiences in a Replacement Battalion in England, buzz bombs and all. In our circles everyone was united behind the war effort and I think that patriotism and unity helped see us all through. But we were excited when peace finally came! In my memory book I have two Time Magazine covers - one of Hitler and one of Hirohito, each with a big X across his face.

COLLEGE IN WARTIME
Gina Dunseth

We were out for our usual Sunday drive following Church. Suddenly, the radio music was interrupted by a "flash" announcement "Pearl Harbor had been bombed." My thoughts jumped to thinking my boyfriend will probably have to go to war. He did, and his family and I agonized 'til the end of the war as to whether that notification from the War Dept. saying he was "missing in action" meant that he was alive or dead. He did come back, but our romance died.

I entered Pomona College in the winter of '43. That Fall all the college men disappeared from the campus, so female companionship developed more strongly and has provided those of us at college during the war years with fast and long lasting female friendships. When the men returned to campus in '45, they were more serious and studious and were in a hurry to get on with their lives. As a result, we women missed the slow growing up (maturation?) of a more normal college life.

My family lived in San Diego so when I returned for summers I had summer jobs related to the war effort. For two summers I staffed as a leader of the Presbyterian Church's Youth Group. I organized activities for the many sailors who came and corresponded with them when they left for overseas. I wrote to about 40 men on a continuing basis. I also volunteered at the Naval Hospital where I read to or wrote letters for wounded and psychiatric patients. Living in San Diego under barrage balloons and in a constant dim-out was part of the war effects. I was in San Diego on August 14th, working at the Church when the news came - "The War Is Over:" I rushed downtown and entered the melee that ensued. A thrilling time in our moment of final triumph.

CIVILIAN REFLECTIONS ON WORLD WAR II
Nancy Ringle
In 1941, I was a newly married, 22-year-old woman, but I hope I can give the reader some insight into what civilian life was like in Southern California and elsewhere during those eventful years of the 1940s.

I was not, nor was any member of my family, in the service. All the men were either 4-F or deferred because of important jobs in the defense industry. Nevertheless, we were all deeply involved in the war effort. I married Bob Ringle in July of 1941, five weeks after I graduated. We should have had a hint that America was gearing up for something when several Pomona classmates canceled plans to come to Santa Rosa for our wedding after being called to active duty.

Bob was working for Douglas Aircraft in El Segundo at the time, so we rented a small, brand-new apartment in West Los Angeles near Pico and Westwood Boulevard. That was where we were four months later on that fateful Sunday morning when a teenage boy ran down the street yelling loudly, "The Japs have attacked Pearl Harbor! "

I was stirring baked beans in my new bean pot, and I have never used it in the 59 years since without thinking of December 7, 1941.

It was a few weeks later that we were awakened in the middle of the night to the sound of cannons. All the military gun emplacements around Santa Monica Bay were firing, and we were convinced the Japanese navy was attempting a landing. We sat in the dark on our front steps until ordered inside by our newly appointed block warden. I remember being impressed that in such a short rime we had a block warden patrolling with a hard hat and flashlight. Civilian defense had moved fast. It wasn't until the next day that we heard that there was a possibility that the Japanese had a submarine patrolling offshore.

In January of 1942, Bob was offered an interesting job in the industrial relations department at Caltech in Pasadena. We found another brand-new spacious apartment on Huntington Drive across from the Sierra Vista Pacific Electric station. This was carefully chosen as we had no idea how long the new war might last, and we could take the big Red Cars to Caltech, to downtown Los Angeles, or to Pasadena. We lived there the entire four years of the war.

One vivid memory is long trains full of Japanese Americans going by night after night, usually after midnight. They were going to the parking lot at Santa Anita racetrack. Quonset huts had been assembled as temporary housing quarters for Japanese Americans until they were permanently interned at Manzanar or other camps. Strangely, this, at the time, did not bother us, because after the "infamous" attack on Pearl Harbor, all of us living on the West Coast were paranoid about being betrayed again. Also, at that time, we were not as conscious of human rights as we are now. I am still embarrassed by our unquestioning attitude.

Bob was assigned to go east for five months to visit various manufacturing plants and report back to Caltech about how improved time and motion studies could increase their production. I was "hired" at no salary to go along to be his secretary and make all reservations, type all reports for Caltech, and write all thank-you letters. I had never been east of Reno, so this was an exciting prospect for me. Off we went for five months of train travel and hotel living.

The trains were unbelievable! Every piece of rolling stock had been taken out of mothballs and some had half-an-inch of soot piled on the windowsills, lots of torn upholstery, and one time our car carried four caskets. The hotels were equally unforgettable. We were on a limited budget, and of course there was no such thing as a rental car due to gasoline rationing, so we tried to stay in hotels near train stations, where Bob could get taxis. Some hotels were priceless; one was obviously a house of prostitution, doing its patriotic duty by renting out rooms. One was a retirement hotel where, each day, I ran the gauntlet of elderly men who occupied chairs in the lobby. Hotel rooms were very scarce, and once we had an unfinished attic room in Ann Arbor, Michigan, with no bath, and when John Reigle, head of industrial relations for the University of Michigan, heard where we were staying, he moved us to the faculty club.

We spent Christmas in New York City and had a wonderful time.

With two friends, Bob, and I went to a Boston nightclub the night of the Coconut Grove fire. Over 450 people perished. My family had a real scare as they knew we were going to go to a Boston nightclub that night. Bob and I watched from our Statler Hotel window as hundreds of volunteers lined up their station wagons to drive victims to hospitals or to the morgue. Again, I was impressed with how quickly the civilian defense organization could recruit volunteers.

In Boston, we had a complete blackout and were caught on the street. It was a dark, moonless night (carefully chosen), and we gingerly felt for the curb and tried to get back to our darkened hotel. No lights anywhere. It turned out the Navy was assembling the armada in Boston harbor and Newport News for the North Africa invasion. Days later, we understood the reasons for such secrecy. Later, we had many occasions to see great convoys leaving San Francisco Bay at the height of the Pacific conflict - very dramatic.

In New York, we contacted Robert Shaw, a classmate of Bob's, who at age 26 had organized The Collegiate Chorale. Little did we guess, when he invited us to a rehearsal that we were hearing the first choral conducting of a man who would later be acclaimed the person who had done more than anyone else to revolutionize choral music in the United States. Another contact with the Shaw family in New York was with his sister Hollace Shaw, who was singing on the General Electric "Hour of Charm." She was dating a young Army captain who was stationed at the Pentagon. She asked him to take us to dinner at the Officers' Club in Washington and we had such a pleasant time that we dined together two more times. That captain would later run for public office and become the distinguished Senator Jacob Javits of New York. Years later when I saw him in the U.S. Capitol, he told me about visiting Jim Shaw's grave in New Guinea.

Finally, our train travels were over and in February of 1943, we returned to Huntington Drive to face rationing and shortages for the first time. It was time to volunteer for the war effort. The rationing was very real: gasoline coupons, ration books, food coupons, shoe coupons. Meat was very scarce, but Mr. Mitchell of "Mitchell's Market" at the end of our block, would often save some ground beef for me. His son had been captured by the Japanese early in the war and was a prisoner somewhere in Pacific. Mr. Mitchell had made a huge sign out of butcher paper and mounted it on the wall behind his meat counter, "We hate Japs." While I thought this was too much of a blanket statement, we all respected Mitchell's feelings of grief and frustration, and no one reprimanded him because, after all, our government still had civilian Japanese-Americans, including children, incarcerated.

Bob was working long hours using public transportation or carpooling. I decided to become a nurse's aide at the Huntington Memorial Hospital in Pasadena. I took the big Red Car from in front of our duplex to McKinley Junior High School, where the American Red Cross had organized its training program. The course lasted six weeks, headed by a retired RN who ran it like a top sergeant! She was very stern and demanding, but really whipped our motley crew into shape. Some were girls who had only attended private school. Some were high school graduates, and all of us were in our twenties. Fortunately, we were well trained because there would be only one RN on each floor at the hospital who administered medication. All other nursing services for the seriously ill and dying would be provided by us aides. Believe me, we saw everything. The air quality was not of prime concern as most of the manufacturing plants were working all three shifts. One day, on the hospital's third floor corridor, I could not see the doors into the surgery section. It was indoor smog.

Everyone was doing something to help the war effort. My brother delayed law school and worked at Douglas Aircraft in Santa Monica. My mother was still in Santa Rosa; after being widowed in 1944, she rented out three bedrooms in the big Victorian house to three Army Air Force officers. Being a school teacher and a strict disciplinarian, she had firm "house rules": no liquor on the premises, no women upstairs, no cooking or kitchen privileges. She also commuted every week to the naval hospital at Mare Island near Vallejo to be a Gray Lady in the wards. She was also chairman of the Santa Rosa USO. Bob's mother, who had never done any volunteer work, went to a Methodist church and cut and rolled bandages for the Red Cross. Our daughter Sallie was born in 1944. There was no softening agent in the wartime soap, and her diapers came off the clothesline as stiff as if they had been starched.

Social life during the war was not normal, but it was busy for the handful of us who had husbands at home. We were frequently invited to farewell parties when friends were sent overseas and to small affairs when they came home on leave. We were all urged to write and to send packages. I have to laugh at some of the things I sent overseas. Not knowing everything was government issued, one Christmas I sent shoelaces to New Guinea and Italy, not to mention cookies that probably arrived as a box of crumbs. I finally learned to send gummy, gooey brownies and date bars. I still have all the letters from all over the world; V-mail from college and high school friends.

Several of us young married women volunteered to go to the Biltmore Bowl where the USO sponsored tea dancing from 3 to 5 p.m. for the boys shipping out.

In 1944, I read in the L.A. Times that General George Patton would be speaking on the steps of the L.A. City Hall, so I took the Red Car to City Hall and was ushered to a seat within a few feet of the podium. He made a bombastic speech, and years later I appreciated what a magnificent actor George Scott was as Patton.

When the war began in 1941, we made a solemn vow with friends, the Cochrans, to meet in the Biltmore Hotel lobby the night the war was over. Four years later, we confirmed our date on the phone. We took public transportation from East Los Angeles, and the Cochrans got a bus from West Los Angeles. We met in front of the Biltmore on Olive Street to find it locked and boarded up as was most of downtown L.A. The restaurants, hotels, and stores were fearful that an overly exuberant crowd might vandalize downtown. The only place we could eat was Clifton's cafeteria. We will never forget VJ day.

WORLD WAR II AS A CONSCIENTIOUS OBJECTOR
T. T. Woodson
The General Electric Research Laboratory in late 1930's

I was a young electrical engineer assigned an instrument development project, out of the mainstream of the basic research being done by the two hundred others on the staff. This was the lab that had produced the first practical x-ray tube in early 1900's, developed ductile tungsten for light bulbs, and silicone rubber. It was led by scientists like Whitney, Coolidge, and Langmuir. It was my good fortune to be rubbing elbows, even if seldom, with the likes of these.

My job then was designing a detector for mercury vapor in air. GE had built a completely new power plant using mercury instead of water, and any leakage of the shiny metal drops and resulting vapor was both expensive and poisonous. The liquid metal looked harmless, but it was evaporating into the air all the time. By 1940 my prototype instruments were working in both the Kearney, NJ and Schenectady power plants. Also, a portable version had been made to carry into felt hat factories like Stetson, in Danbury, CT. Yes, a mercury compound was used to help remove fur from rabbit pelts and mercury poisoning was a continuing threat.

My College Ethical and Religious Background

At Purdue University, the Methodist Student Center had become my recreation site along with an opportunity for after-hours courses in ethics, Bible, etc. The very liberal Student Pastor there had stressed the morals of Jesus. I took these principles seriously enough to quit ROTC when we were beginning to start pistol target-practice. I looked at the gun in my hand and realized its only purpose was to kill people. Simplistically, I didn't know exactly how non-violence worked,, but there were better ways of solving quarrels than by war. You had to get to the TALK phase sometime.

A similar Center was in Columbus, OH, during my graduate work there. In discussion groups along the way, we looked at the C O's (conscientious objector) legal status and at their historical treatment by the public. It had ranged from grudging acceptance, to alternative service (hospitals), to jailing. The experiences of Quakers and Amish were usually cited. But in the end everything was always uncertain.

War Work in 1940-41

Specific war projects were being started and my section boss, Mr. Thearle, called me in. He suggested an assignment on something for a submarine. I told him, respectfully, that I would prefer civilian work. There was no discussion; it was left that way.

A short time later, I was called into the office of Dr. William Coolidge, Director of the whole laboratory. He had heard from Mr. Thearle, and would like now to hear my viewpoint. I went into it in more detail, after which, in a very quiet and dignified voice, he said, "I'm afraid Mr. Hitler won't give us the opportunity to do it that way." Again, it was left at that.

At this juncture, a Mr. George Dunham, from the Bridgeport, CT, plant made a visit to the Lab. He talked to me, among others, about his need for an assistant to help develop a post-war product, a new automatic clothes washing machine. They had made conventional washers before, but no automatics; those had to be "high-tech".

I visited the Bridgeport plant, got the offer and accepted it promptly. Of course, I knew nothing about the business of washing machines, but it was in the right direction. By the time we moved it was March, 1942, and our new home was to be in Fairfleld, a suburb of Bridgeport.

War and Post-war Developments

G E quickly ceased civilian production and converted to military. All of us started on overtime; three or four days a week, I think. All engineers were automatically deferred from the draft, in spite of my trying to register as a C O. Our washer project collected a close-knit team of drafting, shop and test persons that stayed together during the duration. GE was fully aware of the market and of the building up of demand for post-war products and employment.

Starting pretty much from scratch, we developed a new process, mechanism and control concepts, made prototypes and put them to test, both in the lab and in homes. Due to a patent question, halfway through, Mr. Dunham was taken off the job and it was left to me to design the machine. As the war went on, manufacturing planners were added and a whole new plant layout emerged. In 1945, an old Bayer aspirin plant in Trenton, New Jersey was bought and conversion to a mass production line was begun.

GE was tolerant of my views and sent my "Quaker Bond" deduction (vs. war bonds) down to Philadelphia monthly. The first full year's production of the new washing machine, 1947, was 300,000 units. Now they manufacture a million a year.

HEART MOUNTAIN RELOCATION CENTER
Masago Armstrong

December 7, 1941 changed lives world wide and what follows is a brief review of my family in those troublesome times. In December of that fall, after working long and hard for their six children, my parents were beginning to turn over the reins of their business to my oldest brother, Takeshi. He had earned his BA degree from UC Berkeley, married his beautiful and much loved wife, Ellen, and together they were beginning to settle into the family business. An older sister, Madoka, was a second year medical student at Stanford. Chronologically I was next and had just completed my BA and MA degrees at Stanford in history. Employment for a Japanese-American US citizen in teaching or research at that time was not easy so I was able to help my brother in the business. A younger brother, Yoshimaro, was a freshman at Stanford. A younger sister, Manabu, and a still younger brother, Maremaro, were in elementary school. We were all aware of the world situation particularly since my mother had recently returned from a visit with her parents in Japan and told us of her ship being blacked-out every night of the entire voyage.

The attack on Pearl Harbor came on December seventh. The country mobilized all resources for war. We began to hear rumblings about what might happen to the Japanese in the United States - there was talk of removing those who, like my parents, had come to the United States. My parents were not allowed by law to become citizens. The idea of our parents being herded into such a confinement situation was totally unacceptable to we children and caused us unbelievable concern. All Japanese were confined to their homes from 8 PM to 8 AM and not allowed to travel more than 5 miles from their homes. For a period of time our bank accounts and other savings were seized by the government.

Then came President Franklin D Roosevelt's Executive order 9066. We learned that we were, regardless of citizenship status, to be removed from our homes and confined. We Shibuyas worked hard and long to prepare our home and land for this evacuation. We rented our beautiful 16-room home that we had had built in 1935 to the manager of the Los Altos branch of the Bank of America. We asked that a neighbor who lived across the street take care our property for us. Our Taro, a wonderful and faithful dog, had to be taken to the pound. Orders were that we take only that which we could carry - meaning a small suitcase each. We were to report to the train depot by 9 am. A good neighbor with tears in her eyes drove us in two trips to entrain. We boarded the train in Mountain View and with blinds pulled were moved to our destination that turned out to be the Santa Anita Race Track. On a hot summer day under the surveillance of military police we were herded to the stable area, and assigned by family, four to a stable. Then we were ordered to go to the end of the stable area where we would find canvas sacks. We were then to fill these sacks with straw - our bedding, which we took back to our assigned stable. Bathrooms were stalls without doors and the showers used to wash down horses after a race were our bathing provision. Food preparation was equally unbelievable and the hot weather presented problems of spoilage. I was immediately drafted to document this whole phenomenal incident, factually and as completely as possible. Men were assigned to the grandstand area where they were to weave camouflage nets, ad infinitum.

Madoka, of course, had to leave medical school but through her professors at the school was able to find employment with a pharmaceutical company based in Denver. She left our home in Mountain View on a jeep accompanied by the jeep driver and two MPs. While confined at Santa Anita my brother, Yoshi, applied to and was accepted at the University of Nebraska in Lincoln. He departed to continue his studies immediately.

In early September of 1942 we learned that we were to be sent to the Heart Mountain Relocation Center near Cody, Wyoming. We were again herded onto long multi-car trains and then began a long, tough, difficult trip which took many days, a lot of it spent on sidings to allow other trains to pass. We arrived in Wyoming and were taken to the relocation center. Heart Mountain was cold and the altitude was so high the kitchen staff had difficulty preparing food. Tak, and his wife were assigned to a small room and my parents, Manabu, Mare and I were assigned to one room containing 5 cots and a wood-coal burning stove. Dining was in a hall located one to a block of 24 barracks, each barracks housing six families. Bathrooms and laundry rooms were also centrally located in each 24-barrack block. The weather was a shock to us arriving from the heat of Santa Anita. Sears Roebuck did a booming business and we were lucky to still have money to afford much needed clothing.

I with my history background was immediately assigned to Mr. Vaughn Mechau to document the history of the Center. It was a lucky assignment as he showed great sympathy for us. His own father was a German immigrant during WW I and had been held for a time. Mr. Mechau also supervised the camp newspaper. I worked hard and long at my assignment and with a staff of ten issued weekly, monthly and quarterly reports on the over 10,000 people detained there. Because we were not allowed to have cameras, three members of my staff painted in water color many scenes of the Center and this helped illustrate our reports.

Emily Ridgway, a Cody resident, visited the Center and asked if I would work with her to gather a group of internees and form a Girl Scout troop. We did so and this proved to be a very active group especially when Emily would plan overnight and day trips outside the Center. This of course was a great morale booster for the members of the troop and their families.

In February our mother lost her life and we were all saddened beyond description. Madoka and Yosh came from Denver and Lincoln and many, many others including Vaughn came to her funeral. A group of internees who had met my mother stayed up all night the day before her funeral making a casket cover of paper flowers. We Shibuyas were deeply moved but our mother was very loved and respected and we could understand.

Soon after this, Tak and I talked about the very real danger of losing our father, so we decided to try to leave the Center. We moved as fast as we could. I had been involved in a Student Christian Association conference in Estes Park, Colorado and then was invited to a national meeting of this group in Wisconsin. At the suggestion of a fellow student from Stanford, I had also begun to write to a few institutions about possible employment. One of the answers I received was from President Albin Bro of Frances Shimer College in Mt. Carroll, Illinois. I called him from the railroad station in Chicago and he invited me to drop in on my way back to Heart Mountain. He and Mrs. Bro received me warmly and I stayed for several days. He offered me employment as Secretary to the Dean with housing and also offered for Mana space in her class, housing in the residential dormitory, and a scholarship given by Mrs. Walgreen (of the drug chain). We Shibuyas were touched by this extending of friendship on their part. When I returned to Heart Mountain, Tak had found employment for himself and Ellen at Quakerdale in Iowa. Our father and Mare were included in that offer. And so all of us were at long last free of confinement and able to pursue independently our lives outside the three western states.

Directly after VE day, Madoka resumed her studies at Stanford Medical School, completed her degree and residency and was appointed to the Cornell University medical school teaching staff. Yosh was rushed through his BA degree at Nebraska, assigned to the language school at Fort Snelling, and served in the army of occupation in Japan. There he and a fellow GI spent any free time they had going from police station to police station in Tokyo looking for members of the family living in Japan; they were at last successful. After VE Day I briefly brought my father back to Mountain View where he began to bring back the business until Tak and Ellen and Mare could join him after Mare finished school. When the school year ended I also returned to Mountain View, leaving Mana to finish her final high school year at Frances Shimer College.

During the days prior to our having to leave our home, Dorothea Lange, a photographer, visited us in Mountain View and her pictures of us can be found in many museums and occasionally on TV presentations of the evacuation of the Japanese-Americans. James Edmiston was in the San Jose Office of the government agency set up to help the Japanese return to our homes. He did a magnificent job and was honored by the Japanese government for his work. His son was in the film industry and wrote a book, Home Again, novelizing the Shibuya family and its internment.

WARTIME IN LOS ANGELES
Fran Drake

After our marriage, Ted and I moved to a small duplex in Inglewood, California, not far from Douglas Aircraft where Ted worked. We owed $150 when we were married and paid it off the first year. Sometimes I had $10 a week for food and house expenses, but I remember that for two weeks had to manage on $5 a week.

The house was small and required little of me. One day, while washing Ted's socks in the sink, I thought, "Did I go to college for four years just to be doing this? What a waste!" So I bestirred myself and became involved in Girl Scouts for a time, with a troop of girls who met at the Scout House in the center of Inglewood. Many GI's were stationed in the area to guard the Douglas El Segundo Aircraft plant, and wives and mothers began to come to the Scout House for information about their men in the service. One of my friends had been involved with the Red Cross in World War I, and we decided to put up a card table on the front porch, record the questions and requests and refer them to the Red Cross Office in Los Angeles.

In a short time a Red Cross Office was opened in Inglewood. I became office manager in charge of scheduling volunteers, Staff Assistants as we were called, to work in the office and respond to inquiries. We offered classes in Nutrition and in Motor Corps, providing coffee and doughnut deliveries to the soldiers on night duty. The Motor Corp also offered transportation for workers manning the Army Command Center in downtown Los Angeles during the night shift. I remember the half moon was low in the sky one night when I started out to pick up two workers and transport them to the Center. My car was low on gas, and I had to awaken a sleepy garage man to fill my tank in order to get home.

One night there was a blackout. Searchlights were focusing on some small object high in the sky that looked like a moth from our vantage point but might have been an enemy plane. (Later, I think later it proved not to be, but no one was sure.) Although the night was warm, I found myself shivering as Ted and I looked out of the window in the dark night at the spectacle above. It was scary!

Often I took Ted's lunch to the plant and had to pass an army station and show my pass to be admitted. I got acquainted with the soldiers at the station and asked if they might like to have a home cooked dinner some night at our house. They would. From my meager budget I saved enough to feed six or so and was prepared for their arrival. They didn't come. I learned the next day that duty prevented, and so we arranged another night. That night was rainy, and they appeared in their full gear, slickers, helmets, rifles, boots et al. They seemed to like being in a home and were a laughing and jolly group. We all had a good time though I remember spending the next day cleaning up. My new davenport flounce was muddy from the boots. But it was well worth it.

In 1943 a group of Chinese in San Francisco conceived of a plan to build a Chinese owned and operated aircraft factory to aid the war effort and to serve as a starting point of a post-war Chinese aviation industry. The plan was presented to the Chinese and United States Army Air Corps and was approved. The new company was to manufacture a sub-assembly for the Douglas Aircraft A-26 attack bomber. A thousand young men were interviewed and 65 were given employment and trained by Douglas. Along with several others, Ted was sent by Douglas to help the Chinese get the plant started and he became technical advisor to the Chinese purchasing agent. We attended dinners in Chinatown and heard speeches in Mandarin, Cantonese, and English. Our young son with his very blond hair was a minority of one among the many black-haired Chinese children present at these gatherings.

MY WORLD WAR II
Angelyn Riffenburgh

On December 7, 1941, my mother and I were in her bedroom when my father called and told us that Pearl Harbor had been bombed. At the time it was too much to comprehend. I was seventeen and planning to graduate from high school in just over a month. The next day our entire student body marched into the auditorium and seriously listened to President Franklin Roosevelt declare war. I saved the newspaper that came out - JAPS BOMB PEARL HARBOR -- and still have it today. In January I started college at a small liberal arts school in Charleston, West Virginia, living at home and involved with a part time job. Thus, I wasn't to know until much later what happened to many members of my graduating class who were planning to work until fall before starting college. (Most of the young men went into the service immediately.)

I started a major in history and became acquainted with new friends. It took a year or so before the men at the college started leaving for the service. Bond rallies were held and we watched the news at the theaters, but it still seemed far away. My father's two brothers went into the navy and the army and my father, a school teacher and forty years old by 1943, decided that he wanted to serve his country. It was through him that I became more closely involved. He volunteered for the army air corps and was sent to Officers' Training School in San Antonio, Texas. After finishing his training my father, Cecil Kelley, was sent to Ellington Field near Houston. He was involved in public address as a sideline to his teaching and had a large and extensive sound system, the contents of which were sophisticated but impossible to purchase during the war. The officials at Ellington Field proposed borrowing his equipment for the duration of the war. They flew him home in an army plane, picked up all his equipment, and gave him ten days leave to organize his family and take them to Texas.

So we went-my mother, my sister and I. The first month we shared a house with a young family, and had kitchen privileges, while my sister and I slept in a hide-a-bed in their living room. During that time we weathered a hurricane at the house while my father had to stay on the base to help anchor the planes.

At the end of the month we found a duplex which was really a large house redesigned. In addition to us, the woman who owned it had a roomer from Chicago who was working in the Houston shipyards while her husband was in the service. My father joined a carpool to the base as it was seventeen miles away and gas rationing made it impossible to drive alone. I started the University of Houston in the fall of my junior year. There I made friends with twins who told me about the program for servicemen at their church. Each Sunday after church the young people had a luncheon for all those men who came to town from nearby bases. Thus, finally my contact with soldiers and sailors! Life was definitely more interesting.

After one semester I decided to go back to Charleston to complete my education but spent the summer between my junior and senior year in Houston going to school and working. My father was theater officer on the base and we were able to see a lot of movies and buy goodies at the PX. I worked evenings behind the candy counter at a local movie house and I was always at the church on Sunday. During my final year of college, having decided becoming a physician might be an interesting life, I worked on courses to prepare me for medical school. I had thought I might want to become a WAAC but I wasn't old enough. I applied to the Medical College of Virginia in Richmond and was accepted on the basis of completing a physics and chemistry course. So after graduation in the spring of 1945, I went to the University of Houston for those courses. It was particularly difficult because I also met a sailor who came from Corpus Christi as often as he could to be with me.

To make things more complex, my father was sent off to Utah to train for going to the South Pacific. My mother made preparations to return to West Virginia in the fall. It was at this time the atom bombs were dropped on Japan, something we discussed in my chemistry class. VJ Day was celebrated with my sailor on the streets of Houston and shortly after my mother went to Dallas to meet my father as he returned to Texas. He was back but had no house, so when I went off to Richmond, the family resettled in Texas City, on the other side of Ellington Field. They were to live there for nine months until he was discharged from the service. My father was offered opportunities to stay in Texas and utilize his public address skills, but chose to return to the state of his birth.

A RIVETER AT POMONA
Claire McDonald

I was on a yacht sailing around the Palos Verde peninsula with friends when the news of Pearl Harbor came. The harbor was closed and we had to go ashore by rowboats. Later they told us that we had passed through a minefield. I was in high school at the time and we were upset to see our Japanese friends go off to the camps. Many of the boys from my class went into the military. We lived with blackouts and rationing like the rest of American, though the Pacific Coast close to the ocean was more concerned with proper blackouts.

I started Pomona College at 16 in 1943. It was a very small class but there were also army ASTP students in pre-meteorology. These finished in March and were not replaced. Gradually the school became made up mostly of women as the men left. Many faculty members also left for the military and President Lyons was teaching classes for departing faculty.

At Pomona the war was ever a part of life. We would hear about the death of alumni. The teacher of chorus read to the group a letter from the mother of a dead soldier, telling how much the chorus had meant to him when he was in college. It was very moving. We had dances, sometimes importing boys from Caltech. The music was mostly about the time after the war. Movies were about the war and tended to be emotionally impressive.

After the things we heard about our enemies, I was afraid of the Germans but I knew many Japanese Americans so wasn't afraid of the Japanese.

A dear friend whose girl friend was in my class at Pomona was killed in the battle of the bulge, bringing home the war even closer.

During summer vacations from school I worked in an aircraft plant. I was in a group that riveted wing flaps for the C-47 transport plane. Many of the girls spent a lot of time in conversation or in the rest room. Our team of college girls worked very hard and improved from seven to fifteen flaps a shift. Shifts were 10 hours and we were paid 35 cents an hour. On night shift my mother changed our mealtime so that I was able to sleep before I had to return to work. Sometimes we were working six days a week. At the end of the war, the factory terminated many of the women but our team was offered a continuing job. However, we all planned to return to school in the fall so they didn't keep us.

My boy friend, Lee MacDonald, was in the Army. When he was stationed in Northern California, he would come down every possible week-end, sometimes not arriving until eleven at night. This was made very difficult by the dorm rules on being out at night. In 1945, we became engaged and at the end of the school year went up to Oregon on the train for me to meet his parents. The train was very crowded and we had one berth and one seat which we alternated using. Lee had been sent to Texas for a time and I was to meet him at Burbank airport when he returned. I waited and waited and finally go a call that he was at Long Beach airport. He was now a lieutenant and very impressive in officer uniform.

That spring the war was over in Europe but Lee still expected to go to the Pacific. The atom bomb ended that and I saw him for the first time in civilian clothes. He was in an accelerated group at USC which made getting together difficult so we were married before my senior year and Lee came back to Pomona.

Women had been running the college but now the men were back and suddenly we were relegated to our old position and they took over. This was a hard adjustment for many of the women. Everyone was keyed up by the war and adjustment was hard in many ways. It was hard for me with both of us going to school as I was expected to do all the house work as well as study. The career of the returning soldier seemed to dominate the thinking of everyone.

BERKELEY DURING THE WAR
Dorothy Campbell

We arrived in this delightful place in 1940, driving and delivering a new car to San Francisco, never going over 35 miles an hour. We received $50 and had a wonderful time. We thought we had come to Paradise after Ohio.

Then came December 7th and life changed. All lights went out; cars with no lights, checking blackout of houses at night. Art, my husband, became a monitor to see that not a sliver of light would be showing through the shades as he walked up and down the street. The beautiful Japanese art shop on Telegraph Avenue closed because the Japanese-American owner was being sent away. He was also a very popular Professor of Art.

We moved into a house with a view overlooking the Golden Gate and watched our ships coming and going. Art was refused a request to be in "Service" so did double duty, teaching for professors leaving to do research at 'hush-hush' secret places and continuing his own research. He was a part time worker on the Manhattan Project. It was top secret and Art did much of his research at night, teaching during the day. I questioned him about the late nights and all he would tell me was that "if this research works out we could win the war in a few weeks." I never asked him again.

The FBI was always checking. Art had lunch at the men's faculty club. A stranger was introduced and after a week or so he announced, "I am here from the FBI to check on you and I want to congratulate you. None of you are talking about your own research. However, you certainly are talking about everybody else's and you must stop."

Many friends would come and see us as they were either shipping out to the Pacific or just coming back, weary and happy. Friends would say their goodbyes as they left as we were the last friends on the way out. The ones returning really enjoyed home cooking and fresh fruit and vegetables. There was a time when a sailor stopped by and went sight seeing with Art. I was left to press his pants and, horrors, I pressed them wrong. I often wondered what happened to him when he returned to his ship. (Ed. note: Bell bottom trousers were packed turned inside out so the creases were on the sides and pointed inward instead of out.)

Cooking was a challenge with the constant necessity of counting food stamps. We almost lived on 'Spam'. Once I found horse meat for sale. I bought some and cooked it but no one would eat it.

Once we had a fighter pilot from the Philippines who had been a POW for three years. He looked so awed and bewildered, not believing he was still alive and really home. There was a farmer who would bring a truckload of fresh vegetables for sale once a week. Our visitor couldn't believe such abundance. He kept walking around the truck, eyeing all the fresh produce. He came into the house loaded with things he had dreamed about, especially fresh asparagus.

War was changing and research was no longer so pressing. This allowed us to leave beautiful Berkeley for a new position at Oberlin College back in Ohio. Driving across the country on all retreaded tires with two small children was a daring adventure.

We arrived in Oberlin to the news: "the war is over." Everybody was out of their homes, with the children marching, waving flags. It was hard to believe that there was such a thing as the atom bomb.

CHAPTER 4

THE PACIFIC WAR

The main US Army thrust in the Pacific was MacArthur's area, which included the New Guinea and Philippine campaigns. Some Army divisions were involved in the island hopping campaigns through the Pacific but this was headed by Admiral Nimitz and primarily involved the Navy and the Marines.

Starting with the battle of Midway, the Navy gradually reconquered the Pacific with the final battle at Okinawa. Preparations were going forward rapidly for an invasion of the Japanese mainland when the atomic bombs led to the immediate end of the war.

The growth of the Navy was even more impressive than the other services, considering the time required to build a large warship. The battle of Midway was won with only three US carriers, one of which, Yorktown, was covered by temporary patches put on in 3 days after arriving in Hawaii from a battle in the far Pacific. Over 30 carriers took part in the Okinawa campaign. Much of the damage to Japanese shipping and to their Navy was done by our submarines. At the start of the war, torpedoes were not well controlled and frequently didn't go off. By the end, our sub attacks were extremely deadly.

The cryptographers who broke the main Japanese Navy code allowed the submarines to be where the merchant shipping of Japan was going. This also allowed the Navy to foresee Japanese plans and avoid the element of surprise attacks.

With the lack of airfields within reach of the island invasions, most of the air war was in the hands of Navy and Marine pilots, flying off the carriers. Once the islands were taken, airfields could be built and eventually large Air Corps bombers were based on such islands as Tinian and Saipan where they could reach the Japanese homeland with bombs. The Navy planes were a completely different group than those of the Air Corps. They required special stressing for carrier landings and had folding wings for storage on the carrier. Carrier landings, particularly at night or in a stormy sea with the carrier moving up and down, are probably the most difficult flying there is.

The logistics of supplying the combat ships clear across the ocean were demanding. The Navy had freighters, tankers, personnel ships, ammunition ships, and others but even so was very dependent on the merchant marine to bring out material from the United States.

Hospital ships were an essential part of the Pacific invasion fleets. They were excellently equipped hospitals and saved many lives and limbs by the prompt availability of specialist care and advanced surgery.

The Navy is well represented. Bill Dunseth gives us episodes from his service on two different ships. His second ship was damaged by a kamikaze in the invasion of Okinawa.

Jack Tallon was a navy diver, trained in hard hat diving, who salvaged boats damaged in making landings.

Bill Christensen was aircraft maintenance officer on a seaplane tender which was also used in times of stress as a transport. When the war in Europe was over, the ship was converted to a troop transport carrying nearly 2000 men. In this capacity, it made two trips to the Pacific, to New Caledonia and to the Philippines.

When Bob Stafford finished law school, he went into the Navy as an officer. Because of boating experience, he was in the boat division at Pearl Harbor. Much of the small boat work was in air/sea rescue and he went to diving school to work with crashes. He also defended sailors at courts martial, angering his Captain and getting him sent to Midway Island.

Augie Weigle requested the Army when drafted but was sent to the Navy and then offered the "CB's" (construction battalions.) He spent much time on Tinian, building the Naval Air Station there.

Glenn Cornwell was a Navy supply officer. He was on disbursing duty and wandered widely around the Pacific, his group carrying huge amounts of money to pay off military personnel.

The Marines are part of the Naval Service, being the infantry of the Navy. Bob Poindexter was a Marine in the second Marine division and made a landing on Okinawa though he actually never came under fire. He was then in the Army of occupation in Japan.

Ben Souther was an officer in bomb disposal. He taught the handling of ordnance in Navy schools and on ships at sea. He also was responsible for disarming or disposing of stray ordnance, including that brought back for souvenirs.

Burdette Boileau was on a destroyer escort that accompanied one of the small carriers doing convoy duty in the North Atlantic.

After officer training, Don Faust was ordered to the battleship Texas. He spent several months chasing her around the Pacific. Shortly after this the Texas was decommissioned and he went to China to instruct in some surplus landing craft that we were giving the Chinese nationalists.

French Fogle enlisted in the Marines as a private. He was commissioned and served in the invasions of Bougainville, Iwo Jima, and Guam. He returned to Washington as a Major and served in planning until the end of the war.

Art Langdon went to sea on a Navy cargo ship directly out of officer candidate school and spent three years in the Pacific on the same ship, participating in many of the invasions.

Gale Reynolds went in the Navy at 17 and after spending many months in San Francisco Bay as a net tender, went to the Pacific on a new attack transport. He was discharged just four years after enlisting.

DUNSETH'S NAVY

Bill Dunseth wrote an autobiography, "Just One More Band". Two stories are taken from the book. The first is a brief story of his first docking of a new ship. The ship was built in Cleveland and was taken out, only partially complete, before the St. Lawrence froze it in for the winter. The second, longer story catalogues his reaching a new post on a larger ship and its involvement in the Okinawa campaign.

DOCKING 1413

In the Boston Navy Yard we got our first glimpse of how the Navy supported its ships. While some talked with us about our list and a supplementary one we had prepared, others were on board beginning work on some of our projects. Furthermore they worked from reveille until they were asked to leave at night to allow the crew to sleep. Small ship that we were, they made us feel as important as any of the major ships of the line that came to that Yard for assistance.

The captain lived in New Jersey with a wife and a child so he informed me on Christmas Eve morning that he was going home and would return sometime Christmas Day. The Yard was not working on Christmas Day so there would be nothing to do and no one would miss him. Oh, how wrong he was!

In the captain's absence I knew it was essential that I stand by on the ship in case anything unusual occurred so I went to the Yard Christmas morning. Almost upon my arrival we were ordered to proceed to a position outside the harbor for "degaussing" of the ship. That is a process designed to reduce the metallic attraction of the ship to help reduce location by enemy radar and/or sonar. I could not report the captain missing so I, who had not yet undocked a ship of that size, commanded one underway, or docked such a ship proceeded to undertake to command the operation. What was I thinking of? If anything happened to that ship both the Captain and I would have been in serious trouble.

I am not certain that the entire crew was aboard. But at the appointed time we cast off the lines and proceeded slowly astern until we were clear of the slip and headed down the channel. My quartermaster and some of the other experienced crew stood ready to help, which I appreciated very much. I knew enough about the channel buoys and their colors to proceed down the channel to the open sea and my quartermaster gave me the course to our destination. When we arrived we had nothing to do but proceed very slowly to maintain position against the wind and current while several other ships did whatever they had to do. Then we were ordered to return to port and tie up next to the 1414 in a certain slip.

Our ship had two propellers. Degrees of speed were designated as, "All ahead 1/3, all ahead 2/3, all ahead full, and all ahead flank" reading from slow to as fast as the engines would propel us. In reverse, the orders were the same, using "back" in place of "ahead". I am certain that I probably used "Ahead 2/3" when proceeding to the harbor entrance and for some distance up the return channel. As we reached a point from which I could see the entrance to the slip in which we were to tie up next to the 1414, the channel narrowed somewhat so that I could observe the rate at which the structures on shore were slipping past us. I had the feeling we were going a bit too fast, so I cut engine turns to "All ahead 1/3". That was when I learned a very important lesson - reducing or stopping propeller turns does not mean that the ship reacts immediately - it continues to proceed ahead.

I knew I had to have the engines going to control the ship as I turned into the slip but as we made the turn I knew we were going far too fast. I stopped both engines with little effect. The slip was several hundred feet long and I was staring at the end toward which I was hurtling at tremendous speed (it seemed to me) and a court martial and time in Portsmouth Naval prison appeared to be an inevitable result. I went to "All back 1/3" and watched us approach the 1414 whose crew members were now watching us with some concern. Then we went to "All back 2/3". We were beginning to slow down but the perspiration was pouring out of me with increasing volume, regardless of the cold. Finally I did what any experienced ship commander would do: the only option left to me was "All back flank", an order I gave as I grabbed the bridge rail for support during the impending crash. All of a sudden my ship began to tremble and shake fiercely and came to a stop so close aboard the 1414 that my crew just handed our lines over to their crew. I had enough sense and strength left to stop all engines and secure the deck crew.

Several of the crew who had not been on the bridge during the docking congratulated me on a superb job, knowing it was my first time. I staggered to my bunk and lay there, soaking wet, and trying to regain my composure. Ted Emerson brought me a cup of coffee and the doctor gave me - illegally - a small shot of scotch. I learned much about ship handling in a very short time - not a method I would recommend - and the captain learned to never leave his ship secretly again.

OKINAWA

I reported and my orders called for me to report on board a ship for travel into the Pacific. Moreover the ship was sailing at noon. So I went back to the hotel packed my gear and went down to check out. As I got into a taxi for the trip to the pier, I found the cab occupied by a Navy captain who told me to give directions to the cabbie. The captain was looking for a place to stay in the city, had not had much luck, had more than 70 or 80 dollars on the cab's meter, and said he would be happy to deliver me to the dock as the Navy was paying for his ride. I arrived to find I would be on board a relatively small freighter that was not new. Indeed, on the main deck a wooden room had been constructed which turned out to be my quarters. I was the only passenger. That ship was not only old but very slow - almost all of eight days to get to Honolulu. I ate with the crew but the captain asked me to please stay out of the way so I read and slept my slow passage to Hawaii.

All of a sudden life changed dramatically for me. The lazy days of leave, the fall days of San Francisco, and the slow ride to Hawaii ended with a bang. We arrived in Hawaii about dusk and I found my way to where I was to report. When I showed my orders to the transportation officer he looked startled and his words to me were "Where the hell have you been?"

When I told him my story he continued to be very upset but allowed it was not my fault. I learned that I had been issued the second highest priority for travel that was available but obviously the San Francisco district office had not received the word. I was to go to a ship that was in desperate need of another officer. In less than half an hour I was on my way to the Naval Air Station where a plane had been held for me and I was on my way to Saipan. The plane had eight or twelve seats up front - first class in the Navy. The rest of the accommodations were strips of canvas, out from the side of the plane, stretching the length of the main cabin, and attached to pipes which caught anybody sitting there right under the thighs. No more tortuous places to sit were ever invented. However, because of my having the highest travel priority on the plane I was taken to one of the front seats. All the seats were filled by officers who outranked me - remember, I was still a Lieutenant (jg) - but a full Lieutenant was informed he would have to go sit in the back. I was certainly the focus of interest of the other officers and when my only answer as to why I rated such a priority was that I did not know, the consensus was sympathy for the displaced Lieutenant and agreement that the Navy had screwed up again.

I was met at the plane by an officer with a jeep who took me directly to the docking area. There was a small boat that ran mail and messages throughout the harbor with one other officer, a Lieutenant, in it. As soon as I and my luggage were aboard, the boat raced off through the harbor and pulled up beside the ladder of the USS Yokes (APD 69). The other officer and I went up the ladder and reported to the Officer of the Deck and immediately we became aware of another foul up. Only one new officer was expected aboard. After a short wait we were escorted to the office of the Executive Officer, Commander Weed, who had to sort things out. The Captain was apparently somewhat older, had been through several engagements with the Japanese, and was so fatigued that he was leaving the ship in Saipan.

Commander Weed was taking over as Captain and a new Executive officer had been requested. The ship got one - the Lieutenant who had been in the mail boat - and I was excess. The ship was under urgent orders to sail so the Captain went ashore and we sailed with an extra officer - me. Inasmuch as I had just come from Damage Control School, and the officer on board who had been filling that billet was an Ensign, I drew that duty. So I had my wish and was on a ship in the Pacific, going with three other ships of the same type to a destination the Captain would reveal to us in a few days.

I did not get much sleep for the next few days as I had to quickly become familiar with the ship, the color code for identifying what was in each pipe throughout the ship, the location of damage control materials, and the crew members who were assigned to damage control. That meant touring the ship many times, studying the manuals and holding meetings with my crew team. The designation of APD for the ship meant Attack Personnel Destroyer. It was really a Destroyer Escort (DE) hull but the open decks running fore and aft on each side of the ship had been enclosed and bunks and storage spaces installed to accommodate an Underwater Demolition team of about 35 men which we had aboard.

Our job was to arrive at an island three days before an invasion. For three mornings just before dawn we would steam to a designated distance from the shoreline. Our team had three motorized rubber boats large enough to hold four divers and a coxswain to drive the boat. The boats would proceed at high speed toward shore and then run parallel to the shore over underwater obstacles designed to do damage to invading boats and hinder them reaching the beach. Each boat had a designated sector. As the boats proceeded at high speed, members of the team would go over the side at designated intervals, dive to find such obstacles as were present, apply detonating devices, keeping watch on the time. At a previously determined time, each man surfaced to find the boat coming for him at high speed. Each boat had a rubber triangle arm extending from the side. As the boat approached, the team member in the water would extend his arm, catch the triangle, and be flung up into the boat. The boat then returned to the 69, which in turn sailed off to a safe distance and waited to return the next morning.

Our destination was Okinawa. We arrived on time and for three mornings performed our designated task. We received some gunfire from the shore but nothing came close. We were under orders not to return it. The UDT boats came under machine gun fire but there were no casualties. Each day, after the boats returned to our ship, the devices attached to underwater obstacles were detonated. A careful log was kept of the location of each detonation and the boats of the invasion knew just where obstacles might still exist. The main invasion force, including the battleships and carriers, arrived one or two days before the actual invasion. The sight of that huge fleet was certainly awe-inspiring. There was a heavy bombardment of the island by planes and ships. Planes from carriers we never saw flew continuously, dropping bombs and napalm.

The morning of the invasion there were more than 500 ships present, not that we could see far enough to see all of them. The bombardment made the island look as though it was on fire as the smoke from the bombs made it impossible to see. The invading boats finally went ashore - several months later we received word that the ship and our UDT team had been commended for our work in clearing the approaches to the beach. In the days following the morning of invasion our ship was assigned to transport wounded to hospital ships, transfer men and supplies from one ship to another, and odd tasks that had to be done to make the fleet effective. On one occasion we asked for and received permission to fire our 5-inch gun at targets on the beach. I am certain that our one little gun had no major effect on the outcome of the invasion but we did feel that we had been a real part of it all. I, of course, spent most of the days at my assigned station with my damage control crew inside the ship. On one or two occasions I relieved the Officer of the Deck topside for short periods of time.

Although we were part of a huge enterprise, we were a very small part of it and for a period of time our role was such as to find our interest somewhat waning. It became very dull to sit at my station inside the ship, day after day, as we stayed at an alert condition most of the time. But then everything changed - the Kamikazes arrived. The Japanese were becoming desperate as our possession of Okinawa meant bases from which we could bomb Japan around the clock. So now they were assigning young pilots to fly the oldest of their aircraft on one-way missions - to fly their aircraft on suicide flights, ending by diving into our ships. This is something most of us still do not understand - how those young men believed that by killing themselves while inflicting damage on our ships they would earn their way into whatever hereafter they understood to be waiting for them. But they did it. Maybe, if they had known that nine of every ten would never survive our defenses but would crash into the ocean, they might not have tried. But that was not the case.

We first heard of them when they went after our carriers, positioned out of our sight over the horizon. But then they started after ships that were part of the invasion - transports and supply ships in particular. Destroyers were stationed at sixteen positions around Okinawa to serve as early warning sources for incoming attacks and the kamikazes soon learned to attack those ships to prevent the early warnings. As a result a number of destroyers were sunk and others were damaged enough to be removed from the picket line. Suddenly we were assigned a spot in the defensive ring - one of the two positions closest to Japan. The word gets around on board ship with miraculous speed and those of us who were not topside could only sit and wait. I was connected by phone with the bridge but really only heard part of what was going on. Suddenly we were thrown to the deck when something hit our ship. I was immediately ordered to take my team to the main engine room. We arrived midst extreme confusion and later determined that a kamikaze had headed for us but our gunfire caused him to glide into the water just short of our ship. Like a rock skipping across the surface of the water the engine flew out of the plane and into the 3/8 inch metal side of our ship. The engine came right through into the engine room. One man was dead and several others needed immediate medical attention. Fortunately the hole in the side of our ship was about two feet above the water line so we were not flooding. However, water was coming in as the result of waves hitting the side of the ship as we proceeded underway with such power as we could muster. We were immediately ordered to continue our radar watch until relieved by another ship, which, fortunately, occurred within an hour or so.

Meantime my crew was able to rig some sheets of plywood and some mattresses to cover the hole and we were able to continue underway to an emergency repair facility at the south end of the island. One engine was out of commission and the other suffered light damage. Our machinists were able to maintain some power throughout and soon had us proceeding, slowly, under power from our undamaged engine. The injured were removed to the sick bay and a few were transferred to a hospital ship, along with the body of the dead man. It all happened very suddenly and it was not until some order had been restored that some of us realized how shaken we were. But everyone carried on in good order. We had no choice.

At a temporary repair facility they improved as best they could on our own damage control work, principally by supplying some metal sheets that were placed in front of our mattresses covering the hole. But then we were ordered to another repair facility on an island some days away at our slow speed (the name of that facility escapes me now). But they had little time for us when larger ships needed help so we were sent on the long, slow trip to Guam. The trip seemed forever as we carefully watched our wound, hoping our repairs would hold, and by some very judicious work by our excellent crew members we were able to handle minor slippages until we did get there. That facility was too busy repairing the ships that were more important to the war effort than we were so we were patched up a little better and then sent on the long trip back to Pearl Harbor. Every one anticipated much time there for rest and recreation but upon arrival were told the shipyard could take us for just two days to make any repairs absolutely necessary and then we were to leave for Long Beach shipyard where major repairs were to be made. Many of the crew utilized the short time they had ashore in Honolulu to wash away much of the experience of Okinawa. It was good that the captain allowed a very relaxed ship to make the final slow journey to Long Beach where a dry dock was awaiting us. The shipyard workers came aboard and worked round the clock - much faster than many of the crew wanted as we all hoped to enjoy what we thought would be a well deserved rest back home.

And for the time we had, it was a pleasant time when we were off duty. I had to stay on board for much of the time as I had to oversee the repair work, which was going on round the clock. But one of our officers was from Pasadena and I spent a very pleasant day relaxing at his home. He and his parents took me to a concert in the Hollywood Bowl, a real treat. Once or twice I was able to arrange time off to go the Biltmore Hotel where rooms were reserved by the Navy for officers back from the Pacific. I enjoyed the time alone, ate in some nice restaurants, took a bus tour of Los Angeles and got my self back to a fairly normal condition.

Then, repairs completed, we were ordered down the coast to Oceanside to await the arrival of another UDT team and departure for Pearl. We could only guess what our ultimate destination was going to be, and it wasn't too pleasant a thought. The day before our UDT team was to come on board I had some time off so I rode the red cars into Los Angeles. I was on that ride when somehow, we heard that the Japanese had surrendered.

NAVY DIVER
Jack Tallon

At age 18 I enlisted in the Navy and arrived in Farragut, Idaho on Thanksgiving Day, 1942. Even though boot camp was 12 weeks, I was put in Ship's Company before Christmas and assigned to Seaman Guard (the base equivalent of shore patrol) for a couple of months. I was then transferred to the San Diego destroyer base where I was assigned to a landing craft unit for training as a coxswain on an LCM (landing craft mechanized).

During this training period, our unit was sent to Camp Pendleton to help in the filming of "Guadalcanal Diary." In June 1943, we were shipped to Oahu to train marines in amphibious landings. In the process we were losing boats at sea during training exercises and I was sent to the Pearl Harbor Submarine Base to become a diver. The suit with all of its weights was 195 pounds. I was a Boatswain's (Bosun) Mate 2nd class and upon graduation from diving school I was also a Diver 2nd class.

Most of the training was in the Harbor. The only area off limits to the diving school was the area around the battleship Arizona, sunk in the Pearl Harbor attack. About a quarter of the training was done in open ocean, where we did our qualifying dives and also had to dive to requalify when required.

All of my real diving after training was done in the ocean but in relatively shallow water - 30 to 40 feet in depth. The primary purpose of my training was to salvage boats up to 50 feet in length that were lost in landing accidents during maneuvers near shore or off the small islands. I did this when needed for about two years but it was not my primary job.

We did not have the upscale diving equipment that is available today. We used a Victor Berg mask and modified it for this work. We made lead weighted diving belts. It all worked well. There were three support people on a dive: a boat coxswain and two deck hands. One acted as handler to the diver and the other worked the hand pump. This was a double action pump, working on both forward and return strokes. They would periodically change jobs, depending on the depth of the diver, as pumping can be strenuous work. This team did a fair amount of salvage work since I was the only diver on the base. However, most of my time was still spent on my regular assignment.

The diving served me well, not only for the purpose of salvaging our boats but our unit was selected to train what was called at that time the "Underwater Demolition Team", now known as Navy seals.

By this time, I was a Bosun's mate 1st class and on the day President Roosevelt died, I was on board a ship in Pearl Harbor on my way back to San Francisco for reassignment and leave. After a 30 day leave, I was based in San Francisco awaiting orders when the war with Japan ended. I was reassigned to Port Hueneme near Oxnard to a systems support group, as senior non-commissioned officer of 250 men. The purpose of this team was to go to areas around the world as required to evacuate materials, equipment, etc. and return them to the United States or where ever they were needed. The men had to be trained as coxswains, crane operator, truck and equipment operators, longshoremen and many other things.

The day before our ship left, the Commander of Western Sea Frontier issued an order that anyone with a specified number of points did not have to go overseas again. I had this and one quarter point to spare. When I notified our Skipper that I had enough points to meet the requirements, he tried to get me to stay on by offering to promote me to Chief Bosun's Mate as soon as we passed the 3 mile limit. (Captains could promote outside the territorial limits of the US.) I chose not to do that and instead moved out so quickly I left my pea coat behind.

I remained at Port Hueneme and was made junior officer of the day, an assignment normally give to Chief Petty Officers. By now most of the Chiefs who were not career Navy had enough points to get out. I served in that capacity until I was discharged in June, 1946.

DUTY ABOARD U.S.S. ALBEMARLE - AV-5
William M. Christensen, Jr.

The U. S. S. Albemarle, AV-5 was a seaplane tender that spent the greater part of WW-II in the North Atlantic, Caribbean, Gulf of Mexico, South Atlantic, and Galapagos Islands. She was a floating seadrome for squadrons of PBY's and later PBM's which were flying anti-submarine patrols from remote inlets and island bays in the Atlantic and Caribbean. She was pressed into service on several occasions to transport other cargo and personnel to points overseas, such as England, Casablanca, Iceland etc.

I was the Aircraft Maintenance officer for the ship and was responsible for a crew of 150 aircraft mechanics and technicians who serviced the squadrons of planes assigned to the ship. The Captain of the ship when I reported aboard was Capt. Donald L. Mills who was relieved by Capt. Christian H. Duborg on May 11th, 1945. Captain Duborg was an Annapolis and Pensacola flight school graduate, but had not had sea duty prior to becoming commanding officer of the Albemarle.

The ship was in the Navy Yard in Boston for routine repairs, when he assumed command and we sailed from Boston to our home port of Norfolk, Virginia for a short stay before leaving on several cruises to various islands in the Caribbean, including Cuba, Trinidad and San Juan.

When we were deployed, we were usually escorted by two destroyers or destroyer escorts. When we joined a convoy out of New York, in May 1945, bound for England as the lead ship for column number 5, it was a new and unusual experience for both the captain and crew. About the second or third day out we began to encounter drifting fog banks that, when entered, reduced visibility to almost zero distance. At that point the convey commander, on the lead ship of column 4, ordered that each ship trail out a marker buoy to a distance of 300 yards.

Captain Duborg, summoned Chief Boatswainmate Harper to the bridge and inquired if we had such a device and was told the we did not but that given an hour or less, he could build one. It should be explained that a marker buoy is a device made of wood in the shape of a cross with a metal scoop located at the junction of the pieces of the cross that scooped up water. This sent a plume of water up into the air as the cross was dragged through the water. This plume of water could be observed by the following ship in line and allow the ship to keep a safe distance behind the one it was following. An observer in the bow of the following ship could keep it in sight and relay messages to the bridge as to what was necessary, as far as direction and speed were concerned, to keep station on it.

Boats Harper had the spar trailed out and some time later informed the Captain that he had completed the construction of the marker buoy. The Captain then gave the order to "Haul in the boat spar and trail out the marker buoy". Boats Harper did not question the order but proceeded to haul in the spar we were trailing and was ready to trail out the marker buoy. It should be pointed out at this juncture that the ship following us was a Swedish tanker with a typical, no nonsense, Swedish Captain as her master. Everything proceeded well until all at once the crew handling the lines on our stern looked unto the fog to see the bow of the Swedish tanker bearing down directly on them. The Swedish look-out must have seen what was happening about the same time our crew did and he relayed the message to his skipper. The Swedish skipper reacted quickly and his bow veered off and our men reported it missed us by only a few feet. There was supposed to be radio silence between ships but the Swede broke silence and really gave our Captain a few well chosen words of advice.

The war ended in Europe and the Albemarle entered the naval yard at Norfolk to be refitted to transport troops. Our hangar deck, which was located foreword of the main deck aft, about amidships, and had a cavernous interior approximately 80 -90 feet in width by 50- 60 feet in height and 80 feet in depth, was gutted and bunks installed stacked five high and less than three feet apart. There were approximately 1100 bunks installed. Other spaces on the ship were also converted and in the end we were capable of handling probably close to 2000 men.

My wife was expecting our first child in January of 1946 and we were scheduled to go to the South Pacific to bring home troops. We left Norfolk, Virginia and headed for the Panama Canal. This is as I remember the sequence of events. We had picked up a pilot in Colon and made the passage through Gatun Lake. I was officer of the deck stationed in the pilothouse, Captain Duborg and the Panamanian Pilot were out on the Bridge. The portholes to the Bridge were all open. We had had lunch, had entered the Calebra Cut and were passing through it. Capt. Duborg had asked if the pilot would like a cup of coffee and he had said "yes". I relayed the request to the Captain's steward who left the bridge to get the coffee. We had been making a turn to starboard (to the right) which meant that we had had on right rudder. The next order to the wheel was "Rudder amid ships." At that point in time the watch on the wheel changed and a new quartermaster took over, who we later discovered was not told what the prior commands to the wheel had been. While this was happening, the Captains Steward returned with the coffee and I was passing cups out through the porthole to the Captain and the pilot. The pilot then issued the order to "Meet Her" which meant to apply opposite rudder from what had been used in the turn in order to stop the continued swing of the bow and to hold to the new heading. The quartermaster on the wheel had applied left rudder and the bow began to swing towards the left bank. After a few seconds the pilot became aware of the situation and yelled "How's your rudder?" The quartermaster replied "Left rudder". I do not remember the exact amount.

Immediately there was an explosion of orders, "Full right rudder", "Full ahead Port", Full Back Starboard" Then as the bow started to come to the right the orders came "Full Left rudder", "Full back Port" and " Full Ahead Starboard". A short interval passed, then came the orders "rudder amidships" and Full ahead Port and Starboard. In checking the swing of the bow to the left towards the bank, by the first set of orders to the engines and the wheel, the pilot had induced a lateral motion to the stern of the ship that caused it to approach the side of the canal. The second set of orders were intended to check the lateral motion of the stern and keep it from colliding with the wall of the canal. The third set of orders were intended to check the swing of the stern towards the bank. We all held our breath but there was sickening shudder in the ship as the stern collided with the rocks on the wall of the canal.

We limped into Panama on the Starboard screw and tied up at a pier, sent divers over to inspect the damage and found one blade missing from the four bladed port screw and a hole in our hull about the size of a Volkswagen.

Shortly there after it was found that there was a two or three minute difference in the clocks on the bridge and those in the engine room. These discrepancies were corrected and the reports of the accident written up. Captain Duborg entrusted me with the reports of the accident and I was driven across the isthmus to Cocoa Solo to deliver the papers to the proper authority at the Naval Headquarters there.

Temporary repairs were made to the ship and we sailed for San Francisco, traveling at only 8 to 10 knots. We made it to the Alameda Naval Air Station and then into a Navy yard where the port screw was replaced and the damage to the hull repaired. During all this time I was continually kidded by other officers saying that the reason the ship was in San Francisco was because I wanted to see my wife, who lived in Pasadena, again before our child was born. Repairs were completed and we made two trips to the South Pacific. The first to Noumea, New Caledonia and the second to Tacloban in the gulf of Leyte in the Philippines before returning to the Naval Air Station at Alameda, San Francisco Bay on 14 January 1946. As soon as the phone lines were connected, I called my wife to tell her I was back and that within the next day or two the ship would be sailing for Long Beach Naval Ship Yard for some repairs. My wife told me that she had seen the pediatrician that day and he had said the baby would not be born for several more days. So with that information we decided that I would stay in San Francisco and ride the ship to Long Beach.

Anticipating that I would want to have as much leave as possible while in Long Beach, I swapped my shore leave in San Francisco, with other Officers for their shore leave in Long Beach. That evening when the movie had just begun I had a phone call from my Father-in-law to tell me that he was at the Huntington Hospital in Pasadena and that my wife was in the delivery room. Not only was I Officer of the deck until 2:00 AM, but I was the senior officer aboard. The Captain and Executive Officer were both ashore, whereabouts unknown, and the duty officer was junior to me in rank and could not issue the orders I would need to get to Pasadena. I finally tracked down the Executive Officer and he gave the duty officer permission to issue orders for me to have leave.

I got in touch with the airlines, they were scheduling an extra flight from San Francisco to Burbank that was to leave at 2:00 AM. They would hold a seat for me if I could get there. I was in Alameda and fortunately was able to use one of my plane personnel boats, which has a top speed of approximately 30 knots, to get me across the bay to San Francisco, where I caught a cab to the airport. I made the connection with no more than a minute or two to spare. I got into Burbank about 6:00 AM, called the hospital and found that our daughter had been born about 2:30 A.M. as I was flying to Burbank. I came that close to being there.

I had enough points and was released to inactive duty about two months later. The Albemarle, after being refitted in Long Beach, sailed for Bikini Atoll and was the trigger ship for the atomic tests that were conducted there in 1946.

PEARL HARBOR, MIDWAY AND NORFOLK
Bob Stafford

When WW II began, I was in law school in Connecticut and they had given us a full semester during summer session of 1941, so that I could finish school by January 1942, the end of the regular semester. When Pearl Harbor was attacked on December 7th, I wasn't able to reach my family at home in Hawaii. Another Hawaiian student at the law school and I went down to Washington to try to see if we could make contact through the office of the Delegate to Congress from Hawaii who knew my family. Through his assistance we were able to talk to our families.

One day while I was walking along the street in Washington, someone behind me said, "What the hell are you doing out of uniform, Stafford?" I turned around and saw Capt. Lewis, the father of a girl I had dated throughout my senior year in high school and whom I knew well because he was interested in boating. He knew that I had quite a lot of experience in small boats around and among the islands in Hawaii, and that I enjoyed and spent some time in scuba diving and under water spear fishing, as so many kids did in Hawaii at that time. I explained to him that I'd contacted the authorities in Connecticut, but they didn't seem to feel that they could do anything about my entry into the service since I was a resident of Hawaii. He thought he could help and he gave me his card which he addressed to an Officer of the Bureau of Naval Personnel in Anacostia, Maryland. He told me to take the card over there and he was sure that they would be able to work out some way to solve that particular problem.

They were very helpful and went as far as arranging for me to complete my law school exams and take the District of Columbia Bar in February. They told me that I would be commissioned and would receive orders to Pearl Harbor and orders for Navy transportation leaving from Washington and connecting with a ship from the West Coast to the Naval Air station on Ford Island at Pearl Harbor. Meanwhile, I should return to the school and to wait for those documents. I did so and in February received the orders which instructed me to proceed by Navy transportation to the West Coast and then to the ship from Oakland to Pearl Harbor where I was to be stationed.

Marylouise and I had been planning to get married after I finished law school and the departure orders made it possible for us to be married on March 10th at her home in California before I took the ship to Hawaii.

At the Naval Air Station, I was first assigned to the personnel office but asked to transfer to a sea division. When they discovered my background experience in small boats, I was transferred to the boat division. That division had boats that furnished transportation back and forth between Ford Island Air Station and the shore and crash boats that carried out the air/sea rescue functions for the air station and the rest of Pearl Harbor. As part of that work, I was assigned to a deep-sea diving school because, of course, a lot of air/sea rescue work involved airplane crashes in and around Pearl Harbor. This required diving equipment to get people out of the plane and then remove the planes that had crashed in the water.

Several battle ships, including the Arizona, the Oklahoma, and the California had been sunk at their moorings along the west side of Ford Island. The Arizona went right straight down and as you know, has been made into a memorial of the events that occurred on Pearl Harbor day. The Oklahoma received a number of torpedoes along the port side and rolled over before she sank so that her keel was essentially straight up in the air. In order to roll her back upright again, the Navy set up series of winches on the Island. We had to run cables out over the hull and down to the deck underwater on the outboard side so that when they tightened up on the cables, she rolled up straight. The torpedo holes in the hull were then covered and she was pumped out and hauled right side up as she lay in the water and it was then possible to remove her.

Because I was a lawyer, some of the men in our division and later from other units on Ford Island asked me from time to time to represent them when they were charged with some Court Martial offense. These courts almost always convicted the defendants. (This makes me very concerned about the present proposals by our Federal Attorney General to try civilians in military courts for alleged offenses connected with our present world problems.)

I remember once when we were walking down the hall to a courtroom to try a case in which a very serious offense was charged, the Admiral who was to be the senior member of the Judges' panel was walking behind us. I heard him say to another member of the Court, "I don't know why they keep sending these cases to us. The Captain wouldn't send these guys to us if they weren't guilty." Needless to say, the defense lost almost all its cases, but the saving grace was that all Courts martial records were reviewed by the Judge Advocate General's office in Washington and they had the power to reverse the decision of the Court Martial panel. It took a long time but after awhile, we began to get a lot of reversals of convictions.

One day the commanding officer of the Air Station called me into his office and said, "Stafford, I want you to stop defending courts martial!" He had several reversal notices from Washington lying on his desk.

I said, "Captain, I don't think that's a legal order," and cited the Navy Regulation section about a sailor's right to representation before a Court Martial.

He became very angry and said, "What does a blankity blank Ensign know about it?"

Within a month, in May of 1943, I received orders to Midway Island, to the air/sea rescue division at the Naval Air Station there. I was the skipper of a PT boat that was used for air/sea rescue operations both with the training program in the harbor and in the ocean area around the island.

From time to time, the Army Air Force would send a group of bombers over to Wake Island with a fuel stop at Midway. When they went out, the PT boat was assigned to go out about halfway to Wake Island in order to be as close as possible in the event some sort of damage occurred to the plane: if it was having trouble getting back, we would be as close as we could to help.

One time when we were coming back into Midway Harbor from that mission at night, we radioed in to notify the command post that we were coming in and they were suppose to notify the Marines at the gun emplacements along the entrance of the harbor. Something slipped and as we came into the harbor, the Marines fired on us and blew off a part of the transom although, fortunately, they didn't hit the torpedoes. Actually, that's the only time anybody shot at me during the whole war.

In the fall of 1943, I was transferred to Naval Air Station in Norfolk to the boat division there for air/sea rescue and diving operations. We were responsible for aircraft salvage operations up and down the coast as far as the north end of the Chesapeake Bay and down to Pimlico Sound and Cherry Point Naval Air Station in North Carolina. Chesapeake Bay was used by the aircraft carriers of the Atlantic coast and for training of new pilots in landing and takeoff while the ship was underway. If a plane crashed in the water, it was our job to get there in time to get the pilot out before the plane sank and then to salvage the airplane. The oyster bed owners in the Chesapeake Bay were very unhappy when the planes stayed on the bottom very long and the gasoline and oil from the planes caused damage to the oyster bed.

I'll never forget the time that I was called to a salvage operation in Cherry Point in North Carolina, where the American forces were training Russian pilots. A plane had crashed there with several people on board and it fell to us to raise the plane and get the bodies out of the plane in fairly deep water involving deep sea diving equipment. When I arrived at Cherry Point, I was introduced to the Russian Colonel who was the commander of the Russian unit there and was anxious to stay close to the operation. He talked about all of the crew as his "boys," and when we would bring a body out of the wreckage, the tears would run down his face and he would hold the person in his arms for a moment before he was turned over to the medical units. I'll never forget the love and care that he showed for those men.

We were stationed at Norfolk for the rest of the war.

THE C B's

August Weigle

I graduated from Pomona High School in June 1943, with a 1A draft classification. Mid-July I received my "GREETINGS" and in early August reported to LA for induction physical. I requested Army, but while passing through I noticed a Navy Chief stamp "U.S.Navy'" on my records. I asked him what he put there, as I had asked for the Army, he stated in no uncertain terms "that I was in the Navy!" When crossing a hallway, two men approached me and asked me to step out of the line of men. They asked me if I would like the C.B's, about which I knew nothing. They stated that, "they were construction battalions, land based, combat trained, and needed big men." Sounded like what I really wanted. I was then classified as selective volunteer on special assignment.

I reported to the LA train station early morning Mid-August. We traveled five nights and four days. I saw this beautiful country of ours before arriving at Williamsburg, VA. A sailor mispronounced my name and I missed his call. I received a two hour fire watch at midnight my first night in boot camp. In my boot company there were two other men from Pomona, both over six feet as I was, and their surnames started with W's. Guess what men led the columns. Upon breaking boot I was assigned into the 137th Construction Battalion, but what happened to my two Pomona buddies I do not know as I never heard from them again.

My battalion immediately shipped out by train to Davisville, Rhode Island, an advance base depot for combat and specialized training. We arrived mid-October and left in January 1944. A very mild winter according to the natives, but it was snowing when we left and I experienced shoveling snow, for most of a night, on one occasion. They had to give us sulfa pills and some old CCC greens to wear to help make the battalion healthy before we could ship out. Navy regulations were that a battalion of men must be at least 50% healthy.

Our next stop was Gulfport, Mississippi, another advanced base depot. The men from East of the Mississippi River received a 10 day leave. I, in turn, was assigned to public works details. I changed truck tires, picked up trash, pealed potatoes, picked up or moved rocks, K.P. duty, scrubbed out garbage cans till they glistened, and scrubbed cooking pots & pans (mounds of them). Upon the return of the first group, we men from the west received our 10 day leave. Upon returning we made a practice invasion of Cat Island 12 miles out in the bay. We were to stay a week and set up island X type base. The labor unions were strong and anything that we erected had to be taken down. Further, the first day we were there a storm loomed up and by the end of the week a full hurricane was in force. We, the Navy had to be rescued from off of the island by PT boats (rescue for Keesler Field) of the Army. Our battalion, the 137th, along with 4 other battalions was decommissioned. Most of the men in my company were assigned to a casual draft. The latter were quickly outfitted and shipped out. We later heard that they participated in the Tarawa invasion. I personally was assigned to C.B.M.U. #597. The M.U. stands for maintenance unit. Shortly thereafter we shipped out to Port Hueneme, CA., an advanced base depot. At this base we continued our combat training and also received specialized training. I attended a fire fighting and a stevedore school. I did not know at the time but the latter training became very important.

In March we were issued our overseas gear and shipped out to Hawaii. We received jungle training, did some construction work, but most important of all, we did stevedoring full time; unloading and then later loading ours and others' supplies for our island X assignment. My outfit shipped out in May. I was assigned to rear guard duty, loading additional ships, before we then shipped out. We laid over in the Marshall Islands for a few days. What a desolate spot, no trees left standing, dust flying all over. We arrived on Saipan in early August and were transferred by Higgins boats to Tinian, where my outfit had made camp in the Tinian school grounds, a week or so before. Our camp was up a steep hill approximately 1\4 of a mile from the South Beach, where we unloaded all ship to shore material brought to Tinian. The war materials were then transported to central staging or compound areas by trucks, on which we also rode shotgun. As the trucks labored up the hill going pass our camp, we were able to slip off articles that we needed, such as DDT.

The flies and mosquitoes were horrendous. The natives used human waste for fertilizer so there was a plague of flies. We set up flytraps all over, but natives would attempt to let them out. There was some malaria present, through the mosquitoes, but dengue fever was very prevalent. We worked hard, 12 to 14 hour shifts, 7 days a week. The Japanese had built a short cement causeway and C.B's improved it with additional pontoons, so as to enlarge it for additional small boats to anchor. The end of August the annual monsoon hit us. We battled to save the LCFs and LCM's that were caught beached, because of heavy cargo loads that we were unable to unload. We had cables strung all over the beach tied down to dead men (niggerheads), and our heavy equipment. The huge waves would make these cables "come alive" and could very well snap a person's leg off if not careful. We also worked our butts off helping the 9th CB's to save the causeway. We did the bulk of the work (app. 200 men in our unit) to the 9th's full battalion of men being available. The 9th received a Presidential Unit Citation for their efforts, not so for us. We continued stevedoring through October, although the Army took over island command about the end of September and the trucking of supplies was then done by Army personnel.

During this period we were sending work crews to help construct the Naval Air Station. This air base was the purpose for our being here on Tinian. We ultimately would provide the maintenance for this base. In December my outfit moved up to the air base. I again remained in rear guard action, protecting our camp, and still stevedoring. We had a Christmas dinner in our chow hall (the school's classrooms) which incidentally was the first of such on the island and the first to serve hot foods, even if they were C & K rations, or Spam. The Marines and sailors would line up in our chow lines. I helped build the first reefers on the island and had my first experience of working with spun glass. My clothing and skin were punctured, but at least we were then able to get some meat and vegetables on the island. The Christmas dinner was all ours, we ate the chickens (babies) we brought from Hawaii. We had an assigned crew to nurture, feed and to protect. They molted practically all of their feathers by the time they had arrived in the Marshalls. When we got to the island we mixed them up with some "gook" chickens, and had to maintain an armed guard over them at all times, to prevent the Marines from stealing them. Have you ever heard of any other outfit to take baby chickens? Leave it to the Seabees. We, the rear guard, after clearing and squaring away our camp then moved up to the air base.

We were quartered in Quonset huts, but still had open air showers of cold water for the duration of our time on Tinian. The macho AA crew of Marines right across the street lived in squad tents, with open air facilities for everything, all during my stay on this island. This was January and I had obtained the rate of a C/M (carpenter's mate) 3rd Class and was assigned to a crew doing new and maintenance construction. I helped to build a laundry facility. This was great, because upon completion and operating, it meant no more personal washing of my effects.

Tinian was destined to be just a floating air base, and a staging area for advancements against the Japs. We had two B29 bases, our air base and an old Japanese strip. The Japanese were bombing the heck out of Saipan, but did not bother us very much. During the stevedoring episodes, all of our beached ships were flying red flags and Nip planes, as an afterthought of their strafing of Saipan would seem to veer away from us and strafed up the beach, where we were building a desalination plant. We never stopped work, or shut down operations, with all kinds of flood lights and heavy machinery operating. In fact, during the first couple of months, the Marine AA crews were threatened with a Court Martial if they opened up their fire in retaliation. The Command did not want to draw the Japs' attention to what was being constructed on the island.

Agua, a little island just three miles away, was still Japanese held even to the war's end. It provided a means whereby the Jap planes would skim in behind said island (cutting off our radar) and then they would skip bomb the B29 fields, so low that sometimes the bombs failed to detonate. Also, the 20's & 40's could not lower their field of fire, whereas the CB's with camps and work in the immediate area, set up their own special weapons, 50 caliber machine guns, and became very effective in helping to combat these attacks. The Marines on two different occasions attempted to invade Agua and failed. It had extremely high cliffs. For the first couple of months, every day about noon, a salvo of Long Tom (155 millimeter cannon) would fire upon this island, and each time a part of Tinian would shake. To counter the Jap planes skimming behind the island the Navy picketed some ships near the island, so that the ship's radar could detect incoming Jap planes. There were no fighter planes either on Saipan or Tinian. We had to depend upon aid from Guam, if any was forthcoming. In time we received such aid, and could hear a blow by blow description on the ground, of two, three or more bogies being sighted, attacked, destroyed, or chased off. The Japs then reverted to night bombing, but were in for a big surprise because "Black Widow" night fighters had been incorporated in our defense. They could be upon you before hearing them, and then only see their tail exhaust as they blasted away.

Another condition where the island would seem to rock, was underwater explosions detonated at noon. This operation went on for days and weeks, with geysers of water shooting way up into the air; the purpose being to demolish the coral rock to a condition that a dredge could remove it, and in turn to give depth to the harbor. Now, the larger ships such as a Liberty, Victory or an LST, could enter and dock. Before the war was over it was a beautiful harbor, with a breakwater & docking facilities provided.

One night while we were asleep, an instant and blinding, daylight like flash occurred, then a thunderous explosion, knocking us out of our bunks, and then the implosion. We hit our shelters or foxholes, which had not been used for months, thinking that a near miss bomb had been dropped. Next day it was reported that a C.B. ammunition dump had blown up. Scuttlebutt, on the island after the atomic bombings, was that, while assembling the bomb, a minor reaction occurred. Not the ammo dump! Life went on. I received a promotion to C/M 2nd Class. We were sending at least 50% or better of the 1,000 plane bombing raids over Japan from Tinian. We also were sending a lone plane from a very strange bomb group stationed at North field. This group was made a buffoon all over the island for their antics, so much so, that the scuttlebutt was, we were preparing for gas warfare. We knew that the Japs had conducted the same in China. As it turned out this was the bomb group that delivered the two atomic bombs. We heard about the first atomic bombing from Radio San Francisco and that set the island abuzz. 50 thousand men on the island and possible only a dozen or more men knew what was up. We remembered seeing some civilians roaming about, but thought that they were merchant mariners.

Just before the war ended in August, I was made boss of my own carpenter crew. And about that time of year we again suffered a devastating monsoon. There were two results of the storm. One, that the two porches I and my company members had built onto our hut withstood the storm, but that a large nose hanger for repairing aircraft, had been badly damaged. I received the assignment to repair this hanger to its original state. We were just about to put the finishing touches to the roof when our Chief climbed up on the roof and said, "Augie, return to your hut and pack your bag. You are going home." I was very proud of our work, and really wanted to finish the job, especially after the men working below had stated that they did not think we could repair it. This was early December '45.

I was transported by a mail boat to Saipan, where I, with hundreds of other men, was assigned to squad tents awaiting transportation back to the states. On the 13th I received transport on an APA ship. At first we were to go to Hawaii, but it was too full, so we were then routed for San Francisco. Then upon approaching San Francisco, we were rerouted to Seattle. It was miserably cold, damp and wet. I processed in 3 days, having to use my lunch periods to scrounge up a dress uniform with blue cap and a pea jacket so that I could take leave of the base, as my sea bag had not caught up with me. I left on the 21st and traveled on the streamliner. What comfort. What a sight traveling down through Washington and Oregon. It was snowing, streams flowing and the trees heavily laden with fresh snow. I caught one hell of a cold in Seattle. It took almost my full 30 day leave to cure it. I was home for Christmas (just unbelievable) and had papers to report to Terminal Island Naval Base on Jan. 21st for reassignment. I was reassigned to the USS Alabama, which was anchored beyond the breakwaters of Long Beach Harbor. On board, I was assigned to the E compartment (construction). I was one of 13 Seabees so assigned. There was a Chief Carpenter Mate, no 1st class C\M. I was the only 2nd class C\M on board and there were several 3rd class C\M's.

I was assigned a detail to repair a gangway damaged by the skipper's gig. It was made of hard inlaid wood, not my specialty, but fortunately some of the men in my crew were very capable. Most of my work, while on board, consisted of making up shipping boxes for the Officers, and some pine wood caskets.

We had an Admiral on board; the majority of sailors were boots, so everything was strictly G.I. We had to wear undress blues to dine, and to go top side, unless on a work detail. We had to dine by ranks. I had read in a BuPers magazine that if a man was in his immediate discharge district and he had less than 20 days to be discharged, that he could not be transferred out of his immediate district. I and several other men signed a petition and delivered it to the Captain.

The ship was scheduled to pull anchor at 3:00 PM. We, who signed the paper, were allowed to take leave at 1:30 PM. I returned to Terminal Island for discharge. I was scheduled for discharge on March 15th, but was discharged March 6, 1946.

"THEY ALSO SERVE WHO STAND AND WAIT"
Glenn Cornwell

I don't know who made the above statement but I'm sure it must have been someone who had a good overall picture of those in service and their contributions to the total war effort. As I recall, there wasn't a lot of standing around in my WWII experience, but then my contribution was definitely of the non glamorous variety of support to the men who were out in the front shooting guns, dropping bombs, and firing torpedoes.

After graduation in 1942 from Pomona College, I enrolled at Harvard Business School with the expectation of receiving a commission in the Navy Supply Corps. Two months into the year course, I received my Ensign's Commission, but on inactive duty. Upon completion at Harvard, I went on active duty, stationed at the Naval Air Station in San Diego until I returned to the Navy Supply School.

My first billet was as Disbursing Officer for GroPac 10 (Group Pacific 10). We formed in Norfolk, Va. and staged in Iroquois Point, Oahu, Hawaii. My job was paymaster for the outfit and I also paid any Navy ship or group in the vicinity that did not have access to reimbursement. But that required cash. In the staging mode, the future is unknown except we knew we were headed west to some island destination in the Pacific. My office was to be the bank.

Banks need money to operate. One day seven storekeepers (my staff), two armed guards, and I (also well armed) boarded a truck and went to the Bank of Hawaii in Honolulu to pick up $100,000. There was $95,000 in standard U.S. currency with "HAWAII" imprinted on the bills. This was in case the enemy would get a hold of them, they could be declared illegal tender. The other $5,000 was in coin and the reason so many men were required on the expedition. It came in bulk in large sacks-pennies, nickels, dimes, quarters, and half dollars. They were heavy!

When our outfit received orders to sail, as passenger troops, my group kept busy wrapping all $5,000 in the coin wrappers that are still familiar to everyone. I was personally responsible for the entire $100,000 so the cash, whether coin or bills, had to be accounted for exactly. After we got to our destination and we were a working entity. I would pay out one day and receive much of it back the next day from the post office clerk who had sold money orders for the men to send home. The bills were recycled to the point that they were used until I could see light through them and then I would set them aside in the safe and bring out new ones.

This was necessary because our mission was indefinite and the bank in Honolulu was 5000 miles away.

GroPac 10's destination was Angaur in the Palau Islands. We landed in the second echelon of the operation and after our initial squaring away, my job was rather routine. I paid CB's, Coast Guard, and passing ships as well as our own personnel. Angaur, along with Pelelieu, our neighboring island 7 miles to the north, were taken to establish B24 bases. These served as take-offs for operations to neutralize Koror and soften resistance in Tinian and Saipan to make landings possible on the stepping stones to Japan.

As the war progressed there was no longer need for a port facility on Angaur and GroPac 10 was decommissioned. I did wait in Guam for a short while for reassignment to ComServDiv 102 (Commander Service Division 102) as a Supply Officer. I joined the outfit in Eniwetok and after the atom bombs were dropped we went to Tokyo Bay where we were when the peace was signed.

When I returned to the States I was assigned to the 11th Naval District Disbursing Office. By then I did wait (with minimum duties) until I had enough service points to be discharged as a full Lieutenant, Supply Corps, U.S. Naval Reserve.

OKINAWA: THE BEGINNING AND THE END
Bob Poindexter
PROLOGUE:
Sunday morning, December 7th, 1941 started out as a normal weekend day in our college student house at Caltech. We were a week from starting term finals, and were mostly in our rooms studying when urgent sounds led us to the house lounge. There, most of our fellow students were clustered around the radio with expressions of disbelief. How could the attack on Pearl Harbor possibly be happening?

Same time, 1942, I was in my junior year. By that time, we had registered for the draft, had ration books, and the United States was gearing up its military and industrial forces to meet the challenges of War in Europe and in the Pacific. We did not yet have an officer training program such as the Navy V-12 or Meteorology programs in place at Caltech, and the local draft board was beginning to look at us undergraduates to help fill quotas.

Surprisingly, a notice appeared on an employment opportunity bulletin board stating that the General Motors Corporation was looking for several undergraduate Mechanical Engineers to go to work immediately in Detroit as Junior Aerodynamicists. Four of us applied, were interviewed by a General Motors personnel director, and were all hired to report for work in early January 1943.

The projects that we were working on went well until the spring of 1944. G. M. did not get the production contracts that were the objective of our work, and gradually our draft deferment priority faded. By May, I had a notice from my draft board in Pasadena and in early June returned to California.

Induction Day was an unforgettable experience. We boarded a Pacific Electric streetcar in Pasadena and went to the processing center in Los Angeles. There, we were poked and prodded, questioned and examined, given lunch coupons and finally ushered into a large room. Here we were told that each day had its quota for Army, Navy and Marine recruits. Those who didn't initially volunteer for whichever service had the highest quota on that day would arbitrarily be assigned to whatever quota was not filled. Volunteers for the Marines were called first, and for some reason, that I still cannot explain to my own satisfaction, I stepped forward. Perhaps it was because this call came first, and I don't like prolonging decisions. By late afternoon, we were on a bus headed for San Diego and two months of boot camp. Another unforgettable experience! But that is another story.

In late November, I was on the island of Saipan in the Mariana Islands as part of large replacement unit. This was several months after the battle of Saipan and Tinian, and American troops were now within bomber range of Japan. I was assigned as a member of the Intelligence Section, Headquarters and Service Company, 8th Marine Battalion of the Second Marine Division (R-2, H&S Co., 8th Marines, 2nd MarDiv as we were known.)

OKINAWA - THE BEGINNING

Early in 1945, in addition to occasional forays into the heavy growth of Saipan in search of Japanese holdouts, we commenced active training for a new campaign. We were well aware of the invasion of Iwo Jima in January, but were not directly involved. It was also clear that the B-29s stationed here were making more frequent flights to Japan and that there was some reciprocal bombing coming our way. Finally, in late March, we started to load our entire Division onto troop ships of various types. Our unit was part of a contingent aboard an LST (Landing-Ship-Tank) that had a flat bottom, shallow draft, and a large ramp for unloading amphibious vehicles into the water, or tanks and trucks onto a beach. In our case, troops were to go ashore in amphibious tractors (amtracs) which were a steel shell that carried troops and were driven by a propeller and by caterpillar treads. Power came from a very noisy radial aircraft engine mounted amidships.

April 1, 1945 was Easter Sunday, April Fool's Day, and Love Day or L-Day all in one. We arrived offshore Okinawa early, but unknown to us was that the genuine invasion was taking place on the west side of the island while we were taking part in a simulated invasion on the southeast quadrant. One of our Regimental battalions took a heavy blow when one of their ships was sunk and another badly damaged by kamikaze planes; otherwise all went smoothly according to plan. We embarked early in the morning and before reaching shore turned back to our ships to spend the rest of the day and that night at sea. The action was repeated the next morning and then we beat a hasty retreat back to Saipan. During our brief stay at Okinawa, we were considered a floating reserve force in case we were needed, but when the actual invading troops met virtually no resistance in the beginning days, there was little need to expose our Division to further kamikaze action which was increasing in intensity.

OKINAWA - THE END:

After returning to Saipan, we resumed training, not knowing what lay ahead but presuming that in the not too distant future we would be embarking for Japan. But by mid-May, it became apparent that the battle for Okinawa was not going as well as hoped and that Japanese kamikaze planes were becoming an increasing problem. It was determined that two radar stations to the north of Okinawa would be of great help in early detection of incoming flights. The 8* Marine Regiment boarded ship once again on May 16th, to land and take the two small islands of Iheya Shima to the northwest and Aguni Shima to the west of Okinawa. [Shima simply means Island in Japanese]

The reinforced regiment occupied 26 LST's and went first to Iheya, arriving on June 3rd. After receiving no response from shore, the landing was made without opposition - even the civilians had fled inland. Rain and mud were the principal nuisance. By the end of June 4th, all was secure and we had a brief respite.

Nothing quite so pleasant had happened to the Second Marine Division since the occupation of Apamama nearly two years before. For nearly a fortnight, the Marines of the special landing force enjoyed what could almost be considered a resort vacation. True, some units were busy rounding up and interning civilians, and the doctors were occupied with treating the few Okinawans injured in the bombardment. But many of the Marines had little to do. They set up a post office and store and even rode the little Okinawa ponies bareback.

But then we had orders to move south to the main Okinawa engagement and on June 16th made our landing. By early morning on the 18th, we relieved the 7th Regiment of the First Marine Division. I was assigned to lead a small group to establish an observation post at a suitable point on Mezado Ridge that had a clear view of the remaining southern part of the island. We had inherited a large pair of Japanese binoculars from the 7th Marines, but chose to keep these well secluded, so that observations could be made from a prone position, but certainly not a standing one. Unfortunately, as the morning progressed, more and more people began to occupy this area, and were beginning to ignore all of the rigorous cautionary training that we had received as regards unnecessary exposure. In fact, there was distant sniper fire coming our way, apparently from a lone rifleman, who finally did manage to hit one of our men in the foot.

By noon, the binoculars and their tripod were upright and a fair number of troops were also standing on the ridge. Then the Commanding General of the entire Okinawa campaign, Lt. General Simon Bolivar Buckner showed up, and with two other senior officers did have the good sense to go below the brow of the ridge to observe the progress. Buckner stayed for about an hour and remarked finally, "Things are going so well here I think I'll move on to another unit."

These were almost his last words. Whether the Japanese, through their powerful, long-range glasses, had somehow discerned his presence, probably will never be known. At any rate, with the suddenness of a clap of thunder, five Japanese artillery shells struck directly on the observation post. They were big shells - probably 15 cm - and they blasted the coral heads and the men between them.

I personally always felt that lack of discipline in the fundamental training we had received was somehow directly responsible for this incident. The ridge was demonstrably not safe as evidenced by the sniper. On reconnoitering in the land below the ridge the following day, it became apparent that many Japanese troops had been bypassed in their underground positions and were still a threat to us.

By late afternoon of the next day, Marines of the 8th Regiment broke through the last barrier to the southern shores of Okinawa. The battle for Okinawa was over, and as it turned out, these last two days constituted the last major attack of World War II although it was not until June 22nd that the Island was officially proclaimed secure.

I personally was in the unique position of being an observer to these final days without having to fire my rifle or face enemy troops, though I will admit that the two nights we spent at the front were dark and long.

EPILOGUE:

This story is not complete without mention of the implications of the atomic bombs dropped on Hiroshima and Nagasaki. Here are some comments as to what lay ahead if an invasion of Japan had taken place.

A top Navy Admiral described the battle of Okinawa as "a bloody, hellish prelude to the invasion of Japan." As protracted a nightmare as Okinawa had been, every survivor knew in his heart that the next battles in Kyushu and Honshu would be incalculably worse.

In Japan, thousands of suicide aircraft and boats would attack the American fleet, targeting troop transports in an effort to disrupt the landings. Then newly organized defense divisions occupying heavy fortifications overlooking the beaches, would attempt to prevent the landing force from gaining a foothold. Finally, mobile divisions based inland would counterattack toward threatened positions. In August of 1945 Japanese ground forces on Kyushu consisted of 14 divisions and several independent brigades, about 600,000 die-hard troops, most of whom were deployed near the invasion area.

Ideally, an attacking force should have at least a three-to-one superiority in numbers over the defenders. On Kyushu, American and Japanese ground forces would be of almost equal strength. In addition to the regular military units, Allied forces would also face a large citizen militia, armed with whatever was at hand.

But what was Japan defending? Their Navy was lost as was their long-range air fleet. The military defense of each one of the Pacific islands had cost them dearly as had the more recent daily bombing of the homeland, in terms of civilian morale. How much more were the Japanese people willing to suffer? We had asked repeatedly for surrender, though insisting that it be an unconditional surrender. Before the atom bombs the Japanese government sought Russian mediation, hoping to reach some sort of compromise. Despite the success of the Hiroshima bomb, Japan would still not agree to our terms and so the second one landed at Nagasaki, bringing the war to an immediate end on August 15, 1945, when the Emperor of Japan addressed his nation.

If only the development of A-bombs and weaponry had stopped here, think about what a different era would have followed. I sent a letter to TIME Magazine that was published April 1, 1946:

"Is there anyone in this world who really wants another war - who truthfully believes that an atomic war could be won satisfactorily by one nation or a group of nations? Then why are we talking about the next war [WWIII] as a foregone conclusion?"

To end this account, the Second Marine Division landed near Nagasaki on September 23 to begin the occupation of the southern part of Japan - the island of Kyushu. We were soon deployed into small units at various points on the islands and had six months to learn something of the Japanese way of life. I spent some time in an industrial city, Omuta, living in a former ship officers' club with excellent Japanese cuisine, took some weekend trips to nearby resort areas, and took two recreational trips. The first was to Mt. Aso, an occasionally active volcano with a delightful hotel nearby, and the second to the city of Kyoto where we viewed the ruins of Hiroshima from the train windows enroute. But the best experience of all, after about six weeks of idleness at the end was boarding a ship for the non-stop trip to San Diego.

NAVAL BOMB DISPOSAL
Ben Souther

I was at Harvard Business School and we were advised that we could have a direct commission either in Army Supply or in the Navy Ordnance department. I chose the Navy and was commissioned an Ensign. I was called to active duty in September 1942 and sent to Fort Schuyler for indoctrination. Following this, I was sent to Washington, DC to the bomb disposal school for a course in U. S. aviation ordnance. This was located at American University and the course covered American bombs and fuses. After the completion of the course, I was ordered to stay on at the school as an instructor.

One of the extra duties of the instructors was to examine suspicious pieces of ordnance that were found and people suspected were bombs. We examined them and blew them up if necessary. I went on a number of these calls on the East Coast, teamed with a Navy chief petty officer. After a time as instructor, I was allowed to take the bomb disposal course, while still teaching the basic ordnance course. The disposal course covered all types of British, German, Italian, and Japanese bombs; identifying and disposing of them. The course taught us how to dig a crater around the bomb, supporting the edges with timbers, and then disposing of the bomb. This was very similar to the show "UXB", unexploded bomb, which was seen on British TV much later. One of the places we went was to the Navy rocket firing ranges. There were always some that didn't explode. My chief and I carried primacord fuse and quarter pound blocks of explosive. We would place the explosive beside the unexploded rocket, fuse it, and then blow them up.

I was promoted to Lieutenant (jg) while at the school. After a time of teaching directly in the school, I was assigned to travel to various naval bases, mostly Air

Stations, to give concentrated courses on bombs and fuses. These would be four or five days and I traveled widely around the country, returning to the school in Washington as my base. Among others, I taught at the Air Stations at Norfolk, Jacksonville, Florida, and Patuxent near Washington.

In early 1944 I was sent to ComAirPac (commander air Pacific) at Pearl Harbor. I instructed in bombs and fuses to both ground personnel and pilots at various land bases around Hawaii. In November of 1944 I began sea duty. I went to sea on the escort carrier USS Steamer Bay, followed by other ships. I would catch the ship when it was about to leave Pearl and stay on it while it picked up its planes and checked new equipment and sea-worthiness. At sea we ran classes on bombs and I was usually out for four to five days. I was promoted to Lieutenant while on this duty.

Later I joined the USS Independence, a light carrier, at Pearl and traveled on it to Ulithi atoll where there was a large fleet anchorage. I was supposed to go to the carrier USS Franklin at Ulithi and then go to Okinawa and later Japan. At Ulithi the Independence received a new squadron of planes and they asked for me to stay and check out the ordnance on the planes. During this time, the Franklin went to sea and I stayed on the Independence as it operated at sea and went to bomb Okinawa. The Franklin was in the next group of ships and I was able to see the kamakazi pilots attacking it and the fires they started. It was so badly damaged that it was towed back to the United States for repair and I never did transfer to it.

We were off Japan and I had orders to transfer to a tanker and then returned on it to Ulithi. I then flew to Pearl Harbor, via Guam and Saipan. I continued teaching, both ashore and on ships leaving after overhaul. Then I was ordered back to the bomb disposal school in Washington. There was some testing of 100 pound bombs being done in the Chesapeake Bay. One didn't work and I took two Navy divers and went looking for it. They found the bomb and I took it apart with a Stillson pipe wrench. By this time I had been teaching bombs so long that taking them apart was almost second nature. There really wasn't much risk if one knew exactly what he was doing and those of us who had been at the bomb disposal school for a long time did know.

An ex bomb disposal officer I knew was in the Bureau of Personnel so he asked where I would like to go. There were a number of ROTC staff openings but I didn't find that job appealing. I was finally assigned to New York as the bomb disposal officer for the third Naval District. At first I was downtown but then moved to the Brooklyn Navy Yard. I remained here until April of 1946. I met my future wife, Ginnie, on my first day in New York.

Frequently, people found ordnance around New York, often left by returning service people. We were called and had to evaluate and then dispose of it. Once a torpedo was reported and I went to Cape May to go to sea in a big tug that had been built in 1890. The torpedo was caught in a fisherman's net. It broke loose and was never reclaimed, having sunk in very deep water. It was an interesting four days on an unusual ship, though we didn't get the torpedo.

Many merchant ships had sailors bring ordnance back from Europe. They often left the material aboard the ship. When this was reported, my chief and I had to find the material and take it to New Jersey and blow it up. Often they were hidden so that a sudden movement of the ship might blow them up and blow the bottom out of the ship. Handling these was somewhat more hazardous as the type of material was harder to identify.

In April 1946, I was separated from the Navy, married four days later, and after a family visit in Chicago, returned to Harvard to finish my MBA.

USS SNOWDEN
BURDETTE BOILEAU

I finished law school in 1937 and after a time in practice, went to work for the OPA. This government agency controlled prices and my job was in explaining and implementing the rules, not enforcing them. This job did not protect me from the draft and when it came close, I decided I would rather be in the Navy. I went in the Navy in 1942 and was sent to officer training school in Tucson, Arizona. On completion, I was commissioned an Ensign and sent to Treasure Island in San Francisco Bay.

I received training in communications and was sent to the section base for small craft in San Pedro. I was assistant communication officer and we handled various codes and coded messages. Occasionally there was one in the most secret code that I had to take to San Diego to get decoded.

After nine months this base was closed and I was sent to the small craft training center in Miami. After two months there, I was assigned to the USS Snowden, a DE (destroyer escort.) as communications officer. These small ships had many of the duties of a destroyer but were smaller and less expensive. We carried eleven officers and about 200 enlisted men. This was one of six DE's assigned to a CVE (escort aircraft carrier) to screen it. We varied location around the carrier, with one DE in the tail position, where it could pick up any pilots who couldn't make the carrier for landing.

Our ship was homeported at Brooklyn Navy Yard and we returned there intermittently for new, updated gear or for maintenance. When we were to be there a time, my wife came out and we were able to be together and go to New York and see plays or participate in other activities the city offered.

Once I took my wife to dinner at the wardroom on the ship. She wore a white dress that made climbing around the ship difficult. At dinner, she had a napkin with lipstick on it. I asked the steward for a clean one and was told that this was the guest napkin.

While we were out of Brooklyn, the carrier was based in Norfolk, Virginia. After repairs we had to go down to Norfolk and pick up the carrier and often a convoy out of Norfolk. Our first mission out was to search where a destroyer had turned over in a storm and sunk. We were looking for survivors but found only two bodies. These were buried at sea.

The north Atlantic had a lot of bad weather, particularly in winter. The ship recorded rolls of 45 to 50 degrees but always came back up. We would see on our sister ships that the sonar gear in front and the screw in back would be completely out of the water when a wave pushed the ship up. I'm sure they could see our ship do the same thing. It could be very cold in winter but the ship heating worked well and was quite comfortable except when one had a watch on deck. We had excellent cold weather gear and weren't too uncomfortable.

We had to use the carrier for refueling and also for medical care. We had a corpsman but the carrier had a doctor. I was never on the carrier in two years of duty. Occasionally the commodore who was in charge of the whole task force would come and spend some time on a DE to make sure all his ships operated well. I was never badly seasick but spent a lot of time feeling a little odd and it lasted for months after I went ashore.

My wife's father was very ill and the Navy gave me compassionate leave. We were in Baltimore and I took DC-3's across the country to California. I arrived in time for the funeral service.

After VE day it was reported that a group of subs was returning to Germany via the great circle route. We were sent north to look for them but didn't find any. After returning to Norfolk, we were sent to Guantanomo Bay, Cuba for target practice. We had rarely used our guns except in practice. Our warfare was conducted almost completely with depth charges, though I suspect we did more damage to whales than to submarines. My post when we used the cannon was close to one of them. I never used ear protection and have had hearing loss that was permanent.

After the firing training, we went through the Panama Canal to San Diego. From there we went to Pearl Harbor, expecting to join in the invasion of Japan fleet. We understood that DE's were prime targets for kimakazes and we weren't looking forward to it. We arrived at Pearl Harbor to the announcement of VJ day. We didn't get there in time for the celebration but then had two weeks in Honolulu where everything was in a holiday mood. I received my promotion to full lieutenant while in Pearl Harbor.

Then we returned back through the Panama Canal to the Atlantic and Jackson River, Florida. I was separated from the Navy there. On returning to Los Angeles, I was asked to stay in the Naval Reserve but I felt I had enough salt water for a lifetime. The bar put on a legal refresher course in Los Angeles for lawyers leaving the service and after that I returned to my old law firm.

WHAT DID YOU DO IN THE WAR, GRANDPA?
Don Faust

I entered The College at the U of Chicago for what would have been my junior year of high school but was my freshman year in The College. When I became 18 years old, I enlisted in the Naval Air Force, on 19 October 1943. I really wanted to fly but I liked boats much more than I liked carrying 60 lb. packs. I thought I would like the "gourmet food" in the Navy mess (mess is a good word) better than field rations.

In March 1944, almost 5 months after I enlisted, I was sent to Marysville, MO (North West Missouri State Teachers College) in V12 for a year of training in navigation and other subjects. The classes were not very rigorous and I spent most of my time in athletics; on the football team and tennis team.

After Pearl Harbor, the US was desperate for planes and fliers. But by 1944, the Navy Air Force had been very successful in shooting down Japanese MIGs and sinking Japanese aircraft carriers. The Navy decided that it had enough "Flyboys" and transferred me and all others in V12 at North West Missouri State Teachers College to Naval Officers Training Program, V6, still at NWMSTC.

April 1945 I was sent to the United States Naval Reserve Midshipman's School at Fort Schuyler, New York out at Throgs Neck on Long Island. The Japanese were losing badly but no one expected them to surrender. We officers were told to be prepared for the US to invade the island of Japan. I expected to be part of that invasion. My classes at Naval Midshipman Training School were in damage control, navigation, ordinance (50mm guns), US and Japanese aircraft identification, seamanship, and other subjects.

On 22 June 1945, I received orders from the Bureau of Naval Personnel. When I received my commission, I was to proceed to San Francisco for temporary assignment awaiting transport to the battleship, USS Texas, where I was to report to the Commanding Officer for duty. When I was assigned to the USS Texas, I was sure that the USS Texas would be in the first wave of an invasion of Japan.

On 3 July 1945, I received my commission: Ensign William Langdon Faust, (D)L, USNR, 451778. (USNR stands for United States Naval Reserve.) On the Training School report I was described as "Pleasing personality, quick, alert mind. Outstanding candidate." The report continued, "Duty recommended LCS (BB-CA)." This is a landing craft, the type which were being used to take soldiers from a troop transport ship onto the beach in invasions of the islands in the Pacific. I did not get an LCS. I got a battleship, the USS Texas.

Getting to the USS Texas, I received 10 days leave that I spent in Chicago at with Mom and Dad. I paid for the train from New York to Chicago myself. I was lucky to get a ticket without a high priority but since I had my orders in hand they had to give me transport somehow. On 18 July 1945, I took a train to San Francisco. This time I had a first class ticket from Chicago to San Francisco furnished by the Navy.

When an Officer has Orders to go somewhere, the Navy will provide or help with the means of getting there. Each time a unit of the Navy helps, they add an "endorsement." The endorsements state when you reported, what facility (sleeping quarters) was provided for you, what your next orders are, and says that you are detached (sent somewhere else). The endorsements are numbered to show sequence. They are given to you about the day you are detached and dated with the date you reported and the date you were detached. Following is a sequence of endorsements to my Orders to report to the U.S.S. Texas.

My Orders: I was to proceed to San Francisco and report to the Commandant, Twelfth Naval District for temporary active duty awaiting first available government transportation to the U.S.S. Texas (BB-35) where I was to report to the Commanding Officer of that vessel for duty. I was given ten days leave. The 1st endorsement, by the US Naval Reserve Midshipman's School at Fort Schuyler, N.Y. "Detached from duty at Fort Schuyler on 3 July 1945."

The 2nd endorsement, by the Commandant of the 12th Naval District, San Francisco indicates that I reported 21 July 1945 to the Commandant. Of course, I never saw the Commandant but I did see a clerk in the District Staff Headquarters, Twelfth Naval District in San Francisco who processed my papers and gave me a place in the Bachelor Officers Quarters (BOQ) in a hotel in downtown San Francisco. I was awaiting first available government transport to the U.S.S. Texas.

I remained "attached" to the Twelfth Naval District until I reported to the U.S.S. Texas. The Twelfth Naval District, San Francisco covers a large territory, land and sea, and so the various endorsements were made under the Command of the Twelfth Naval District but were not necessarily endorsed in San Francisco. The transportation ships signed endorsements Twelfth Naval District even if they were going to Hawaii.

From 21 July to 9 August 1945, the Commandant of the Twelfth Naval District (actually quite a few aides in many different places) was trying to get me to the U.S.S. Texas. Much of the time the U.S.S. Texas was at sea and the USS Texas did not want me badly enough to have me flown by sea plane to report aboard at sea. Sometimes there was no transportation available for such a low priority as mine. And sometimes I think that the Commandant had more pressing problems than mine.

The 3rd endorsement by Office of Commandant Twelfth Naval District in San Francisco, California, detached me as of 9 August 1945, and I finally got orders that transportation was available and I should report for "duty" as directed. The "duty" was being transported on the USS Long Island.

From 9 August 1945 to 8 September 1945, the USS Long Island transported me to Hawaii. The 4th endorsement by U.S.S. Long Island indicates that I reported 9 August 1945 to the USS Long Island. I was transported and subsisted on board without cost to me. The U.S.S. Long Island was a small aircraft carrier being used as a transport. We left from San Francisco heading for Hawaii. Just outside the Golden Gate it was rough. I was lying in my bunk, top of a triple decker, when everyone around me started to throw up. In about one minute I was very ill and I crawled up on deck in the fresh air. I recovered quickly and did not spend any more time than I needed below decks. That was the only time I got seasick and it lasted only a few hours.

The war was over. I was at sea on the USS Long Island when news of Japan's surrender came through. When I got to Hawaii, I discovered that the U.S.S. Texas was not in Hawaii but at sea heading back to the States. From 8 September 1945 to 24 September 1945, I was ashore in Hawaii. I shuttled from one receiving station to another in Hawaii while "they" tried to find transportation back to States. The war was over and hundreds of thousands of service men with years of duty in serious fighting wanted to get back to the States. They had priority.

The 5th endorsement (No. 1 of 2) U.S. Naval Receiving Station, Navy Number 3149 c/o Fleet Post Office San Francisco, Calif. It says that I reported 8 September 1945 in Hawaii. The endorsement says I was "transported." Really I was just assigned Government quarters. I furnished my own general mess: I had to find my own food. I was to proceed as orally assigned. I was detached 10 September 1945

The 5th endorsement (No. 2 of 2) US Naval Receiving Station Navy Number 3964 c/o Fleet post Office, San Francisco, Calif. indicates that I reported for transportation 10 September 1945 still in Hawaii. I moved from one receiving station to another. I was assigned to BOQ, Bachelor Officer Quarters. I was to proceed as orally assigned. Detached 24 September 1945

These two 5th endorsements are by two different Receiving Stations, both in Hawaii. What I discovered was that since the U.S.S. Texas was heading back to the Mainland, I would have to find transportation back to San Francisco.

The 6th endorsement by Receiving Station Navy NO.926 c/o Fleet Post Office, San Francisco, says that I reported 28 September 1945. I was still in Hawaii, awaiting transportation, and I was assigned Government quarters, and I was furnished general mess from 28 September to 1 October. I proceeded as verbally assigned and was detached 1 October 1945.

The 7th endorsement by U.S.S. Teton (AGC-14) indicated that I reported 1 October 1945. The U.S.S. Teton was a Communications Ship fitted as a Flag Ship for Chiefs of Combined Forces (Navy, Marines, Army, and Air Force). From 1 October - 16 October I was on the USS Teton being transported from Hawaii to San Francisco.

The 8th endorsement by District Staff Headquarters Twelfth Naval District, San Francisco says that I reported 16 October 1945, in San Francisco. On my original orders there is notation that on 16 October 1945 that the DPTO, Twelfth Naval District, San Francisco furnished transportation from San Francisco to San Pedro, Cal. via SP(LA)PE, the Southern Pacific to LA and the Pacific Electric to San Pedro.

Twelfth Naval District Staff Headquarters ordered me to report to Port Director, 242 West Seventh Street, San Pedro, Cal. for transportation to the station [USS Texas] as indicated in basic orders. I was given no quarters or transportation but was sent to the Port Director in San Pedro. Detached 17 October 1945

The 9th endorsement by Port Director (NTS) San Pedro, California indicates that I reported 17 October 1945. I was ordered to proceed immediately and carry out the unexecuted portion of my basic orders. However, the U.S.S. Texas was not yet in port so I was assigned BOQ to stay overnight. From 17 October - morning 18 October, I hung around waiting for Texas to pull into the harbor. Finally on 18 October 1945 at 1245, I reported to the U.S.S. Texas.

The 10th endorsement is by U.S.S. Texas in care of Fleet Post Office, San Francisco, California. The ship was in San Pedro but mail came through the Fleet Post Office so that mail from home would not give away where the ship was.

The war being over, the U.S.S. Texas was assigned to pick up returning service men in Hawaii and to bring them back to the States. So I sailed on the Texas from San Pedro back to Hawaii.

On the ocean blue, on New Years day Jan. 1, 1946, the Duty Officer informed me, as an Ensign on watch, that some enlisted man had been reported being drunk. He ordered me to "check all lockers and places where a bottle of liquor could be hidden." I immediately called the petty officer and told him that there would be an inspection, in a couple of hours, at 17:00 sharp. He and I searched diligently but we found no bottles of liquor in any locker. Every locker was clean, certainly much cleaner than I had ever seen them before.

Then the Navy decided to decommission the USS Texas and give it to the state of Texas.

On 8 January, 1946, I received Orders which detached me from duty on the USS Texas and directed "You will proceed to a port in the United States, and upon arrival further proceed to San Francisco, Calif., and report to Commandant, Twelfth Naval District for first available government transportation to the port in which the Commander of the Seventh Fleet may be, and, upon arrival, report to the Commander Seventh Fleet for temporary duty pending further assignment by him."

My transportation from Hawaii to Mainland US was on the USS Texas. We returned to Long Beach and I was detached from the USS Texas. I received 15 days leave.

Since thousands of returning servicemen were trying to go east, no train tickets were to be had. I joined two other officers and we paid a person who had a car and could get gas to take us in his automobile to Chicago. (Do not ask where he got gas. I asked but didn't get a satisfactory answer.) I spent my leave in Chicago and then, flew by plane, United Air Lines, back to San Francisco at my own expense.

I had left the Texas in Long Beach and after leave went to San Francisco to Twelfth Naval District for transportation to the Commander of the Seventh Fleet. From 6 February 1946 to 26 February 1946, I was waiting in Frisco for transportation. I spent 20 days in Frisco waiting for the Twelfth Naval District to find transport to the port where the Commander of the Seventh Fleet was based. I then reported to the U.S.S. General H. W. Butner, a transport ship carrying troops around the Pacific.

The U.S.S. Butner and I set forth out into the Pacific to find the port in which the Commander of the Seventh Fleet was based. The General Butner stopped in Hawaii and I felt as if I was going in circles. When we left Hawaii, on the General Butner, there was a barrel sitting in a passage below with a dipper hanging on its side. Everyone who came on board from shore leave in Hawaii brought a bottle or two of some kind of liquor which they poured into the barrel. Most of the stuff was rot gut and it tasted terrible. Everyone who passed the barrel would take a dipper of the contents. Somehow we would gag it down, smack our lips, and declare it was the "best stuff I ever drank."

I was detached from the Butner and left on some island, somewhere out in the Pacific, to find transportation. I flew to Guam. I stayed a few days and then flew to the Philippines in a PBY seaplane. When we landed on the water in the bay, a small boat (tender) came to pick up the passengers. As we motored toward shore we looked back and saw the PBY taking on water through the "hatch" (door) through which we just left the plane. The pilot and crew pushed a raft out the hatch and paddled away. We watched the plane slowly sink.

On the last lap to Shanghai, I went by boat, the U.S.S. General H. W. Butner. I had definitely been around this block before. The Butner delivered me to the Commander Seventh Fleet and "the Commander" gave me orders to report to Commander Chinese Amphibious Training Group (C.T.U. 70.4.3) in Tsingtao, China.

Again I reported to the General Butner for transport to Tsingtao (in those days the town was spelled Tsingtao and pronounced Sing-taow; now spelled Qingdao and pronounced Ching-dao). I reported 28 March 1946 to the Commander Chinese Amphibious Training Group (C.T.U. 70.4.3) and was assigned quarters and mess on board the U.S.S. LST 993.

I moved into a house in town, owned by an English couple. He had a responsible position in the Port Authority. Tsingtao was on a beautiful bay. The land almost enclosed the harbor so the anchorage was well protected from storms. I worked as an instructor at the Naval Base, teaching semaphore and other subjects of which I had little knowledge. My students were third and fourth sons from wealthy families; the first son inherited the family wealth and might, to increase the family wealth, enter service for the Emperor; the second son could become a monk; the third or later sons might be placed the army. My students, boys 18-22 years, were very bright and worked hard but they were very immature. They spoke little English so I had a translator for the first few days but that was not very successful. The translator understood and spoke British English. We could barely communicate. I learned some Chinese and we struggled along without translation. Since the students spoke little English, they sent and received semaphore letter by letter without knowing what the letters were and certainly having no clue as to the content of the message. The officers who sent and received the messages had been trained in the US and they did speak English.

The Chinese Communists were at war with the Chinese Nationalists. The US was on the Nationalist's side and therefore, of course, I was on the Nationalist's side. The Nationalists controlled the town of Tsingtao. The Chinese Communists had the town surrounded on the land sides. They would make forays into the town every once in a while; a car would race through the outskirts, shooting wildly, and then fade away.

The US was giving the Chinese Nationalists some landing craft (LST's and LCI's which, since the war was over, we did not think we would need). A number of Chinese Naval Lieutenants had been sent to a Naval Training School in Florida and they were on the base ready to man the landing craft. They were very able. However, each LST or LCI was commanded by a Chinese Admiral who didn't have a clue about seamanship; the Admirals came from powerful families and were appointed Admiral with no training. The Admirals expected to be obeyed immediately, with no back talk. One day we received news that the Chinese Communists were going to attack Tsingtao by sea with 100 junks armed with rifles and maybe bows and arrows. The Nationalists sent their landing craft which had 50mm guns out to engage in battle. We, Americans, thought that the battle might last 20 minutes before the Nationalist gunners sunk every junk. Hours later the landing craft returned and the Admirals claimed victory. We were told that the communists also claimed victory.

We heard the story of the battle from the Chinese Lieutenants; the Admirals were afraid to get their LSTs or LCIs close to a junk. They did not know seamanship and they had given orders that were stupid. Often two landing craft would be on a collision course and the Admiral in charge of each vessel would refuse to change course. When informed that a collision was immanent then the Admiral would stalk off. A Lieutenant would quietly change course enough to avoid a collision. Avoiding a collision was OK. But no landing craft could be taken close enough to a junk to hit it with a 50mm gun. I really believe that Admirals believed that a junk could damage their ship and they would lose face. The junks could not damage a landing craft with a rifle so the Nationalists should have sailed right up to the junks and sunk them. They could have even rammed them with no damage to the landing craft. While each side claimed victory, neither side had damaged the other. The Lieutenants were angry and very embarrassed.

For a while, in addition to teaching, I was in charge of the transportation pool; that meant I assigned jeeps to officers. The trouble was everyone had more seniority than I did, so after I filled all requests I seldom had a jeep. Once, when I did get a jeep, some friends and I drove out into the countryside. Going out into the countryside was exciting but foolish as the town was surrounded by Communists who were trigger-happy. All we saw was the Chinese countryside, no shooting.

I spent time shopping, and looking around in town. One morning as I was walking to the base, I saw a man lying in the middle of the street. There was a policeman nearby so I hurried down to the base to teach. I was told by the Chinese Lieutenants that I should not interfere; the police would not be pleased. When I went home that evening, the man was still there. When I got to the house, in which some friends and I were renting a room, I asked the English owner what was going on. He said, "The man would be left there until he died." The man lay there for days. No one helped him or moved him; even for a day or so after he died, no one moved him. I was shocked that a person would lie in the street for days and die.

One of the US officers had an auto accident in which he injured "some peasants" and killed a cow. No Chinese Officials seemed to care about the injured peasants but they cared about the cow. The officer had to pay five dollars to the man who owned the cow.

Often, some of the Chinese Lieutenants would invite us to a restaurant for a party. The food was wonderful. There were musical groups: a woman to sing and one or two string players whose instruments were tall and thin with only two or three strings. As I remember, the strings were plucked. The songs were always about ancient battles.

The Lieutenants always thought that they would get the Americans drunk and then the party would be a success. They would put two Chinese between each American. Small bowls would be filled with liquor. Then the Chinese Officer on one side would "gombay" (this is spelled the way we pronounced the word, which meant bottoms up). So you both empty your bowls. The bowls were refilled as soon as they were empty. Immediately, the Chinese Officer on your other side would say "gombay" and bottoms up again. They were drinking one cup of liquor to our two but they still got drunk and we didn't. The parties would end with the Chinese drunk and asleep. We, Americans, paid the bill and took our Chinese friends to their homes. The bill would always be larger than the Chinese Officers received in pay per month and the bill was very modest for us. However, the next day they would be embarrassed because they had lost face when we paid the bill.

One evening a Chinese Lieutenant awoke as we pulled up to his house. He insisted that we come in and have tea. His family slept on the floor in the living room. We waited outside the door as the family was awakened and dressed and all the mats were set aside. Then his wife made tea and we sat around and drank it. A very quiet party but he saved face.

On 6 June 1946, I received orders that I was released from duty and was to return to the States for discharge. I must say that the duty had not been hazardous thus far but the trip back was HAZARDOUS.

I reported 6 June 1946 to the U.S.S. General H. W. Butner. Join the Navy and see the world on the U.S.S. General Butner. This voyage began in a very big storm, the biggest storm anyone could remember. The Butner was a communications ship with communications towers and aerials stretching high into the sky. In the storm, it rolled on its sides and pitched bow up and then bow dove and it would dig deep into the next wave.

The ship would roll over on its side so far that you had to walk with one foot on the bulkhead (wall) and one on the deck to walk down a passage. Then the ship would roll slowly to the other side. You could walk on the deck for step or two, then you had one foot on the other bulkhead and one on the deck. The ship would hang on one side so long you were sure that it was going to turn turtle, upside down. We were all sure that it was going to roll over and sink.

Most of the officers who were being transported were seasick; very few officers came to meals, but I never got seasick in this storm. At mealtime the captain took a heading which gave as little pitch and roll as he could get. During meals, the ship might be stable for a few minutes but, just when you relaxed, the ship would pitch or roll. Those diners who were not holding on to their plates and glasses saw them slide away. The worst place to sit was at the end of the table where all loose plates and glasses came sliding. The unlucky officer, sitting at the end of the table, had to try to fend them off. Most of the stuff landed in his lap.

The passage home took 18 days and I was ordered to proceed immediately to the Separation Center at Great Lakes, Ill. and report to the Commanding Officer. No government transportation was available so I made my own way. I took the train to Chicago.

I was examined 28 June 1946 and the "Civil Readjustment Process" completed 28 June 1946. The Navy did not do much to rehabilitate even those who needed such. I was given four days leave. I was honorably discharged at Officers Separation Center, Great Lakes, Illinois 2 July 1946.

A MARINE IN THE PACIFIC
French Fogle

In 1942 I was just back from a traveling fellowship with Columbia University. With the war, studying in Europe had not been an option so I spent the time at the Huntington Library in California. Now I was teaching freshman grammar at City College of New York while doing graduate work at Columbia. With the world situation, I didn't find the work rewarding. It seemed superficial after Pearl Harbor and I decided I must go into the military. I went to the Dean and he said, "Young man, do what you must do. Don't consider Columbia."

I went to the Marine enlistment station. The sergeant found I had had a manslaughter charge and said that I would have to wait until that record could be cleared. I had been driving an oil truck out of Beckley, West Virginia about 10 years previously and a child had run directly into the path of the truck. I was completely exonerated because the parents had seen it and reported that I couldn't have seen the child, but the investigation was on my record. It took about a month or more and when I went back I found that I was four days too old to go to OCS. "The Navy next door can take you into OCS." the sergeant said. But I wanted the Marines so March 4, 1942, I was sworn in and sent to Parris Island for boot camp. I was past thirty in boot camp and my larger view and general experience were helpful. I seemed to accept the treatment better than many of the younger men.

At the conclusion of boot a group of us were sent to New River Marine Base (later Camp LeJeune). I became a machine gunner in a light weapons platoon. I was actually a pretty good gunner. O. C. Caldwell, known to all as "Speed", commander of the 3rd Marine Regiment , called me into his tent. He said, "I see you were teaching at Columbia. I don't have teachers for boots. If you will stay with us a time I can get Washington to give you a commission." I asked for overnight to consider and the next day refused. Our group had now bonded together and I wanted to stay with the others.

Before dismissing me, he said, "That's the trouble with you young guys. You want to stick to your unit and get your guts blown out."

We were sent to San Diego and then on a ship. We weren't told where we were going but we sailed west. I remember standing alone on the bow of the ship and wondering what would happen. I felt that it was meant to be and that it would be a positive experience. We landed at Pago Pago in American Samoa. As we approached, we could see a beautiful, lush green island. I worked at unloading and it was dark by the time we went to our billets. We passed a group of natives sitting and chanting. The island and the people were all so new and exciting. We were told they were welcoming us to the island and I was touched. The singing was beautiful. Later we found out that the chant said, "Eat shit, Marines." So much for the welcome to Samoa.

We were at Vitez Bay. The talking chief there was a great person. He loved playing dominoes but always wanted to play the black side. Many of the people moved out of their homes, fales, so the officers could have a place to stay. We were there for the annual circumcision ceremony. All boys eight or so were involved and this time they had the Navy corpsmen and nurses do the actual surgery. The treatment afterwards was salt water, so the boys went into the ocean with their lava-lavas. They had to hold them out as the penis was sore. The girls came and sat on the beach and laughed at them.

American Samoa was religiously divided into almost equal numbers of Catholics and Mormons. The children sang hymns and the singing was very beautiful.

After a month in Samoa, I was called to the battalion commander's office. I didn't know why I was singled out; had I messed up with my shooting? He handed me some orders and said, "You are now a second lieutenant. Get some bars." "Speed", Brigadier General Caldwell, had sent in the papers the day he offered me the commission and hadn't recalled them when I refused. The commission had gone through the Washington red tape and had just caught up with me. I became platoon leader of my old platoon. The men accepted me well and I didn't have problems. We, the third Marine division, trained on American Samoa and practiced an amphibious landing on Western Samoa, British controlled at that time. Next we were sent to New Zealand. After a short time in New Zealand we were again on ships and went to Guadalcanal with a couple of island stops on the way. I remember at one island the Navy was putting on an amazingly good musical show that we were able to see.

Guadalcanal had been taken by this time, though a few Japanese soldiers were hiding in caves and we had to be careful away from camp. We were training for the next invasion, not knowing where we were going. It turned out to Bougainville. This was the dirtiest campaign I was in. We landed on the beach at Empress Augusta Bay. Several of the boatloads of invading Marines were all shot up but many of us made the beach. Only a few feet from the beach the ground was covered with tidal pools and jungle vegetation. The land was always wet and the vegetation rotting and slimy. It was a most unpleasant place to be. We established a beachhead and stayed one month. We were relieved by armored troops who were to clear an area near Empress Augusta for a fighter strip.

On Bougainville, we were using Navajo Indians speaking their native language for communication so the Japanese couldn't interpret our messages. This was the precursor of the Navajo code talkers, widely used by the Marines.

We were relieved and sent back to Guadalcanal to prepare for the next attack. This one turned out to be Guam. The second Marine division had previously landed on neighboring islands and was having trouble controlling them. The planners didn't want us to land until these islands were controlled, so we stayed on the ships for 54 days before going into Guam. By this time I was executive officer of the company. We went ashore with 407 men and 7 officers in the company. When the island was secured we had 138 men and 2 officers fit for duty. Guam was a rough fight, including Bonzai attacks.

On Guam, when the battalion had set up its perimeter, four or six light Japanese tanks appeared at dusk with machine guns blazing. We had no antitank weapons, only light machine guns. The Marines killed the infantry guides accompanying the tanks and the tankers became confused in the dark. One came up to 10 feet from my post. We were effectively trapped and the battalion commander asked the three Captains what they felt we should do. One of the sacred rules of combat was: don't leave your foxhole at night. Two of the Captains said, "Wait until daylight."

I felt this would be suicidal: the tanks would destroy us at first light. I suggested that we withdraw to some higher ground about 200 yards away. The commander replied, "OK, Frenchy, lead us there." I led us up, quietly, in single file, and all three companies made it without a shot being fired. We had been unable to reach the artillery before but from the higher ground were able to do so and they promptly wiped out the tanks. The commander felt I had saved the battalion and I was awarded the Silver Star.

We approached Agania, the capital of Guam, from the back side. There were many caves along the hills there and we found caches of liquor stored in the caves by the Japanese. Some tank troops came along and loaded whole cases in their tanks but the poor infantry could only take as much as they could carry. That night I found many troops were beginning to be drunk and I had them dig a pit with rocks in the bottom. All bottles were to be thrown into the pit. Some of the Marines suspected what was coming and buried bottles in the sand for future retrieval.

Those of us who had been in combat a certain time were given a months leave and flown to the United States for Christmas. I visited at Columbia and the whole departmental group came to see what had happened to me. I was telling the story of the Bonzai charge and one elderly professor said, "Oh yes, I know the story. It is just like the British longbows at the battle of Agincourt."

On returning to the Pacific, we started preparations again. This time it was to Iwo Jima. I was intelligence officer of the 2nd battalion of the 3rd division. The 9th battalion was already ashore and we were in ships expecting to go ashore. Ironically, after all this, we spent several weeks on the ships and never did make the landing but were sent back to Guam.

About this time a rule came out that those with three years in the Pacific must go home. I was one of two who wanted to stay with my buddies and unit but there was no choice. I went to San Diego and then to Washington DC where I was in the plans and policies section. I was sitting in a bar in Washington, having a drink alone, when VJ day was announced. I was overcome and put my head down on the table and wept. I was discharged as a major but stayed in the reserve and eventually retired as a Colonel.

THREE YEARS AT SEA
Art Langdon

I graduated from Pomona College one morning in April 1943 and that afternoon went to the railway station in Los Angeles. Here I took a train to Chicago for the navy 90 day officer candidate school. Here we were taught drill and the fundamentals of being a naval officer but most of what we needed to know was left for on the job training. Commissioned an Ensign, I took a train to San Francisco to join a ship, AKA 9, the Alhena. This ship, the largest attack cargo ship in the

Navy, arrived the day after I did. It had been bombed at Guadalcanal and under repair for six month in Australia and was returning to the United States.

I was assigned to work with the ship's pilot where my minor in astronomy was very helpful in learning navigation. I also had a second job of decoding secret messages that were sent to the ship. We loaded and left for the invasion of Bougainville. We carried troops as well as supplies. I was soon approved to stand watch as the pilot and continued in this job for my time in the Navy.

The ship was steady in storms because of its size and I was never seasick. It also was fast for a transport, making 15 to 18 knots. We had lots of storage, some refrigerated, so the food was good on board. Saipan was now a staging base and we went back and forth from there to various islands that were being invaded. Occasionally we went to New Zealand to pick up troops and once I had a day off to sight-see but I was rarely ashore for three years. Our Captain was an excellent leader but after about a year he was ordered to other duty. The new Captain was dumb! Among other things, he would have me awakened in the middle of the night to code an ordinary, non-urgent message. We made one trip to San Francisco and the executive officer found someone in authority and reported the Captain's incompetence. He was replaced before we left. The new Captain had been a merchant marine captain and really knew ship handling.

When we left troops for an invasion, we would stand off the area for several days. We had three doctors on board and cared for many of the early casualties. We had facilities for initial care and then we would take them to the big shore based hospital at Saipan. The true hospital ships often came later to the invasion areas.

Our ship has anti-aircraft guns and two three inch guns. On landings we used the three inch guns to cover the troops and I was in charge of one of the guns. I had been promoted to LT(jg) and near the end of the war made Lieutenant. Once I was piloting the ship and a Japanese aircraft attacked us with bombs. This was dangerous as we had a deck load of high octane gasoline. Fortunately a destroyer escort nearby was shooting heavily at the plane and threw his aim off so the bombs fell safely astern.

We were in the invasion of Okinawa. The size of the fleet and the number of warships was truly amazing. The kamakazi planes flew into the fleet but they aimed for the heavy combat vessels like carriers and ignored us.

At the end of the war we loaded troops at Okinawa for the occupation of Japan. As we sailed up the channel to Japan we could see the devastation of the atomic bomb. We then went back to Pearl Harbor for another load of troops for Japan. At the conclusion of this trip, we took the ship through the Panama Canal and up the coast to Norfolk, Virginia where I was separated from the Navy.

A YOUNG BOY GOES TO WAR

Gale A. Reynolds

Most of the non-school talk by the young boys at Whittier High School in the Fall of 1941 related to the war then raging in Europe. We argued the relative merits of the Spitfires of the British and the Messerschmidts of the Germans and debated the "draft" to which we would soon be subject. We questioned our government sending 50 World War I "four-piper" destroyers to Britain in the lend lease program. It had been much the same at Phoenix High where I had attended my junior year. There we had argued about the strength of the German Siegfried and French Maginot defense lines. We were shocked when the Germans went around the Maginot Line and attacked France through the Low Countries.

At Phoenix High I was in the Army ROTC, and most of the boys were looking forward to joining the Army or National Guard when we graduated the next year. I was one of the few who wanted to be a sailor. That was in part because a friend who we looked up to as an Eagle Scout had joined the Navy. When Ken came home on leave he visited his ROTC friends in his Navy uniform. We were greatly impressed and it gave the "Navy Boys" a boost. He had been assigned to serve on the battleship named for our state. How we envied his service on a real battleship. Other boys came to visit from Fort Huachuca in southern Arizona where they were on duty in the National Guard. They were soon to leave for duty in the Philippines under General MacArthur.

On a chilly Sunday morning three days after my seventeenth birthday in early December, knowing, that with parental permission, I could now join the Navy, I was practicing semaphore signaling with my homemade signal flags. I dreamed that I was on the signal bridge of a "four piper" destroyer during the icy trip to Britain to deliver the destroyers. The wind was freezing cold and the decks slippery with ice as the wind whipped my flags.

The backdoor slammed as mother ran down the steps, headed for my aunt's house across the alley. "The Japanese have bombed Pearl Harbor and several ships have been sunk," she yelled as she ran. I dropped my signal flags and ran in to listen on the old Atwater Kent radio. The Arizona had been sunk and the Japanese were invading the Philippines. I remember having a horrible sinking feeling in the pit of my stomach.

In the days that followed I began to pester my parents to let me quit school and join the Navy. They were against the idea, but after a week or so of constant pestering they finally said that if the Navy would accept me they would sign the papers. I learned later from relatives that my parents were dead sure the Navy would not take a boy so small, young, and immature.

On Monday, December 22nd, I caught the bus to Los Angeles with very mixed emotions. I remember feeling very small and alone as I approached the Federal Building in Los Angeles. There were hundreds of men and boys in many lines snaking into the many doorways. The Navy lines were very crowded, as men were trying to avoid being drafted into the Army to be foot soldiers. I got into one of the Navy lines and slowly worked my way into the building and up to a recruiting desk. The huge, scowling man, sitting at the desk, looked up with surprise. With a voice that seemed to boom throughout the room he said, "What the Hell are you doing here? We're not enlisting Sea Scouts. Get out of here and don't waste my time." Laughter seemed to fill the room as I turned, fighting back tears, and walked to the door. It was a crushed young boy who walked the streets of L.A. trying to figure out what to do. I went into a theater and watched "Gone With the Wind", barely hearing the words and trying to tell myself that a boy old enough to be a sailor was too old to cry.

What would I tell my mother? She asked me what had happened and I quickly answered that they had been so busy that I was told to come back the next day. I didn't really notice the look of disappointment that crossed my mother's face. The following morning I returned to the Federal Building. Scouting the long lines, I avoided the bo'sun mate whom I had been confronted by on the day before. I approached the recruiting desk of my new line filled with fear and anxiety. The recruiter began asking questions without looking up. After a minute or two he handed me several papers and told me to go get in a line leading to an inner room. There I was punched, prodded, and probed, took vision and hearing tests, and was weighed and measured. An hour or so later I found myself in a room with about forty or fifty other men, each clinging to a sheaf of papers. Finally an officer came in and said we were all being sent home. My heart almost stopped. "But" he added, "You will report back on January 2nd to be sworn into Navy service and those of you who are seventeen are to bring your signed permission slips from your parents." It was a happy and proud boy who rode the bus back to Whittier.

As I entered the living room, mother seemed to fall into a chair and sat silent for a few moments. I thought she was overjoyed with my news. There was a deathly silence at the dinner table except for questions from my younger sister and brother, who were quickly shushed. I fell into a deep and exhausted sleep that night dreaming of the Navy and possibly Annapolis some day. The following morning was silent around the house. Nothing was said about my papers being signed. Fortunately, Christmas and New Year's occupied much of my time. The day before New Year's my parents had a long talk with me trying to convince me I was too young to go off into the Navy. In the end they handed me my signed papers, saying they had promised and felt honor bound to follow that commitment, despite their concerns.

On January 2nd I headed back to the Federal Building for the last time with my toothbrush and a few possessions in hand. I reported to the assigned room, where there were several hundred boys and men in various moods of excitement. We were sent to rooms for retesting and waiting, lots of waiting. Around noon we were mustered in groups of about a hundred and marched down the street to several restaurants for our first meal on the Navy. As we emerged to return to the Federal Building, crowds had gathered to cheer us on and thank us and wish us safety. It was all very exciting..

Back at the Federal Building more than five hundred men were called to attention. A door opened and a tall gray haired man, with four gold stripes on his sleeves and more gold on his hat than I had ever seen, entered the room. We were told to raise our right hand and follow him in the Pledge of Allegiance and be sworn in as members of the U.S. Navy. What a happy moment. His assistant then explained that the Navy training stations were overcrowded and were rushing to build accommodation for us. We were to be placed on paid leave ($21 a month) and to wait until recalled by telegram to go to the San Diego Naval Training Station.

The days of early January moved slowly as I withdrew from Whittier High School. Some of my friends questioned if I really was in the Navy. The telegram finally arrived and on January 20, 1942, I reported to the Federal Building and was transported in one of several buses to San Diego. What a thrill as we passed the Marine Guards at the gates and saw thousands of sailors marching and mustering in front of hundreds of temporary tents on the parade grounds. Our bus pulled up in front of one of the old Spanish Style barracks where we were told to disembark. The barracks' previous occupants had finished their training that morning and luckily this would be our home for the four weeks of recruit training (which had been six months in peacetime). No tents on the blacktop for Company 42-32.

After being marched to the mess hall and "chowed-down" we were marched to the barber to have our hair shaved off, to the clothing locker to be issued our clothes and other gear, and to various and sundry other places as we got established. We were constantly reminded by our company commander, Chief Turret Captain L.L. Hogge, who had been recently recalled to active duty, that we were a sloppy lot but would soon become sailors.

After four weeks of mess cooking, marching, mess cooking, gunnery training, mess cooking, marching, naval rules and regulations, and marching, always marching, we had "completed" our orientation. After graduation, to which many of our parents and friends came, we were told to be packed by 0600 the following morning to be assigned for further duty.

By 0600 (not 0601) the following morning we were packed and mustered in orderly ranks in front of the barracks along with our clothing militarily stored in our "sea bags", which were lashed within our rolled mattress and hammock (with its seven half-hitches for the seven seas). We boarded several buses, which took us to the train station and train car assignments. Our newest word was "scuttlebutt," and it got a good workout over the next twenty-four hours as we tried to figure where we were going. The train moved slowly as it carried its cargo of 500 to 1,000 new sailors north. Scuttlebutt had it we were stopping while each bridge was checked for possible sabotage.

The following morning we arrived at the foggy and cold Port of Oakland, California, where we were taken by bus to the middle of the Oakland Bay Bridge and the Island of Yerba Buena (Goat Island), where we were mustered on a large parking lot. Almost immediately names were called out and men were organized into several "drafts." Each draft would then board a bus with their gear and be driven off. No information was given as to what was going on or where the men were being taken, which we were to learn was a usual Navy practice.

My name, along with several of my buddies of Company 42-32, was finally called and we dragged our "sea bags and hammocks" over to the bus and boarded. We went down a road to the man-made Treasure Island (T.I..) which was connected to Goat Island. It had been built three years previously for the World's Fair of 1939.

Several buses pulled into the large blacktop area called a "grinder" and disgorged their cargoes. Names were called to form several companies of men. We were told to grab our gear, weighing 70 to 80 pounds, and proceed to assigned buildings. It was an exciting sight to see the "sailors" throw their seabags up on their shoulders, just as I had seen in the newsreels. I tugged and lifted as best I could. Finally getting it up on my shoulder caused me to immediately fall over backwards in a heap of bag and boy. I got up and dusted myself off and tugged and pulled my gear over to the barracks.

We remained at Treasure Island for several days awaiting further orders. The second afternoon I was given a six-hour "liberty pass" to San Francisco. I felt very important and patriotic walking down Market Street, a member of the U.S. Navy. I'll never forget the admiring glances, nor the three older ladies who passed. One of them commented, "Isn't that a cute little Sea Scout, he's dressed just like a sailor." Rather deflated I went to a movie and returned to the transportation area and to T.I..

Several days later some of us were told to pack our gear and muster on the grinder. From there we carried (or pushed and shoved) our lashed sea bags and hammocks down to a dock where we loaded them on the aft deck of a waiting tugboat. The sailors "cast off" the lines, and the tug slowly moved out into San Francisco Bay. As we sailed west, one of the deck hands pointed "off the port bow" and showed us the island of Alcatraz. After about an hour and a half, the tug began to slow as we approached a dock in a small inner bay. On the opposite side of the dock was a camouflaged old riverboat without its paddlewheel. Thirty or forty of us worked together to put our gear up on the dock and gathered for muster.

A short, stocky man in a khaki uniform and an officer's hat came out and began bellowing at us. We learned later this was Chief Warrant Officer Norvelle. A crusty old sea dog who had spent forty years as an enlisted man in the "old navy", he had been recalled and commissioned as a Chief Warrant Officer assigned to the United States Naval Net Depot at Tiburon, California. He was to be our mother, father, and "whatever" as long as we were on the base. We learned to greatly respect and like him. He knew how to chew a person out but also fought for and supported his sailors. We never wanted to let him down.

Norvelle and a couple of his bo'suns led us across the dock and into the cargo deck of the old riverboat. There were about a hundred or so two-level bunk beds in orderly rows in the large room. We were told to find an empty bunk and place our unlashed hammock, mattress, pillow, and blankets on it and our sea bag with our clothing and belongings at the foot of the bed. This was to be home for quite a few months. The officers lived topside in the former cabins on the old Delta King.

The Delta King, along with its sister vessel the Delta Queen, had been party boats before the war, plying the Sacramento River between Sacramento and San Francisco. Now it was without paddlewheel and tied up to the pier at the "Net Depot", serving as a barracks for the sailors who would build, patrol, and repair the anti-submarine nets protecting the entrance to San Francisco Harbor. Here nets were to be made and crews trained to handle them and shipped throughout the South and Western Pacific as the war progressed. Hundreds of anti-submarine and anti-torpedo nets followed the advance and protected the Navy and shipping in ports as they moved toward Japan.

The work was hard and backbreaking, and the hours were long as we worked around the clock in twelve-hour shifts. Four days on and thirty-six hours off. We worked in the open on a large blacktop area (the slab), about the size of a football field, pulling one- and two-inch cables into a giant net with a six-foot mesh, measuring the size of the slab. The cables were pulled by man power and two tractors, and each joint was fixed with special "U" bolts and nuts, all done by hand and wrenches. No power tools in those days.

Once the net was completed and attached to huge buoys, it was lifted and dragged by a huge "Gantry" crane and the tractors to the dock and lowered into the waters of the bay, where special vessels called "Net Tenders" towed it several miles out to the net, which stretched seven miles between the town of Sausalito in Marin County, and the St. Francis Yacht Harbor in San Francisco.

The Net Depot had been a coaling station for the Navy during World War I and during peacetime had served as the base for the Roebling Wire Company as they built the Golden Gate Bridge. As the war in Europe had progressed, it had been reacquired by the Navy and commissioned as the Navy Net Depot. Now they were building housing and the infrastructure necessary for several hundred men and officers. After about six months we moved into the two large, three-story barracks that had been built for the enlisted men. The old Delta King was towed away to have its paddlewheel replaced and be reincarnated as a troop-mover around the bay for the remainder of the war. We were happy when a larger, "modern" mess hall was completed along with a theater and larger "sick bay" for the sick and injured sailors.

After a few months working on the slab, I was called up to Norvelle's office one day. I was very apprehensive and a bit frightened, wondering what I might have done wrong. In his gruff and salty way he told me I was being assigned to "the boats." I would be a crew member on one of the old yachts that patrolled the nets day and night, seven days a week, in all kinds of weather. I had only dreamed of such an assignment. The "boat crews" were special, sort of an elite group on the base. They tended to stay while others came and went as new nets were completed and crews took them overseas to the far off islands recently captured by our troops.

The patrol boats used by the Depot in the first year and a half of the war had been commandeered from their civilian owners, who were paid $1.00 a year for their use. They ranged from about twenty four to thirty six feet in length and were usually powered by gasoline engines. They were stripped of their fancy furnishings and painted in Navy gray. I spent most of my time on a former diesel fishing boat called the St John Bosco. Most boats slept four to six people. There were four men assigned to each twenty four-hour shift. Two men stood watch at a time, two hours on and two hours off, day and night. While not on watch during daylight hours we were expected to keep the boat ship shape and study our advancement books. For meals we went to the gate-tending vessel and dropped two men off at a time where they ate in the ship's mess.

Being on the boats was both fun and exciting. We would leave the base around nine in the morning on the relief boat and travel through the strait between Tiburon and Angel Island and past Alcatraz in the distance. We usually began at the

Sausalito end of the net and replaced the seven crews, moving eastward to the San Francisco end near St Francis Yacht Harbor. We served four days on and one day off, when we got to go ashore on liberty.

San Francisco Bay can be quite dangerous because of thick fogs, storms, and very strong tides that tore at the nets and often played havoc with the huge suspending buoys. Some nights the fog was so thick we had to tie up to one of the buoys until it was safe to continue. This had to be a judgment call as none of the boats had radios. Our only method of communication was by yelling from boat to boat or, for a few of us, the use of semaphore flags during daylight. Signal lights were sometimes used by the gate vessel to call us alongside.

In early June of 1942, I was granted a three-day pass to go home and receive my high school diploma. When I went to pick up the pass the yeoman on duty informed me that my name was on a draft to be sent to Treasure Island with further transfer to the fleet in Honolulu. He told me to go ahead and he would delete my name and add someone else. I had mixed emotions, wanting somewhat to be in the "Fighting Navy." After hitchhiking for about twelve hours, I arrived home the day before graduation. I had made up my mind that I wanted the transfer and told my parents I couldn't stay for the ceremonies the following evening. I went down to Whittier High and met with the Principal. She gave me my diploma and wished me well. The following morning I headed back to the base, again hitchhiking. When I arrived I learned that the draft had been sent the day before and I could not be added. I did go over to T.I. and visit my friends. I was a little sad, as I felt their excitement at going to join ships of the line.

Several months later one of the men from the earlier draft came back to visit us on survivor's leave. His ship had been sunk in the South Pacific. He told us that they had joined up with about five hundred other sailors at T.I. and been shipped to Honolulu. There they were assigned to several ships that had lost men in earlier naval battles. Assignment to ships had been alphabetical. Those with last names beginning with "R" had gone aboard two light cruisers, the U.S.S. Quincy and the U.S.S. Astoria. Both were sunk within the next few months in the Solomon Islands off Guadalcanal with very few survivors. I was no longer sad I had missed being on the draft.

In August of 1943 Norvelle told me to participate in a series of academic tests for a fairly new program to send sailors to college to provide officers for the growing Navy. I was later advised that I had been the one selected from our base and would be transferred to the Navy V12 program at the College of Pacific in Stockton, California, for the fall semester.

My first semester was very interesting. There were very few men from the fleet, as I was. Most of the boys were recent graduates from high school, and generally from the top of their classes. It was tough competition for a boy who had dropped out of school with average grades. However, my grades were a high C average, and I was retained for the next semester and would room with another fleet sailor who was a good buddy. When we returned from a short leave between semesters we learned that my friend had been reassigned to the fleet following review of his academic record by the Navy in Washington, D.C. I was very unhappy and felt that he had been mistreated and that I'd probably be the next to go. My attitude was to leave the books closed and not study, even when the Chief Petty Officer in charge of our company urged and cajoled me. Shortly after the first six weeks' grades were sent to the Bureau of Naval Personnel in D.C., I got what I deserved and was returned to the fleet.

I was assigned back to T.I. for further assignment and then to Bremerton, Washington, for assignment to what was called "new construction". This meant I would be in training to become ship's company on a ship then being built. I was assigned to a group being formed as the crew of a ship to be named the U.S.S. Oconto, an amphibious attack transport being built in Vancouver, Washington. We began to form the crew with men coming from many ships and stations and many raw recruits coming from training stations. Because of my eighteen months' service and rate as a third class petty officer, I was treated as an old hand.

After a couple of weeks of training on the ship's larger guns, and procedures of shipboard life, we were transferred to Astoria, Oregon, to await our ship. In a couple of weeks it arrived from the shipyard with a civilian crew. We took over the ship and in a few days sailed off for San Pedro on a "shakedown" cruise. Before long we were declared ready for combat and headed for the Pacific from San Francisco with a load of Army troops. I was quite excited as we passed through the anti-submarine net and headed for the far Pacific. The young boy was now a young man and off to fight the war.

I served on the Oconto for fifteen months. We carried troops all over the South and Western Pacific, participating in several reinforcement operations and invasions with Army and Marine troops. Our landing craft landed invasion forces twice in the Philippines and in the second wave on Okinawa. On all these invasions we were under constant enemy aircraft fire. At Okinawa on April 1, 1945, we learned the term Kamikaze, as we saw many Navy ships destroyed by the suicide pilots. I spent several days on the beach working with the "Beach Party" from the Oconto. We unloaded supplies brought in by our landing boats. It was an exciting time. The troops were about a mile inland so we had no small arms fire, only an occasional mortar or artillery shell.

In late July we were anchored in the Atoll of Ulithi in the Western Pacific waiting to load troops for the invasion of Japan. There was a bit of somberness as we had heard there were over 400,000 Japanese troops waiting for us.

One day I was called to the bridge to speak to our Captain, Paul Jackson, a three stripe Commander. I didn't think he even knew who I was. He was sitting in his command chair on the bridge as I arrived and he asked me why I had bilged out of the Navy V12 at COP. I stammered and sputtered something; then he asked me if I could make it if I went back. I said I'd give it a darn good try. He then informed me that I had scored second highest in some recent tests for the Western Pacific Fleet and was being returned to the States the next day.

After sixteen days on a slow Merchant Marine ship, I arrived back in San Pedro and was shipped off to Farragut, Idaho, where the fall contingent was being gathered for pre V12 training. Late one night as we crossed the Washington plains, the car steward came through calling out that the war was over. A sailor leaned down from a top bunk and knocked him cold with his shoe because he thought it was a practical joke. The next day, when we arrived in Spokane, we decided we deserved a forty-eight hour liberty and did not report to Farragut until two days later. Everyone was so elated with the war's end that we were not punished. However, several days later, orders came to immediately reduce the size of the program. Several of us who had been in V12 previously were the first to go and were sent off to Lake Union Naval Station in Seattle until we were sent home for discharge on December 31, 1945. It was two days short of four years since I had enlisted. We were all glad the atomic bombs had caused the Japanese to end the war and that our buddies had not been called upon to invade those Islands. It was a happy family who welcomed a young man home from the war.

CHAPTER 5

WOMEN IN THE MILITARY

There are records of women taking part in wars as far back as the Bible and the Greek histories. At least 400 women served as Union soldiers during the Civil War, passing as men. In World War I, women were used as nurses, ambulance drivers, and a few similar roles. However, in World War II a large number of women served in the armed services. Besides the nurses, there was a wide variety of occupations represented in the WAVES, WACs, and the women's divisions of the Marines and Coast Guard.

The use of women in active military service was a pioneering move that has developed since that time to the point where women now fly combat, serve on active warships, and are promoted to general and flag rank. There was a huge resistance to this movement and many men resented having to serve under women officers.

Marjorie Raymond was an enlisted WAVE who worked as a Yeoman. (a military clerk or secretary). She took screening tests to become an officer and then was commissioned in the supply corps. She worked in Washington, canceling contracts, as the war had just ended.

Florence Cromwell applied for a WAVE commission and was sent to OCS. She spent a year teaching in the officer training school. She then was trained in airborne radio and was sent to Washington DC to a group that planned for the supply and maintenance of airborne radio and radar within the fleet.

Ruth (Nikki) Blackman was commissioned in the WAC and was one of the few women to be stationed overseas. She was an officer with a group of telephone operators first sent to North Africa. Later, her unit was transferred to Italy, after that invasion.

Frieda Yakish was a civilian with the Navy Bureau of Ships in Washington. Her senior officer felt she would make a good officer in the WAVEs and encouraged her to take the tests. After commissioning, she spent the rest of the war in Norfolk, Virginia, coding and decoding secret messages.

Bernice Nutt joined the women marines and was trained as an aviation maintenance mechanic to allow men to go to combat but she was never used as she was trained and no one was relieved for combat.

Helen Crawford was assigned by the Waves to be a hospital corpsman and worked in Navy Hospitals. She gives us some stories of her conflicts with the military system.

Frances Randau joined the WAC to travel and was successful in getting an overseas assignment and spent the war in Cairo.

WAVE, ENLISTED TO OFFICER
Marjorie Raymond

On June 15, 1943, along with sixty eight other recruits, I reported to the Union Station, Los Angeles, expecting to leave in the afternoon for Hunter College, Bronx, New York. Once we checked in, we were told there would be a delay. This was during the Zoot Suit Riots, Los Angeles was off limits to Navy Personnel, and we were to stay within the station. Even though we were not in uniform, we were considered Navy Personnel.

At nine o'clock that evening, we left on our cross-country trip. As part of a troop train we were sometimes diverted from the main line to drop off or pick up soldiers. From St. Louis on, I really don't remember our route. We arrived in New York City early in the morning of the sixth day, and went by subway to the Bronx.

At Hunter we were housed in apartments near the college. For the next month, there were more shots, drilling, issuing of uniforms, and classes, which included ship and aircraft identification. I'm not sure if any of us were called on to identify ships or aircraft, but we were prepared! There were batteries of tests for aptitude and interest. We were told that at that time the Navy needed clerical workers, so that is where most of us were assigned.

I was sent to Yeoman School, University of Oklahoma, Stillwater. There we were housed in college dormitories. Classes included typing, shorthand, and naval correspondence. I remember the time there as being very pleasant. The churches and civic clubs in the small town made us feel very welcome. There were other military groups on campus, including Navy Radio School, Army ASTP, and SPARS (Coast Guard Women). Saturday mornings we all took part in a Regimental Review on the college field. Often the local citizens came out to watch, and many of the dogs in town joined the parade. A regular Norman Rockwell scene.

At the end of three months, I was sent to Naval Intelligence, San Francisco. That assignment sounds impressive, and I did work as an indexer, so I probably handled classified material. I need to add that at times my duties included operating the switchboard, running the elevators, and sifting cigar butts out of the sand jars.

WAVE Quarters were at Sutter and Mason in a building that had been a women's residence club. Many of my best memories of being in the Navy are of my time as an enlisted WAVE. Sometime during those months, I took the test for Officer Candidate School, and went to Arlington, Virginia for training. This was in 1945, and the school at Northhampton, Massachusetts. had been closed. After being commissioned an Ensign in the Supply Corps, I was assigned to the Bureau of Supplies and Accounts, Washington, D.C. At that time the office was in barracks type building, along the Reflecting Pool. (They were temporary from World War 1, I heard.) The section where I worked handled contracts, records and distribution for paint ingredients under allocation by the War Production Board.

I lived in a rented room in a house near Dupont Circle. It was the most elegant place I have ever lived, even though my room on the fourth floor was probably servant's quarters at one time. There were rumors that summer that WWII was coming to an end. One morning, early in August, I was waiting for a bus, when a man ran out from the radio station and told the newsboys selling papers: "Start shouting, you're ahead of the extras. The War has ended." It was nearly a week later that the end really came. After the President's announcement that evening, my roommate and I were in the crowd in downtown Washington. People in the park across from the White House were shouting: "We want Harry". President Truman did appear briefly on the balcony.

It was exciting to be in Washington during the weeks that followed. At work we were canceling contracts. I went to a two week class at the Pentagon in Contract Termination. If I remember correctly, I was sent because I had a low point score. In February 1946, I finally had enough points to my credit to be eligible for "Separation from Service," and I was sent to San Francisco to be discharged.

My experience in San Francisco and Washington D.C. was tame in comparison with the dangers and hardships endured by the women and men who served overseas. However, I am proud to have been a part of WWII as a Navy WAVE.

A NAVY WAVE IN WASHINGTON
Florence S. Cromwell
In February of 1942, the Navy began to make plans to enroll women. By summer they had picked the organizing officers, leaders from academia and business, and planned for training and housing. The leaders were outstanding, picked for particular jobs. The head of the WAVES, Mildred McAfee, had previously been President of Wellesley College. She unashamedly robbed women's Ivy League colleges of many of their key women to make the WAVE leadership outstanding. Classes for officers commenced in October of 1942 at Smith College, Northampton, Massachusetts. Enlisted women trained at Hunter College in New York.

The basic uniform was designed by a well known French designer, Mainbocher, and soon had the reputation of being the best looking among the women's services. The Lieutenant in charge of uniforming the officer recruits at Smith had been head of women's apparel at Filene's Department store in Boston. She supervised the outfitting and made sure each woman was clothed properly; hems the right length and no hair touching the collar. She also taught etiquette and other things to make the WAVE officer present herself well. The head of the Corps at Smith had been president of Wilson University and the head of Physical Education at Vassar took the same position in the officer training program.

I was a senior at Miami University in Ohio when I learned of the Navy plan for women. I went to Cincinnati to apply and be tested for officer training over my father's objections since I was not yet 21. I graduated and was accepted and reported at Northhampton on July 3,1943 for basic training. Smith College was unable to handle all the officer candidates and half, including me, were sent to nearby South Hadley to Mt. Holyoke College. Though not yet "uniformed", we were issued clod-hopper shoes and Navy hats and were immediately started on drills in 90o July weather in the humid Connecticut River valley. We lived, military style, in dorms - now barracks - four to a room and were immediately immersed in courses to learn about the Navy ways; organization, history, law, ships and aircraft, and communication! We were seaman for one month, Midshipmen for month two, and finally graduated and commissioned by the end of August to await orders for our first assignment. But through it all, the drill instructors, all men initially, enjoyed pushing us to the limit. We daily marched to all classes, meals, and of course to graduation. By then I had progressed from platoon leader to company commander, so obviously I had learned at least how to march.

My orders, long awaited, assigned Ensign Cromwell to stay at Northampton to teach naval organization. With mixed emotions I faced new challenges but happily found I could at last live out of quarters with a friend in a town apartment. We took meals at the Officer's Club which was operated in the former bar and restaurant of the Hotel Northhampton, a prized local eatery. We thought we had it made!

The hard part was yet to come; facing 3 to 4 classes a day of new recruits. In my very first class were two Lieutenants, women who had been pre-commissioned for special assignments. Even with that exalted status, they still had to take all the basic officer training and classes. One was former Dean of women at Temple University and the other a top administrator of the Merchandise Mart in Chicago. Despite their former status, they were exceedingly gracious and cooperative to the rigor of Navy protocol.

I stayed at "Hamp" for a year during a time of considerable change in military training of women. These two women were examples of those changes since they were destined to jobs related to housing, feeding and equipping of women's billets. One major change spoken of was that chow had to be altered from that usually given to men, both dietary plans and amounts to better accommodate women's food needs and wishes.

In October 1944, I was sent to Ward Island, part of Corpus Christi Naval Air Station in Texas, for airborne radio and radar school. We studied the equipment and its maintenance and were trained in its use in flights from the Air Station over the Gulf of Mexico. Then, after two months, I landed in the Radio Maintenance Section of the Bureau of Aeronautics (BuAer) in the Navy Department in Washington. Our group had thirty officers, including ten WAVES, and no enlisted persons. The commander had been a business man, commissioned for the war but most of the rest of the men were former Chief Radiomen who had been commissioned as Ensigns. They had the technical know how for us all. But together, we did the paper planning for the supply and maintenance of airborne radio and radar equipment throughout the fleet. I stayed in that position in Washington, with some travel to airbases for orientation, until the end of the war.

Living places were hard to find in Washington and at first I had a room in the home of a retired lady and had to eat all meals out. A group of five WAVE friends located a marvelous rental house on East Capital Street just five blocks from the Capitol). There was a real estate office at street level and living quarters on the three floors above, comfortable furnished with a great kitchen, dining room, and two living rooms on the second floor. Four bedrooms were on the third and fourth floors. Rent with utilities paid was $175 per month. We only paid rent and phone - a great bargain.

Washington was full of interesting and lively people, war or not. We all worked long hours, many on shifts, but our house soon became a WAVE social center for friends and families. There was a small mom and pop grocery close by and they sort of adopted us to help with our provisioning. Two of my former Hamp roommates were now admiral's secretaries, one for Admiral King's, the other for the chief of Submarine Service in the Atlantic. High powered friends with good contacts. One of our housemates was a home economics graduate who instantly became the manager of food for our establishment. She became an expert with SPAM; amazingly good as she prepared it for dinner parties.

Washington was a great place to live and get about. It was extremely friendly and everyone was helpful. One would take a ride from anyone who stopped to offer. It was completely safe for someone in uniform. By this time the WAVES and civilians were a majority of the personnel of the Navy buildings in Washington and three quarters of the "communicators" and mail handlers were WAVES. I remained there until I was discharged in March 1946 as a Lt.(jg). Having celebrated both VE and VJ days with all the rest of the crazy folks out in the streets it was sad to leave.

All of my graduate education, starting in September 1946, was made possible by the GI Bill but those war years provided the important beginning to my professional life in occupational therapy which formally concluded fifty years later!

A WAC OVERSEAS
Ruth Blackman

I was assistant office manager and preparing the payroll for 350 employees at the William Carter Company in Barnsville, Georgia, when Pearl Harbor was bombed. The following May, the organization of a Women's Army Auxiliary Corps was announced and I immediately decided to join.

I had to go to Fort McPherson in Atlanta, 60 miles away, several times to fill out forms, take aptitude tests, and have a physical examination. Character references and a birth certificate were required. Gaining 6 pounds before I could pass the physical and obtaining my birth certificate from Belmont, Massachusetts, caused frustrating delays in my acceptance. Finally on October 2, 1942, I reported to Fort Des Moines, Iowa, the first WAAC training center. It was an old cavalry post and the stables had been completely renovated to become women's barracks. Enlistees poured in from across the country. . Nicknames were common and my maiden name, Nichols, was soon shortened to 'Nicky' which I've been called ever since.

The WAAC uniform was good looking and we loved our unique "Hobby Hat" but there weren't enough small sizes. The "Peewee Platoon" had to wear the seersucker P. T. dress until more smaller uniforms arrived. When an early snowstorm hit, we were issued men's overcoats. Mine hung to the ground, the sleeves completely covered my hands and it weighed a ton. Basic training was rigorous; our day started at 5:30 AM and ended with bed check at 10:45 PM. We had classes, an hour of drill every day, K. P., and latrine duty and our barracks had to be kept ready for inspection at all times.

Following a month of basic, came assignment for special training and I spent 8 weeks at Administration School. Our pay was $21 a month. Soon after, I went to O.C.S., graduating on April 3, 1943 as a third officer. We were not given the normal army rank designations until September that year when we became the Women's Army Corps and part of the Army of the United States.

The day after graduation, I was on my way to Ft. Devens, Massachusetts, where a new training center was being activated. I was thrilled. The first twelve years of my life were spent in the general vicinity of Boston and my Grandmother Wright, an aunt, cousins, and friends were still living in the area. However, I served there only a brief time, organizing and training a new company. It was hard work but excellent experience. When company officers were needed to serve overseas, I volunteered and was transferred to Ft. Oglethorpe, Tennessee. There, we hiked, swam, practiced abandoning a ship at sea, studied map reading, carefully sewed identification labels on every item of clothing, made other preparations, and waited. Finally orders came sending us to the POE, Camp Patrick Henry, Virginia. It was early November - cold, foggy, and muddy and crowded with G.I.s waiting to go overseas. Guards with fixed bayonets were posted, around the clock, outside the women's barracks. I'll never forget our boarding ship at night, no lights anywhere, tense and excited and loaded down with over-stuffed barracks's bag, helmet, gas-mask, canteen, and mess kit - destination unknown. The Empress of Scotland, a former cruise ship converted to troop carrier, provided few comforts - we sat on the floor for our two meals a day, played cards, or wrote letters. We were required to stay clothed at all times and to carry our life belt and canteen everywhere. After a jittery but uneventful crossing, we landed at Casablanca.

Two days later, I left for Algiers with one other officer and 35 enlisted women. It took 4 days on a third class French train, with bench-like wooden seats and minimal bathroom facilities. For food we had C rations, eaten cold out of the can. Water was for drinking only and we slept on the floor, the benches, or in the overhead luggage racks, with one army blanket and long-handled woolies under coveralls to keep us warm. We joined a company of telephone operators and other communication specialists and I was assigned as Special Services and Post Exchange Officer and shortly as Personnel Officer also. Company headquarters was in a former museum built on a steep hillside - the Orderly Room, Mess Hall and Day Rooms were on the top floor with sleeping quarters for enlisted women on the floors below, with 300 steps in between. The 17 company and operational officers were billeted in a small villa with no furniture, no heat, and a big hole in the rear wall from a bomb earlier in the war. Our beds were made of 2 by 4's, chicken wire springs, and mattress covers filled stuffed with straw. Innovation became a way of life.

At Christmas, trees in the Mess Hall and Day Rooms were decorated with bits of colored paper, tops of tin cans, cellophane cigarette wrappers, and even a few lights using flashlight batteries. They were beautiful. Initially our women had almost nothing to read and no radio. When I went to Theatre Special Services with a request for one, the Major on duty told me the only one in stock was promised to a chaplain in exchange for a jeep. Even simple needs, such as a comb or bar of soap were not available at the PX and had to be sent from home

Though the war zone had moved into Italy, there remained the threat of air raids and often at night, during the first few months, we were awakened by sirens and heard the smoke trucks rumbling through the streets. Water shortages were not uncommon, creating bathing and laundry difficulties. In the spring, swarms of locusts caused misery for everyone.

Algiers was an interesting and colorful city, but had suffered terrible bomb damage. The casbah and black market restaurants were off limits but proved too tempting to many despite that. On my one leave while in Algiers I spent five days at Bou Saada, an oasis on the edge of the desert. It was sheer luxury with a real bed, eggs for breakfast, and steak for dinner. Two friends, also on leave, took me camel riding - the saddles were primitive and when a race was suggested, I discovered it was not a mode of travel I preferred. We went shopping in the market place that was teeming with men, had tea with a rug merchant, and bought a hand forged dagger.

The highlight of my stay was our visit to the "Holy City", where they cared for the blind, lame, and feeble-minded.. It was arranged by the manager of our hotel, an American officer, primarily to see the school there. It was unlike any we had ever seen, or even imagined, one large room, dim, crowded, and very noisy, like bedlam. The students, all male and all ages, sat cross-legged on the dirt floor, reciting from the Koran. They attended school from 5 AM to 10 AM and then from 2 PM to 7PM, every day, until they had memorized the entire book. Nothing else was taught.

Our host, the Marabout, invited us to his home for coffee and it was impressive, with beautiful china and silver. There was dark, rich coffee and delicate cookies called "Gazelle's Horns", filled with chopped locusts. He invited us to return for lunch the next day. We were treated as honored guests by the marabout and his family members. Virginia, an American civilian employee at our hotel and I were the only women present. The 'lunch' was a feast with many delicious courses, elegantly served. A whole roasted lamb, complete with head and tail, standing upright on a huge silver tray was spectacular. We ate the delectable meat with our fingers - messy but fun and afterwards the servants bathed our hands in warm water. By the time fruit and coffee were served, the meal lasted nearly 3 hours and I was exhausted. It was one of my most unusual experiences while overseas.

In July 1944 we moved to Caserta, Italy, the new headquarters for the Mediterranean Theatre of Operations. It was very hot and dusty but our living conditions were more comfortable. I was assigned as temporary commander of a new company being activated and received my promotion to first lieutenant.

At Christmas that year I flew to Rome with friends to attend the Pope's first public mass since hostilities began. None of us were Catholic but we looked on it as an historic event. It was a mob scene and frightening - thousands of hysterical Italians pressing in from all sides. Finally my husky Texas escorts shoved and elbowed our way to safety. We never did see the Pope.

In January I spent three weeks on temporary duty in the Appenines with a small contingent of WAC telephone and teletype operators, stenos and clerks assigned to the 5th Army. Their commanding officer was on emergency leave. The enlisted women took their snow-bound tent accommodations for granted but it was a new experience for me. My tiny tent with its fractious pot-bellied stove, proved cozy, however, and I truly enjoyed my brief assignment there. One day was extra special. I knew members of the Barnesville National Guard were with a regiment close to the front and not too far away. They could not come to see me, so I obtained permission to visit them. I was given a jeep and driver and told we must be back over the road by a certain time because the Germans bombed it every day at that hour. Seeing friends and neighbors again, and under such circumstances, was an emotional high. We talked a blue streak, exchanging news about home and families and the time passed much too quickly. Shortly after returning to Caserta, my request for transfer to the Adjutant General's office was approved and I went to work at theatre headquarters in the Royal Palace. In April, a plane on a routine flight from Bari to Caserta crashed, killing all on board, including two WAC officers with whom we had lived and worked, and two enlisted women. It was a devastating loss to everyone.

May 8, 1945. V. E. Day. Impossible to describe. Joy! Laughter! Tears! Relief!

The redeployment of troops began immediately; home, to the Pacific, or to Germany with the Army of Occupation. It would be months before completion. On July 1, I was assigned to the Theatre Special Services Section as Operations Officer. On reporting I was surprised to find my new C. O. was the same Major I had met in Algiers 18 months earlier, about a radio. I had leave coming and was allowed to take six days before starting work. Another WAC officer and I flew to Lake Garda to stay at a rest facility for women officers. It was certainly different - an elaborately decorated and furnished small villa which had belonged to Mussolini as a love nest for his mistress. The next few months were very busy.

The surrender of Japan in August meant the war was really and finally over, but it had little effect on the continuing responsibilities of our Special Services Section. Maintenance of morale during the transition period was a primary concern and there were several conferences to discuss programs and activities and how best to implement them. On a return flight from Venice to Caserta, following one of these conferences, the pilot suddenly announced he had just received notice of my promotion to captain. What a thrill!

Tours into Switzerland had already been proposed and approved by the command, and representatives of the Swiss tourist, hotel, banking, and transportation industries visited our headquarters to finalize plans and details. Since I was the only woman officer in the section, I acted as hostess. The young woman secretary to the delegation and I became friends and have exchanged many letters over the years and have enjoyed a few wonderful visits. The tours, one 5 days and one 7 days, were an outstanding success. Thousands of GI's poured into Switzerland for the experience of a lifetime. I took both tours and fell in love with that beautiful country.

I had also fallen in love with Italy. Who could forget Capri and its shimmering Blue Grotto, the Bay of Naples, Sorrento, and the Amalfi Drive. Pompeii! Beautiful Florence, climbing the leaning tower of Pisa, Venice from a gondola. These I'll always remember; the grim reminders of war I would like to forget.

When at last I was on orders home, there was no transport. Because of bad weather, all flights were carrying only litter cases and the necessary care-givers. Three nurses and I were stranded until officers from my section met the Captain of the ship on which they were returning home, over hot chocolate at the Red Cross, and convinced him to take us too. The USS Monterey was a light aircraft carrier, and not equipped for female passengers, but the Captain gave us his below-deck quarters and did everything to make us comfortable. It was a stormy crossing but we enjoyed our "cruise" in spite of that - we were going home. We landed at Camp Patrick Henry, Virginia, on New Year's Eve, 1945. It was no more attractive or welcoming than it had been in November, 1943. Camp personnel were all involved in plans for a big New Year's Eve celebration and we were not included. It was a rather flat homecoming, but only temporary. After all, the war was over and we were home!

THE WAVES
Frieda Yakish
It was June in the summer of 1942, I had just graduated from Simpson College, a small liberal arts school in Indianola, Iowa. I had previously taken a Civil Service exam and had procured a job as a clerk typist at $1800 a year. My destination was Washington, D.C. Since I had a friend from my hometown who already had gone to Washington to work, I was thrilled, even about the long train ride by myself.

I was assigned to the Bureau of Ships, housed in temporary buildings on Constitution Avenue close to the Washington Monument, and worked for a Naval officer, Ensign Ryan. I was sharing a room with my friend who rented from a family in a nice brick residence at the comer of Mass. and Wisconsin Avenue in northeast Washington. Taking the bus each morning down Mass Avenue past a lot of embassies and mansions, I was awestruck and excited about all I saw.

In August, the Navy organized the WAVES (Women Accepted for Volunteer Emergency Service). Since officers were needed first, the Officer's Training School was scheduled to open October 1 at Smith College in Northampton, Mass. My boss, Ensign Ryan, turned to me and said, "Frieda, you qualify for the WAVES, why don't you apply?"

Being the adventurous soul that I was, I said it sounded like a good idea to me. I passed the written exam and the physical and on September 30 boarded a train in Washington, D.C. bound for Northampton, Mass. Though all the women were friendly and conversational, I soon felt "out of my class". The East Coast train carried all the fervent patriots from mostly prestigious Eastern Colleges, Wellesley, Bennington, Vassar, etc. Whenever I said Simpson, they would invariably say "Simmons. Oh yes, I know that". (Simmons is a small college in Boston). I finally just let it go.

We were all billeted at the Northampton Hotel. This was "the" hotel in Northampton and a super place to dine. At that point, the only Navy appearance was the bunk beds. Though we were served cafeteria style, we were privileged to have the regular hotel cooks. To this naive midwestern girl who had never had blueberry muffins or swordfish or numerous other New England dishes, I was impressed.

We had no uniforms for the first six weeks we were there. Though we had to form ranks and learn to march, our time off was not regulated. We went to the football games at nearby Amherst and mingled with civilians. We had a ball!

Though we were told we would all be in communications, the path to get there was not clear. Nobody seemed to know what we needed. We started a course in how radio works that was soon discontinued. We studied naval history and ship recognition.

After we finally got uniforms, things began to tighten up both in Navy discipline and in courses we needed. Strange as it seems, it was decided that everyone needed to be able to type. (We were to find out that most coded messages were sent on ECM machines that required typing 4 letter group code words.) My morale rose; here was something I could do well while most of my cohorts from the fancy Eastern Colleges had never typed at all!

We always had to march to class in company ranks. One very cold morning as we were "falling in", books in one hand, we asked our company commander (one of us) if we could put our other hand in our pocket. She gave the command. We were warmer, but our leader was relieved of her command the next day. The Navy had taken over!

Since the objective of the WAVES was to relieve men to go overseas, we were told that most of our class would be sent to Washington, D.C. where the largest communications center was. I was hoping to go back there where I had friends and living accommodations. "T'was not to be." After getting my commission as an Ensign in January, 1943, I was sent to the 5th Naval District Communication Office at the Naval Operating Base in Norfolk, VA. Now this was not all bad. There were only 8 of us sent there. We lived in a very nice BOQ (Bachelor Officer Quarters) which housed not only men but a few female Navy nurses too. We walked to work to the code room located in the center of the main operations building.

We worked around the clock shifts, encoding and decoding messages. Norfolk was a big harbor and in 1943 many ships, from aircraft carriers to submarines, came and went under tight security. Many of the messages we handled were top secret. We felt very important. We also learned about the Navy ships by going aboard - mostly by invitation of male officers who had never seen a WAVE officer before.

After about a year, more WAVES, both officers and enlisted personnel were assigned to the Communications Office and I was promoted to assist the Communications Officer in charge, Commander Swanson. Shortly thereafter, two new male officers reported to the Commander. He turned to me and said, "Frieda, here's a couple of new bachelors for you". I was embarrassed, but not enough that I didn't go out with them. Six months later I was married to one of them, and our Commander was instrumental in getting us officer housing quarters on the Base, the first married Naval officer couple to live there. We were lucky; our quarters were lovely and convenient. I could walk to work and my husband continued to work there in the harbor area. When war was over we both had enough points to get out of the service and were released in October 1945. It was a great ride!

I had attained the rank of Senior Lieutenant (2 stripes) and my husband was a Lieutenant Commander (2 1/2 stripes). But my stripes were blue and his were gold. That has since changed and women too now wear gold stripes.

A WOMAN MARINE
Beatrice Nutt

One had to be 21 to join the military women organizations. After my birthday, both the Army and the Navy had stopped recruiting women so I joined the new women Marines. I was going to Glendale J C and a photographer was sent out there to take pictures of those going into the Marines. The group of enlistees was sent by train across the country to Camp Lejune, North Carolina. The train was slow and had to give way to other trains. We thought we would never get through San Antonio as they stopped, changed tracks, stopped and waited. I remember how impressed I was when we crossed the Mississippi River. Finally we arrived and coming into the base I saw the white sand and thought it was snow. I had never been in snow but then I was told it was sand. To compound this failure to get in the snow, I heard two weeks later that it had snowed in Glendale and Los Angeles for the first time in my life.

We were issued uniforms and my shoes didn't fit. Finally they sent me to another portion of the base for fitting and I saw the Atlantic Ocean for the first time. Mostly boot camp seemed to be learning to march. The humidity was high and it wasn't very comfortable. They tried to indoctrinate us as Marines and showed films about the war in the Pacific with Japanese snipers. Morale was very high in the group. I sang in the choir and we got liberty for that so I was able to go to the movies occasionally. We learned to live in the barracks and generally to be Marines.

After boot camp I hoped to go to Washington and to get to see more of the east coast. Due to a desire for unit cohesion, our whole class was sent to Norman, Oklahoma for the school for aviation maintenance technicians.

I wanted to get into photo work but didn't have enough experience to get a transfer to this. They taught us how to dope fabric wings on training planes. In addition, we had mess duty. I drew the coffee supply. I had to climb on a ladder to clean the huge coffee machines. We liked to go into the town and buy a local specialty - half a cantaloupe filled with ice cream. Once at Norman we were marching to breakfast and passed a group just back from the Pacific. They marched singing cadence counting, "Left. Left. Left a wife and 49 children all sick in bed in a starving condition and nothing but gingerbread left. Left."

We had a sergeant who was outstanding. She was very calm and inspired everyone. She also told ghost stories in the evening with a chilling effect. She went on to officer training. On completing the course, the whole class was sent to El Toro Marine Air Base in Orange County, California.

El Toro was a new base and was out in the country, with many orange groves. Most of the girls had never seen oranges grow before. They didn't have a job for the group and we never did get to work with planes. We were supposed to "free a man for combat" but the same men continued doing their jobs. Some of us were given jobs scraping paint off the windows of the new buildings, as they spray painted the buildings without covering the windows. The barracks here had two double deck bunks made into a cubicle with some separating material.

We also had mess duty. On this I was able to take ice cream out and we ate ice cream in the barracks for two meals some days. To this day I do not enjoy ice cream. We also had some guard duty which was uneventful. One girl was on a radio program and won the prize money. When asked what she would spend it for, she said, "for a manure spreader for the family farm in Wyoming". This was the joke of the barracks. "Hey, Romanski, how's the manure spreader?"

Finally I was transferred to North Island Naval Air Station in San Diego. I thought I would get to do more useful work here. They did put me on a job of electroplating parts as I had done this on swing shift while going to Glendale J C. One of our girls had emotional problems and I worried about her. Finally I went to the Catholic chaplain (she was Catholic but I wasn't) and told him she needed help. It seemed that she was in love with a married man and couldn't handle it. She did get help and it turned out well.

My mother used to mail me packages and everyone said, "Oh, you are lucky to get a package." However, she just sent her empty cigarette packs to remind me to get her more cigarettes.

At North Island I went into town and sang in a church choir. I think it was five cents to go in on the trolley. I also went to dances at the Hotel del Coronado. I found a guy I liked to dance with but my bunkmate said, "You can't marry him." and kept breaking up my dancing with him. I had no idea of marrying him. He was just a good dancer.

We still didn't get to do any work on the airplanes and no men seemed to be freed up. When the war ended, I was separated at North Island and came home. I enjoyed the experience with the Marines though I was disappointed not to be given more important work.

A WAVE MEDIC
Helen Crawford

I came from a singing family and out of high school I was living in Hollywood studying voice. In 1944 I was told that I had nodes on my vocal cords and wouldn't be able to have a career singing. I was very discouraged and didn't know what to do. I suddenly decided to go into the Navy. I went home to Minnesota for a week and was then to report to Hunter College in New York for boot training.

I reported in wearing a suit and heels. I immediately met two college girls wearing plaid skirts and penny loafers. We became friends immediately and still are 60 years later. We were issued uniforms and found them attractive and a good fit. The stockings were cotton and were ugly and uncomfortable. The buildings at Hunter were tall and we stayed in dorms that had extra beds added to each room.

We were given the same courses as men who were going to sea with lots of ship recognition. The largest amount of time was spent in drill. I was not good at this and was called MM - "marching moron". One of our girls was made acting drill master. She couldn't remember the commands and we marched over benches and into trees.

There was only one place where smoking was allowed, on the fourth floor of the barracks building. We would run up the stairs, get a quick smoke and try to get back down during a ten minute break between classes. At one point my two friends and I were taken out and photographed for recruiting posters. Recruiting was stopped shortly after this and the pictures were never used. At one point, the doors were taken off the toilets and showers as in men's barracks. The girls resisted and wouldn't take showers and eventually the doors were replaced. We studied for tests in the stalls. The watch would look in the rooms and see if there were feet showing under the doors so we had to prop our feet up on the door. The three of us studied this way and made good grades on the tests.

We had bed inspections daily and the beds had to be made so tight that a quarter would bounce. Most of us learned to do this but one girl had a lot of trouble. One day she finally got a beautiful job on her bed. She then just left it made and slept underneath the bed so she wouldn't have to remake it.

Once in boot camp I was called in by an officer. I was scared and wondered what I had done. It turned out that she was dating a man from my home town and she wanted to know if I knew his family.

Being in New York we were able to do things on weekends. Once we decided to go to the Starlight Room. On the elevator on the way up I asked a well dressed man if he thought we could afford this place. He smiled and didn't discourage us. When we asked for the bill the waiter said that he had paid for us.

I went to a military review that my friend Betty was in, held in the New York Armory. I couldn't find a seat until finally I peeked in a box with seats. It was empty so I slipped in and sat down. Each group in the review saluted as they came to me. Later I was called in by the officers. The box was reserved for the president of the country. No one knew what to do as there weren't any rules for this type of offense. Finally they took Betty's weekend liberty away and didn't do anything to me. Military logic!

We were now winning the war and there wasn't such an urgent need for people so they decided to give us better training. Our boot camp was 8 weeks instead of the previous four. Finally we finished and our group was all sent to Bethesda Naval Hospital in Washington, DC for hospital corps school.

Corps school was very demanding and we were there for 6 months. I was in front of the White House when FDR's funeral transport emerged. Near the end of my time in Bethesda, my father died and I went on leave for the funeral. Because of this I was given first choice on where to go after finishing school. I remembered that there was a big military hospital in Pasadena so I looked for a Naval Hospital in southern California and took Corona, thinking it was the one in Pasadena.

When we were coming toward Los Angeles on the train, they said this was the nearest stop to Corona. I said, "No. I'll go on to Los Angeles and just take a cab to the hospital." Someone then explained that Pasadena was an Army hospital and Corona was elsewhere. I had a terrible time getting to Corona Naval Hospital. There were no buses to the area and it was out in the countryside. There no transport out except very expensive taxi or hitching.

Corona had a lot of very badly injured men. They needed a lot of support and the work was very draining. We were told to give some of them penicillin when it was new and we poured it on the wound. Then the nurse showed us how to inject it.

The WAVES did all the cleaning and most of the work on the wards. There were a group of men corpsmen back from the Pacific who did nothing but play cards. One evening there was a serious accident and motorcycle victims were brought in. These men suddenly went to work, cared for the injured, and did a terrific job. We realized then that they had been in battle and really knew how to do the difficult things and we had a lot more respect for them. But they never did do their part in the work on the ward.

Once in Corona I was told to fill in at the switchboard with two civilian ladies. They showed me how to plug in the phones, said two to three was very quiet and went on break. Suddenly the whole board lighted up. I started at the top and just answered what I could. The Captain's phone was at the bottom of the board and he came in furious. I was removed from the job immediately. So my resume included switchboard but didn't say for only one hour.

Another job I had was getting people up for night watch. I would get some out of bed, ask if they were awake and going to work. When they seemed awake I left but found they went back to sleep and didn't remember getting up. I go chewed out for not having awakened them for work.

A friend at Corona took me with her to her aunt's home in Claremont for Thanksgiving. Her aunt was housemother at a dorm at Pomona College and showed us the college. I fell in love with it and was sure I would go there after discharge. (I did)

I lost my cap in the theater in Claremont and when I got back to Corona they said I was out of uniform and must not be in the Navy. When I finally proved I was, I was threatened with the brig. We sat around the quarters in the evenings on our bunks as there wasn't anything to do in Corona. One evening we were talking about hair do's and I fixed several of the girls' hair with peroxide, making them blonde. The Navy said this was illegal as the hair color was part of the identification and we were called on the carpet.

A group of four of us were ordered to the dispensary at the Marine base at Mojave. On the bus out I complained all the way out. No one else said anything. When we arrived, the Marine Colonel in charge of the base had been on the bus. He took me aside and said, "If you still feel that way in three months, come to me and I'll get you transferred." There were no quarters for the women and we had to find beds, blankets, etc. It was terribly windy. Some days we were driven to work in a truck, covered by a tarp to keep the blowing sand out.

By three months I had fallen in love with the desert. About this time a Navy woman officer came to review our situation. She only stayed an hour and we didn't meet her but we heard that she was extremely shocked by conditions. We were told to pack and were moved out the same day to San Diego Naval Hospital.

The end of the war came and went. Most military personnel were no longer needed but medical workers continued to be needed for all the sailors and marines in the hospitals. I continued to work on the wards at San Diego Naval Hospital. Now combat was over, the Navy became more formal and reverted to more emphasis on rank and on inspections.

Once at an inspection I was called on the carpet by a woman officer for having a run in my stocking. She sent me to the quarters to fix myself up and return. I didn't have another pair of stockings and the only thread I could find was navy blue. I mended the tan stocking with navy blue thread and returned. She was furious but couldn't find anything in the regulations to charge me with.

Once we had a very important retired Naval admiral in the hospital.. He was very elderly and had syphilis affecting his brain. He would wander onto our ward and say "Cokes for everyone here." He would stay until someone brought cokes. He frequently told me that "I'm going get you a feather bed in heaven." I still use the expression.

Just before an inspection by the Captain I was hurrying down the ward and knocked over a bottle attached to a patient from the first World War. It was filled with bloody urine and went all over the floor. Someone diverted the Captain from this area. I was so shocked that I can't remember anything that happened after that.

I was released in the summer of 1946, in time to start Pomona College.

A WAC IN EGYPT

Frances Randau

I graduated from Pomona College in 1941 and one of my ambitions was to travel. When the formation of the WAAC was announced, I decided this would be a good way to get to travel and signed up. I took basic training at Fort Des Moines, Iowa and then was sent to Camp McCoy Wisconsin where I was doing office work with personnel records. My goal was to go overseas so I found the things they looked for when picking those to go overseas and changed my own record to show these entries. I was one of the few picked.

We were sent to Hampton Roads Virginia, where we took a ship to Naples. We stayed a week in Naples, bunking in sleeping bags on the floor. They did however get a truck and took us on a tour of Naples. Fighting was still going on and Rome was still in German hands. We could hear shelling in the distance. From there we trained to Brindisi and then took an old Polish ship that the British were using for troop transport. It took us to Port Said, Egypt. We arrived shortly after Rommel's defeat and the GI's in Cairo now had a relaxed, country club attitude. They thought it was most amusing to see a group of women GI's march in with hard helmets, gas masks, boots, and full equipment.

We soon entrained for Cairo. We were taken to the "New" Hotel in Cairo that was now a billet for women troops. It had its own American mess for women only and the food was quite good. The hotel was in downtown Cairo and a short walk to the Headquarters of the Middle East Service Command where we were assigned. The larger group was sent to the airport to work. I was doing personnel work, largely issuing travel orders. We covered the whole Near East and most of East Africa so I typed many exotic places on the orders. The whole atmosphere was relaxed and pleasant.

The American and British headquarters were close together and the British had a much larger staff than the Americans. The British had been there a long time and had things well organized. They set up tours for troops and we were eligible to go. I made one trip up to Luxor and was able to see the temple of Karnak and the Valley of the Kings. On one occasion, four of us were picked for a recruiting film and were sent to Jerusalem. We had some time there and were able to see much of the country, including Tel Aviv and Bethlehem.

I worked for a variety of officers but was really responsible to the WAC officers. (The WAAC and now been integrated into the Army and became the WAC.) We weren't allowed to date officers but often did. I had been promoted to technician 5 but was busted back to private first class when I was found to be dating an officer.

I had a copy of Life magazine with an article on American fashions trends. I bought some yellow cloth and made a simple dress, sewing at the local Singer sales center. I was dating a British officer at this time and when he would come to pick me up, I would leave with my raincoat buttoned clear up. I would get in the car and when we arrived I would take off the raincoat and my date's driver would put it in the car. We would have dinner and dance with me as a civilian and then put the raincoat back on to go into the billet. We were not allowed to wear civilian clothes.

A favorite recreation of both male and female American soldiers was to rent a felucca (a small oared native boat) and go out on the Nile, taking beer and hot dogs from the mess for a picnic. We were also able to play tennis at some of the local sporting clubs.

A friend of mine married a pilot. She was Catholic and wanted a big church wedding. She arranged for the cathedral at Heliopolis. She manipulated bridesmaids' dresses from a British officer. She found white cloth for a wedding dress and made veils out of mosquito netting. It was a fine wedding.

I remained in Cairo until the war was over, nearly three years. We had a huge celebration on VJ day. Going home in November 1945, we went directly from Egypt to New York. We went on a horrible, old Liberty ship that was very slow. I then went to Chicago by train for discharge. Cairo was a fine place to spend the war. It was interesting but also pleasantly relaxed and the British were pleasant and helpful. The food was good and there was a fine social life.

CHAPTER 6

MILITARY RESEARCH

One of the most essential developments of the war was the use of new and innovative technology. The most striking example, of course, was the atomic bomb. Radar and sonar also had a great influence on the Allies ability to become victors in the war in the air and at sea. Research in explosives, new weapons, the accuracy of torpedoes, navigational equipment, and many other things were important as well.

There was extensive research in replacement for vital materials that were unavailable, such as rubber and certain metals for alloys.

Other types of information were sought, such as the psychological handling of prisoners of war and shell-shock victims. Efficient forms of quick food for battle situations were studied. The invasions required the development of new knowledge of logistics and the handling of massive amounts of materiel. New packaging and preservation methods were also developed.

The developments of military research during World War II led to the extremely accurate guided bombs used in the Gulf War and those even more fine-tuned in Afghanistan. Rocket research during the war helped lead to the exploration of space. Some of the researchers were criticized because they weren't in uniform but they ultimately made very significant contributions. Willis Lemm worked with a mobile rocket launcher and then was instrumental in the development of a facility to test and improve torpedoes. His final assignment was an air conditioning unit to protect the electronics of the atomic bomb during its delivery flight.

Bob Feeney spent his time at Oak Ridge, working on the atomic bomb. The secrecy there was an important part of the effect of the work.

Charles Barbour spent his entire war time in the development and improvement of radar.

Leonard Dart was a graduate student in physics when the war started and decided he wasn't comfortable working on a bomb. He stayed at Notre Dame, working in the thermodynamics of rubber and plastic, as well as teaching physics.

Homer White was a chemical engineer with Dow Chemical and planned and supervised the plants that made artificial rubber to replace the natural form no longer available for military needs.

Fred Arndt worked with the development and testing of sonar. Later he instructed Navy personnel in its use.

ROCKETS, TORPEDOES, and THE ATOM BOMB
Willys Lemm

In August 1939, friends visiting in Austria sent me a photo of Hitler riding by in his Mercedes. They felt that we would have another war. Wanting a change in jobs, I went to March Field and volunteered for the meteorology officers' course. However, the physical standards were very rigid and I wasn't accepted. I went to work for Dupont on a project to make vinyl cyanide and acetone cyanhydrin.

After Pearl Harbor, wanting a more challenging job that would allow me to do defense related work, I visited Caltech and Ernest Watson hired me to work with Dr. Fred Lindvall at the Kellogg Radiation Laboratory. Rocket manufacture was underway and launchers were needed. I was asked to design a rocket launcher to fit on a two and one-half ton truck. I designed a launcher that was all made from sheet metal, spot welded together, and fitted together like a puzzle, held together by one bolt. Two men could disassemble it and then reassemble it either on the ground or on the truck within three minutes. It had to work fast as it was to be used within 3000 yards of the enemy lines.

The launcher had twenty four rails, each holding one rocket. It was fired electrically so that all could be fired at once or individually or in rapid-fire sequence.

When the launcher was finished, I drove with a companion eight hundred miles, to take the launcher to Dugway Proving Grounds, Utah, on the Army truck. When the two of us safely arrived with the truck, I parked it in front of headquarters and reported to the Colonel. I told him what we had and he looked out; there was no truck. As a civilian, I told him he would be responsible for the loss but the truck had merely been moved to the nearby official parking lot. One key fitted all trucks.

The tests were extremely successful and I returned to Pasadena. Shortly I was called to go back to Dugway for a final test firing with all the brass assembled. The test was a failure as one of the soldiers had run the truck with the launcher into a Quonset hut and the launcher didn't work at the firing. I had to repair and realign the launcher en situ. The contract for manufacture was then given to the Pacific Railway Equipment Company. The chemical warfare service tried to take me away from Caltech, but Caltech had higher priorities and was able to keep me.

The launcher design and development had been started in December of 1941 and was delivered in the spring. After completion of the tests, a full technical report on the launcher was filed, including its plans and its development.

By now the war in the Pacific was going on and they found that torpedoes launched from aircraft didn't reach the target. They went various directions when launched instead of the direction aimed. If they did hit they often didn't explode, and the delivering planes were frequently shot down. The torpedoes had to be delivered from within 4000 yards as that was the range of the steam driven, 40 knot Mark 13 torpedo. It also couldn't be launched if the plane was going over 125 knots. A retired Captain and a Rear Admiral were in charge of the Navy research program at Caltech. They wanted a torpedo launching facility for research and development and it was decided that Norris Dam and Lake was a suitable location. I was assigned to work with them and put in charge of building a launch station. The goal was to make torpedoes that could be launched at higher speeds, as well as making them more accurate and reliable.

A large compressed air tank was installed on a hill adjoining the lake. The 300 foot launch tube took 30 tons of steel for which we had the highest priority. Air compressed to 250 pounds per square inch filled the tank. This was supplied with six air compressors, three large and three small. These were placed in sequence so that work could continue if one failed. A pump house was built for this equipment.

The launching tube was manufactured, 22 ½ inches inside diameter and installed in a trench in the hill, slanting down at a 19 degree angle. This was cemented with steel and concrete reinforcement. A keyway ½ by ¾ inches was required in the bottom of the tube to guide the torpedo down the 300 foot length. I found that Bethlehem Steel, who was making destroyers, had the tool needed for the keyway. A similar keyway was cut for the outboard bearings of destroyers. Our tubes were 6 feet long, and we had ordered 50. The tubes were sent to Bethlehem Steel, the keyways cut and the tubes delivered back to us in two weeks. They had to be put together with a transit so they would be straight. A flexible steel support had to be placed at each section junction. The terminus of the tube ended 75 feet above the lake.

An office and service building was built near the pump house. Water was needed, so a barge with a pump was placed on the lake to pump up water to the site. Recovery of torpedoes was accomplished by building a pier and having a boat on the lake with a crane. After launching, the torpedoes were found with a magnetometer and then a diver went down the 110 feet depth and hooked a cable on them so the boat could pull them up.

Hydrodynamic information was needed, so special high-speed cameras, taking 3000 frames per second, were utilized. A hydrophone range was built with a number of stations installed in the water so that the trajectory of the torpedo under water could be recorded. An electronics man from Pasadena Junior College built the first decade counter to record the signals. A torpedo traveling at 250 knots recorded a force on hitting the water of 3000 G's and special pressure sensors were installed in the torpedo head.

When it was finally tested, it was found that the fins and propeller blades were being damaged on the impact. A metal ring around the propeller prevented the propeller damage and was found to stabilize the torpedo so that it was much more accurate. Flares were placed on the tail of the torpedo and the photos showed the flare and then the water surface at the time of entry.

I was responsible for the design and construction of the mechanical elements of the whole Morris Dam facility. I was test director for a time after completion and we launched 850 torpedoes. Later, I returned to the research facility in Pasadena. I worked for a time on a means of finding the torpedo without dragging the whole lake with the magnetometer. My next assignment was under Dr Royal Sorensen and C. H. Sanderson on a rotating 90 horsepower electric motor to drive an electric torpedo. It was a unique design containing two counter rotating shafts. When this was completed, the motor was tested at Caltech and at Westinghouse.

About this time, the thrust of our research became secondary to all atomic bomb development. I worked on a project to make an air conditioning unit that would fit within a B-29 and keep the electronics of the bomb at stable temperature in flight. This took compressors, air conditioning equipment, and other specially designed to fit parts.

At this time about half of all metal shops in the Los Angeles area were working on parts for the bomb. The "Fat Boy" bomb was assembled at a facility at 3202 E. Foothill Boulevard in Pasadena. After the bombs had been used, we disposed of excess records of the bombs. There were rooms full of paper; plans, records, etc. Only the essential final materials were kept. Tons of paper were incinerated. In addition, metal supports and other materials used in the assembly of the bomb were smashed with a wrecking ball. My work of scientific creation ended with the bomb work completed.

OAK RIDGE
Robert Feeney

At the start of the war I was working in Boulder City, Nevada at the U.S. Bureau of Mines. My work was in developing a process to utilize domestic chromium ores for the production of chromium. This would have been needed if the German U- boats were successful in cutting off supplies of chromium ore from South Africa. Finally we sank enough of the U-boats so that this was not a problem.

In 1943 a personnel man came to Boulder City (a town of 2500 people). He had already been to all the bigger towns. Anyway he was recruiting for an important war project in the east. "It was of the most importance," he said. So since my work at Boulder City was leading nowhere, I took his offer. We drove east to northeastern Tennessee. When we got to the town, we were surprised to see that we were coming to a group of armed military police in front of a gate with barbed wire all around. We had a pass so we got in. This was Oak Ridge. It used to be a little town of 28 people. Now it was a big reservation, 10 miles wide and 20 miles long, surrounded by barbed wire. Anyway we got in, went to the house that was assigned to us, and I went to work.

My FBI clearance had not come through yet. We started work in a big building. We were assigned to rooms, really classrooms. I was there for about two weeks until my FBI clearance came through. These first weeks (not inside the Tennessee Eastman compound at Oak Ridge) were just make-work, until we could get to our real job. One day, I was asked if I knew algebra. I said, "Yes." So I was assigned to teach all the men algebra that day. But finally my FBI clearance came through and I reported to work inside the Tennessee Eastman compound. The first day on the job, I was told what we were really doing; making uranium 235 (one of the isotopes of uranium, in quantity 0.69 % of the total uranium). It was very secret; we did not tell our wives what we were doing.

Initially I worked for the chief engineer on a special two man team. We were given special jobs and worked on them. One day we were asked to reproduce a small chemical plant, just like the one we had. We needed to double the capacity. Normally this would have taken the engineering department about three months to do. But we didn't wait for drawings. We started immediately, using sketches drawn by hand. We did finish in 10 days!!

With about 80,000 people living that close together and other towns being farther off, we had to use our time off (We worked six days a week, only 8 hours per day.) in Oak Ridge. They constructed beer halls, where lots of people went during their time off.

But Oak Ridge was in a dry county of Tennessee. Major General Groves, who ran the place, went to the State of Tennessee and asked what % alcohol beer had. They replied that beer was 3.5% alcohol and up. So the General went to the beer refinery and got them to make a 3.35% beer. Oak Ridge was enormously important and the general did not have any trouble getting his special beer.

While most of the people were satisfied with beer halls, the engineers and scientists wanted something more. So they started an adult school at night. They would give courses on just about anything that people were interested in. They suggested a course in the Russian language. This had 100 people come the first night The instructor said he would teach us to talk Russian, to read and write Russian and we would learn Russian songs and so forth. He said he could not have 100 people in a class, so he promised to hold one class a night for the five week days. So we came back on our day the next week. There was a different instructor! I never found out what happened to the first one. But someone at Oak Ridge looked at him - and then he was gone.

We had two other instructors, Alexander Walensky and Peter Bondar. Peter had learned Russian at the language school in Boulder Colorado. But they had a surplus of Russian instructors so he came to Oak Ridge. When you asked him a question, he knew the answer right away. When we asked Alexander a question, he would stop and think. After all he knew Russian from his earliest days, but he didn't know the answers to our question without thinking about what he knew. One night I was talking to a fellow about the atomic physics class. It turned out that all of the fellows in his class were from Oak Ridge. They had another atomic physics class for the men who worked at Union Carbide. The authorities went to this much trouble to keep friendships between men working at Oak Ridge and men working at Union Carbide to a minimum.

One day riding to work, John said he heard something about lie detector tests being given. I said, "I had mine yesterday". They did not give lie detector tests to all the workers; only those who had access to the building where the final product was handled. A number of men initially failed the lie detector test, when asked if they had ever used an alias. It turned out that they had used an alias when going to a motel with a girl. So the man running the test rephrased the question to exclude this. I don't think anyone then failed the lie detector test.

The greatest shock that I had at Oak Ridge was on VJ day. I could not get over the talking about U238 and the bomb. We NEVER mentioned those words when working at Oak Ridge or anyplace else.

RADAR DEVELOPMENT
Charles Barbour

In the fall of 1936, I entered Northeastern University, Boston, Mass, as a freshman seeking a degree in electrical engineering. Northeastern is a cooperative education college, which involved a five-year curriculum composed of 13 weeks studies alternating with 13 weeks of employment. Early in 1937 I had several interviews with potential employers including a music recording studio that didn't make any offer. Some time later I had an interview with a firm that had a long established history in under-water sound developments both commercial (fishing industry) and military (Navy) submarine warfare. That interview at Submarine Signal Co., in downtown Boston was successful and I was employed as a student laboratory technician to maintain the engineers' instruments and to assist in constructing development models of new sonar equipment.

Submarine Signal Co. at that time was one of the most important Navy contractors in under-water sound technology, having emanated from MIT during World War I early antisubmarine warfare efforts. During the co-op years I was exposed to many advanced sonar activities including a new emergency FM-modulated under-water (sonar) communication system. This would permit submariners to talk to rescue personnel in case of disabling accidents such as had occurred with the submarine "Squalus" off Cape Cod when the whole crew had lived for many days only to finally perish.

Interestingly, I had unusually acute hearing in those days and was the only person who could discern resonance in the company's magneto-strictive sonar transducers (about 18000 cycles/second) and so had a side job of dealing with them when needed.

Submarine Signal Co. was perhaps most famous for holding the patents controlling the "Fathometer" depth sounders used world wide by the Navy and the commercial fishing industry and to this day by many boaters who know it as the depth sounder. The company was always innovative and sought proprietary products to sustain their business. In the early 1930's an effort had been made to apply their same depth sounding principles using pulsed radio waves and patents had been issued for a so-called "Radameter" device to bounce radio waves off objects and measure their transit time to determine distance. They were ahead of their time and couldn't arouse any serious interest in the development equipment and so quite literally stored the equipment in a closet. This equipment launched my career in radar development, for in early 1940, when the USA was quietly supporting Great Britain in the early days prior to our entry into World War II, it was decided to resurrect the "Radameter" and see if now it would be useful to the Navy. I was chosen by a recently hired nuclear physicist (Harold M. Hart) to be one of two men to assist him in secretly updating the stored equipment to initiate demonstrations of its usefulness. We were ensconced in a highly secured top floor of an unused six story building on Atlantic Avenue on the waterfront of Boston harbor. We spent several months updating the system to use 'lighthouse' vacuum tubes (250 megacycles and peak powers of 1000watts) and constructed a large, tripod-mounted twin horn-antenna (each horn about 3x6 feet) on the roof above. We succeeded in making the system operative and spent several months demonstrating it to Naval officers by tracking aircraft taking off from the Squantum air base about 8-9 miles away. Note that this was 6 to 9 months prior to Pearl Harbor! Unbelievably, they could not see its usefulness or did not want it because of the "NIH" factor or perhaps the fact that we were a commercial concern.

Simultaneously, although we were not privy to it, secret development work was starting at MIT under the guise of 'LAB 4-133', later known as the "Radiation Laboratory", of microwave (3000 megacycles and higher) radar. The Germans had not seen the need for radar and did not know that microwave radar was even possible. Thus the whole MIT activity was cloaked in highly secret conditions; even the very word 'radar' was classified! Great Britain meanwhile had been desperately forging ahead with the technology and once the MIT activity was underway, a very close clandestine relationship emerged to utilize the essential British developments, in particular their revolutionary 'cavity-magnetron' tube (with peak powers of 50,000 watts), in conjunction with the Radiation Lab to further our mutual war effort.

In early 1941 the U. S. Office of Scientific Research and Development established a program to involve the engineering and production capabilities of selected US industries in the vital development efforts at MIT. Submarine Signal Co. was included in the group and immediately ceased its private development. I graduated in June 1941 (now as a full time engineer at Sub-Sig) having earlier been designated as a company representative to MIT where I had begun working and learning at the top-secret MIT laboratory, a hastily constructed wooden building on the roof of MIT's Building 6. One of my first experiences there was to walk across the roof to an improvised pedestal carrying a parabolic dish with an optical telescope mounted at its center through which I viewed a target airplane clearly centered in its cross-hairs as it circled high over Boston! After our own rather cumbersome huge horns it was really an exciting experience.

I was assigned as the company engineer to the group responsible for 'Indicator Display and Ranging'. My job was to develop the circuits and to design a producible version of a new Navy 'surface-search radar' system for small ship use in combating the extremely serious U-boat menace in the North Atlantic. Our initial radar was designated the "SF" and operated in the 10 cm. (3000 M.c.) microwave frequency band. Our small group of three at Su-Signal mushroomed to several hundred in a matter of a month or two. In early 1942, about 8 or 9 months from a cold-start, we delivered and installed our first shipboard units.

Among some interesting sidelights was that our principle source of electronic parts (in those days our equipment used discrete components and vacuum tubes) was a little walk-up store a few blocks uptown called "The Radio Shack", which had been a haunt of radio amateurs and hobbyists. Over the next few months in the interest of speed we found ourselves placing very large orders, sometimes several hundreds of thousands dollars, with that small store and it eventually launched the enterprise now widely known as "Radio Shack". I also recall having a quiet lunch one day with my friend and boss Harold Hart, who was a well-known nuclear physicist, when very softly he said to me "Charlie, something really unusual is going on. You know all of a sudden I can't locate a single one of my old physicist friends"!

We surmised that the nuclear bomb development was starting but he never brought up the subject again. This sudden disappearance of the nuclear physicists is pointed out in the book "Tuxedo Park" by Jennet Conant.

A fascinating aspect of our work at the Rad-Lab was that we were privy to a great deal of top-secret information about Great Britain's war efforts and difficult experiences. We had evening seminars covering both the technology and the practical situation. Immediately after the disastrous retreat from Dieppe the British found that there were two mobile radar units apparently left behind that would reveal the microwave state of the art if the Germans were to find them. They knew they must be found quickly and be destroyed or evacuated. British paratroopers were dispatched during the next several nights behind the enemy lines. Under cover of darkness they finally located and destroyed both units! These evening seminars were often technical lectures by the various Rad-Lab sections on their latest developments and by British and U.S. scientists lecturing about the rapidly transpiring science of microwaves and its rapid deployment in actual combat situations.

One of our first production SF units (1942) was on a converted private yacht employed as the anti-submarine net-tender at the entrance to Boston Harbor. Around the end of March 1942 I was asked to accompany the civilian adviser to the Navy Secretary aboard an uncomfortable "Admirals Barge" for a 45 minute trip in very choppy waters to this net-tender for his first viewing of the new microwave shipboard radar. I recall I was verging on seasickness; the weather was deteriorating rapidly, the "sea-clutter" radar returns all made for a questionable but more or less satisfactory demonstration.

In any event, 4 months later (July 1942) we were producing the completely new "SF" radar at a rate close to 75 per month and had 3000 employees including a field engineering organization operating worldwide. As production increased I was assigned to the design of another display and ranging unit for a much-improved radar to operate at 3 cm (10,000 Mc.) designated the "SU" and intended for installation on the new DE class destroyers and other Navy ships. After another few months we started producing these new more advanced SU radars at an additional 25+ per month. Many people have forgotten that the civilian effort in those war days was extremely motivated and frequently nothing short of heroic. I recall working many weeks as many as 100-120 hours. Submarine Signal Co. maintained a suite in the nearby Hotel Manger and when we became too exhausted we would go there and 'cat-nap' for a few hours before returning to our work. I often didn't see my bed at home for 6 or 7 days.

After VE day, I was briefly considered by the 'OSS' to go to Germany to interrogate their scientists and engineers but my company quickly intervened and insisted that I continue where I was. I was rather frustrated that I wasn't involved in the 'real' action in the Pacific and I quietly signed up for a Navy commission (at the Navy recruitment office at MIT) but when my company's Naval Inspector saw the application come across his desk he quickly vetoed that move. At about this time I was made responsible for a completely new gunfire-control system called the MK39 to upgrade prior naval ship-borne systems to the new 3cm microwave technology. We had just gotten this new system to the formal pre-production type-testing stage, prior to production, when VJ day occurred and everything came to a rapid halt.

Simultaneously with the fire-control system development work I had become involved in a 'crash' program with Applied Physics Laboratory of Johns Hopkins to adapt our SU system for use as an anti-kamikaze gunfire control system. This was to be mounted directly on top of the 20 mm gun mounts of Pacific fleet ships. The kamikaze had become an extremely serious threat because all other low altitude target tracking was ineffective and the only defense was massive gunfire at the approaching planes. The use of the SU system was also just starting when the atomic bomb was dropped and it ended.

Because of my continuing radar development assignments I had been deferred from the draft throughout the war years. To my chagrin I had no sooner asked my wife to be my bride, May 1946, when all such deferments were abolished and my draft number (72), was called! That's when I certainly appreciated President Truman because as we were debating whether to continue with our wedding he declared a draft moratorium for 30 days. Then, when that moratorium expired just before our wedding date, I received a second more ominous draft notice when behold; President Truman called a permanent end to the draft and we could relax.

DURING WORLD WAR II
Leonard Dart
On Dec. 7, 1941, Pearl Harbor Day, I was in my second year of a PhD program in the Physics Department at the University of Notre Dame. There were four of us at that level of the program and we formed a quartet, singing in our spare time and learning the proper barbershop numbers as well as our math and physics. The department had three special areas of study: the Physics of Electronic tubes, Nuclear Physics and High Polymer Physics. When the United States entered the war, the electronics group turned to the development of radar. The nuclear group was building a new high energy accelerator (atom smasher) and began studying the

nuclear properties of uranium. Nuclear fission had been discovered a couple of years before in Europe and the theoretical possibilities were well known. The nuclear group joined the effort to develop the conditions for sustained nuclear reactions and the US effort to build a bomb. We knew at that time that in principle a single nuclear bomb could destroy a whole city in a millisecond blast. I decided that I did not want to put my efforts into such destruction. Some of my classmates did join the effort, went to Los Alamos for bomb development, and one of my teachers was on the observation plane that watched the destruction of Hiroshima.

When I was called to register for the draft I decided to register as a Conscientious Objector. Every spring I was required by the Draft Board to take a physical exam and be classified. One time I was assigned to a Civilian Public Service camp and was ready to go. However, each time the University intervened, saying that I was needed there. The university supported me in this, even giving me only civilians in my teaching assignments. I took up the third option, High Polymer Physics, and completed my degree, remaining at Notre Dame. We studied the thermodynamics of natural and synthetic rubbers and the development of many of the plastics that we now use. After the war I took a job with a textile firm, developing new fibers and fabrics.

WAR SHORTAGE IN STRATEGIC MATERIAL
Homer White

When World War II broke out I was working as a salesman for the Dow Chemical Company in the Los Angeles Sales Office. Early on, I applied for a commission in the Chemical Warfare Department. At that time they were not commissioning any new people into this service. Like all the young men of my age at that time I was put into the draft. One day my big boss called me into his office and asked if I would be willing to let the management put me where they could make the best use of my education and skills during the war. This would of course depend on the company getting a deferment from the draft. I accepted, not knowing what would happen next.

Shortly, I was assigned by Dow to the Defense Plant Corporation (DPC) Styrene Contract Group. The DPC was responsible for all types of vital products need for the war effort. Dow Chemical had patents on a process for making Styrene monomer. This product is a liquid that can be polymerized and made into crystal clear plastic. At that time, polystyrene was used to make housewares, toys etc. In the early stages of the War it became apparent to the government that the supply of rubber from the Far East would be cut off. This would leave the country without a source of rubber. Rubber was a strategic material very vital for the war, in the defense industries as well as for other essential uses such as transportation. There had been research work going on to find a substitute for rubber.

One of the products that could be produced from chemicals was called Buna "S" rubber. This was produced by the polymerization of styrene and butadiene. Dow Chemical made available to the government the use of the Dow patents on this product for the war time production of Styrene. The Defense Plant

Corporation contracted with Dow Chemical and other companies to build plants to produce styrene, butadiene and for the manufacture of rubber. Dow was to build and operate styrene plants in California, Texas and Sarnia, Canada.

Prior to leaving Los Angeles, I was part of the team to find a site for the plant location in Southern California for the project. A site was in chosen in Torrance at Figueroa and 190th Street. Plants would be built at this location for Styrene, Butadiene and Buna S rubber manufacture. My next assignment in the program was to move to Midland, Michigan, Dow's headquarters and a major plant of the company. I was assigned to become familiar with the DPC-Dow contract in detail and to get training in the Styrene production plant. After four months I returned to Los Angeles as Administrative Manager for DPC-Dow during construction of the Los Angeles styrene plant.

On arriving at the bare site with only a construction office, we started from scratch to expedite this urgently needed production for the War effort. My job at this point was to coordinate the contractor, Stone and Webster, with Dow Chemical in Midland and through them any contacts with DPC. As the construction got under way there was need for all kinds of construction materials and equipment that were not available. They had to be allocated to our operation by the DPC. Expediting these needs along with the contractor became an every day job.

Time was critical to get this plant on stream as soon as possible. The rubber supplies in the country were getting low! At the same time all the other related plants on this site were under construction. One of the real major problems we had was the inability to get large steam boilers manufactured in time for the plant start up. The government solved this by taking ship boilers out of World War I destroyers in the ship graveyard at Suisun Bay in the San Francisco Bay area. Eight of these boilers arrived in time to meet our construction schedule.

As the construction progressed there was a need to transfer additional Dow technical and other employees to the site. This brought a number of new operations, getting ready for the start up. As we neared the plant completion, employees had to be hired from the local area. This was a real problem, as most of the skilled and young people were in military service. As a result we had to get along with the best applicants we could find. For example, we were hiring people such as streetcar operators for plant operations.

As the permanent management arrived on site, I was transferred to be plant superintendent of the styrene finishing units. One of my first jobs was to follow the construction and the final instillation of the equipment and product lines. The styrene plant and the others in this complex came on stream only six months after breaking ground. This construction timing could never have been accomplished in normal times. Our production got under way and we met the needs for the local rubber plant as well as shipment to other plants in the country. There were times when we had problems getting all the raw materials that we needed. Since technical people were very short, many of us were moved to other jobs in the plant. During the four years, in addition to plant production, I was Manager of Maintenance and Service, and on the plant production staff.

During the years of operation, we met regularly with the other styrene plant operators looking for ways to increase and improve production. Once a quarter there were technical meetings for the DPC staff and other styrene producers. Getting to these meetings was not easy. Air and rail travel during the war was limited to the needs of the war effort. You had to get a government priority approved for the trip, either by plane or rail. Even with a priority, it did not always get you directly to your destination. At the last minute or even at intervening stopovers, you might get bumped off the plane or train by a person with a higher priority. Then you had to wait for the next plane or find other means of transportation.

During the construction period, an important event happened to me. I met Louise Nancarrow through a friend at the plant. He had gone to Pomona College with Louise. It took us awhile to get acquainted as Louise was working at Douglas Aircraft on the swing shift and I was working 12 hour shifts at the plant. In 1943 we tied the knot and had a short weekend honeymoon at one of the local beach resorts. Monday it was back to work. When you had to move during this period it was difficult. It meant looking for furnished places. You could not go out and buy much in the way of new furniture or appliances. Not many were being manufactured and the inventories were long gone. People learned to cope. They went to garage sales hoping to pickup what they needed. Louise's job was in the personnel department, processing potential applicants for the aircraft factory. This was challenging work as there was a shortage not only of men but of skilled workers. We use to kid Louise that they were hiring any "warm body" that walked in the door. One big change was the hiring of women for all kinds of jobs. "Rozie the Riveter" was a popular name used for all the women that worked in the war effort in all kinds of jobs. Despite the inconveniences of short supplies, rationing, car pooling, etc., we recognized that these were small sacrifices compared to those that served overseas.

SUBMARINE SOUNDS
Fred Arndt

I graduated from Caltech in 1931 with a degree in electrical engineering. This was at the height of the depression and there were no jobs available. Not a single company sent recruiters to our class. I spent three years doing any kind of work, trying to make a living. Then a professor with whom I had done some graduate work introduced me to the head of the sound department at Warner's studios. I was hired as a sound engineer and went to work improving the sound equipment. Sound movies were recent enough so that the equipment was not good. I received a patent on synchronizing the background projection with the camera on the film. I was given one dollar for this and the company owned the patent.

Columbia University started doing war work as we got into the war and had contacted Caltech, looking for engineers with sound experience. I was recommended and started work in the sonar lab operated by Columbia but located at New London. At first we worked on the active sonar which was used to track

German submarines. With this and with the new radar that allowed finding the snorkel on the subs, there was enough improvement that I started work with our subs. We were losing subs to the Japanese and the research hoped to make them quieter.

Our team consisted primarily of physicists and engineers, some with a PhD degree. Most were young with little knowledge of the specific work but were bright, hard working, and eager to learn and contribute. They were a pleasure to work with. Recruiting had also included oil exploration people with experience in high temperature and pressure work as the cables and instruments were subjected to this.

We designed a microphone, called a self-noise monitor that would go outside the ship and allow the crew to hear what a surface ship would hear. Then they could find the equipment making a particular noise and turn it off. The lab had also developed new directional finding equipment. These were installed in New Haven and the crews needed to be taught about them. Toward the end of 1943, I was sent to Hawaii in charge of a group to instruct in using the new equipment. We went on trips out to sea and worked with the crews as they used the equipment. We were supposed to use safe lanes but sometimes the Army didn't get the message and we were shelled as they practiced. We had to try to contact shore immediately and get the Army to stop shelling our areas.

Once on a special test mission, I went to the head when we were 200 feet underwater. While I was there, the ship dived to 400 and the compression locked the door in place. The captain had to come back up to get me out of the head. He wasn't happy about this. Another time, on a first test after a refit, someone dropped a wrench on the battery terminals, starting a battery fire. The black, chemical filled smoke was terrible and is dangerous to the lungs. I had nothing else available for protection, so I urinated on a cloth and breathed through this to save my lungs. After this I always avoided going out on the first dive after a refit.

Once our navigator made an error and we were outside our area. Destroyers found us and depth charged. I thought this would be the end of me. Fortunately, depth charges aren't very accurate and we got back.

Another lab developed noise seeking torpedoes. The sub would launch the torpedo and it was attracted by the propeller noise of the target ship. I was asked to observe a test on an old surface ship. The torpedo was fired at our ship but didn't have explosives in it. Three engineers from the lab that had developed it were to conduct the test. I was used to submarines, where there is much less bounding motion, so I took a Dramamine. Since the other engineers were used to surface ships, I didn't tell them. Later all three were lying on the deck with a bucket while I conducted the test. They were irritated when they found I had used the pill without telling them.

On Wednesdays the officers club at our base had a British rice table lunch with Malaysian food. Being from Indonesia with similar food, I liked it but some of our group from New England wouldn't try this strange food and went off the base for hamburgers.

After six months in Hawaii, the Navy had trained enough people and was familiar enough with the equipment so that my group was no longer needed and returned to New London. The Navy was having a problem with acoustic torpedoes. They would be unable to find the target so they would turn on their own ship. We worked on trying to find a way to prevent them from doing this.

When the war ended, I was offered a job with APL (applied physics laboratory) at Johns Hopkins, working on missiles. I spent much of my career in missile work, later with Hughes Aircraft, and was in charge of missile testing at Hollaman Air Base for Hughes.

CHAPTER 7

AIR CORPS

The Army experimented with airplanes early in the Wright brothers' time. Aviation became important during World War I, but not until World War II did it become a major factor in Army operations. The Air Corps was so big and important that it became almost an autonomous element of the Army. And after the war, this led to it becoming a separate service.

The Air Corps participated in all theaters and carried out one of the main strategies of the war - the bombing campaign. It also was an important tactical part of the ground campaigns. In addition, there were the major elements of reconnaissance and transportation. Lesser functions included map-making and protection of convoys (most of this was done by Navy air, both land based and carrier planes). Logistical support and maintenance of all the equipment, including many different types of planes, varying from Piper trainers to B-29 bombers, required many people and much materiel.

One thinks first of the pilots but there were others involved as air crew: gunners, navigators, mechanics. There were actually fewer serving in the air than on the ground.

The airplane and its manufacture came of age during the war, and these experiences and the knowledge gained led to the development of modern air transportation. Military aircraft have continued to improve to the point where activities are beginning to be carried out without the need for a pilot. Missiles have replaced most of the guns on planes and also many bomb functions. The electronics of navigation, target finding, missile control, and the actual control of the plane are almost unbelievably complicated and accurate.

Hal Johnson was a radio operator and gunner on B-25 bombers in New Guinea. After being grounded for a deviated septum, he was sent to OCS and supervised radio operators and maintenance personnel in the Philippines.

Bob Thorne was navigator on B-24's in Italy. He tells the story of a mission where the crew was forced to bail out and landed on a small island in Dalmatia.

Rachael Schreiber tells the story of her husband, Ivan, who was a pilot on a B-24 and also had to parachute out of his damaged plane. He was found by Yugoslav partisans and eventually returned to duty.

Fred Blair was in charge of maintenance for a group of war-weary B-17s that were sent to Brazil to map South America. Eventually the maps were used by Rockefeller oil interests rather than for military functions.

Don Stoll was trained as a navigator on four engine bombers and sent to Europe. He ended up leading the navigation for huge fleets of bombers in the strategic bombing of Germany.

Paul Smart was trained as a pilot and transitioned to light bombers, the B-25. He was sent to the China, Burma, India theater. The pilots in this area felt they were not important and weren't of any interest to headquarters. He was able to fly evacuation missions of wounded soldiers in a C-47 transport in addition to his combat missions and found this more rewarding.

Bob Bills was in the Air Corps before the war started but developed vertigo. He asked to be transferred where he could use his bacteriology training but this was too complicated for the Army of that day and he was discharged. After Pearl Harbor he went in the Navy and was commissioned out of OCS. He spent the war on destroyers in the Atlantic.

Lee MacDonald went in the army out of ROTC and was able to transfer to the Air Corps where he learned to fly. He qualified in B-24's but the war was over before he was able to go overseas.

IN THE AIR CORPS BY A NOSE
Hal Johnson

I was married in 1939 and when the war seemed close, decided I wanted to be a pilot and applied for flight training. At the final physical I was found to have a deviated septum and turned down. I then waited until I was drafted in 1942. I had basic training at Ft. McArthur in San Pedro. I was assigned to the air corps and had my indoctrination at St. Petersburg, Florida. They then sent me to radio school in Chicago. We used the Conrad Hilton Hotel for our barracks and took classes in the hotel. Following this I took gunnery school for B-25 bombers in Florida.

Assigned to the 5th Air Force, I was with a B-25 group that was sent to Port Moresby, New Guinea. My New Guinea service was my most memorable time. I served several months there, flying missions nearly every day. I was radio operator and belly gunner on a B-25 light bomber. They were primarily interdiction missions on Japanese installations in northern New Guinea and on Japanese troops who were trying to move south. The Japanese had no fighters in this area so the gunners were used primarily for strafing. Port Moresby was very small, with almost no facilities and was a very primitive town. There were hastily constructed quarters and almost nothing to do except work. There wasn't much contact with natives but they were a remarkably primitive people.

After several months and over fifty missions, I passed out during a flight as my deviated septum blocked oxygen flow. I was then grounded and applied for OCS, being offered in Brisbane Australia. Brisbane was a nice town with pleasant people and seemed like a great city after Port Moresby. The OCS course was 90 days and I came out a second lieutenant. I was then assigned to a B-25 group as radio officer, supervising the radio operators and maintenance people on the island of Leyte.

When General McArthur invaded the Philippines, my unit was transferred forward to Mindanao. We went in fairly early and the field where we were was still a target for the Japanese to reclaim. The infantry blocked the Japanese attack and it didn't reach the field. As the conquest of the Philippines advanced, the unit was moved to an airbase near Manila and was there when the war ended. By then I was a first lieutenant. Right after the end of the war, shipping back was overcrowded and we had to wait a time but eventually were put on a ship and returned to the States.

I prearranged a time and place to meet my wife: Los Angeles Grand Central Train Station. I came off the train, saw her, and ran towards her. As I came close, she looked at me strangely and didn't come to me. Then she did and I held her. We went to Palm Springs for a week of recuperation and "getting to know you" again. She then told me she didn't recognize me at first as I was so thin and was completely yellow from the medicine they gave us to prevent malaria. I was discharged in late 1945.

MISSION TO BAD VOSLAU, AUSTRIA
Robert Thorne

After our group (461st) completed training at Hammer Field in Fresno, California, we flew a B-24 H bomber (Lt. K.G. Bush, pilot) February II, 1944 from Hamilton Field, Marin County, California to West Palm Beach, Trinidad (where we picked up the squadron's supply of rum, a very valuable cargo), Belem and Forteleza, Brazil, and across the south Atlantic to Senegal. From there our orders took us by way of Morocco and Tunisia to southern Italy to join our unit (767th squadron, 461st group, 15th Air Force) at Torreta near Cerignola south of Foggia. Incidentally, we got stuck in the mud on landing at our home field. After arriving at Torreta I rejoined my own flight crew with 1st Lt. Matias Torres, pilot. After training missions, we started bombing raids in early April.

On April 23 the 461st left on a seven and a half hour mission to drop fragment bombs on Bad-Voslau Airdrome between Vienna and Wiener-Neustadt, Austria. As we came off the target, our new borrowed plane, No. 71, was badly hit by flak near Weiner-Neustad. Flak fragments from near misses riddled the wings and tail, destroyed the hydraulic system, knocked out our #3 engine and set it on fire, put holes through our #2 engine, cut the gas lines in the bomb bay flooding it with gas, and generally pelted the fuselage. Several chunks of flak came through the nose, one just missing my nose and ear and going through the map on my navigation desk. I pocketed it as a souvenir and still have it. Another spent chunk hit the bombardier, Lt. Lima, on the leg. Fortunately none of the crew was injured. We prepared to bail out but the pilot got the flames out in #3, feathered the propeller, and we stayed as best we could with the formation, losing altitude and falling behind.

Since bomber crews bailing out near the target sometimes got lynched, we decided not to bail out until we crossed the Sava River into Yugoslavia where the partisans might rescue us. When we crossed the river, we decided to try for the Dalmatian coast. And when we got through the mountains to the coast, we thought we would try to cross the Adriatic and crash land at a forward airbase. We had had no experience with parachutes and were not thrilled with the idea of bailing out. However, our cut gas lines caused our #1 and #2 engines to run out of control. We had only #4 to hold us up until we could bail out. I suggested to the pilot, Lt. Torres, that we head for the nearby Dalmatian island of Vis which I knew was held by Tito's partisans. All the other islands adjacent to Vis were in German hands.

Graden, Lt. Lima, and I had cleared the nose. Graden and I were in the bomb bay where I had cranked open the bomb-bay doors. When we neared the island at 9000 feet, Lt. Torres told us to bail out and I nodded to Graden to go first. The island looked awfully small to him and he shook his head. I bailed out and, disobeying recommendations, pulled my ripcord while in the slipstream. The opened parachute wrenched my back but saved me from drowning because the wind was blowing toward the island. We ten bailed out in order. Sgt. Hudson second out and next to me, and all landed on the island except the navigator.

Instead of slamming into the steep cliff, I dropped into the Adriatic just short of the island and had to swim in dragging my parachute behind me like a sea-anchor. Exhausted and in a state of euphoria because I hadn't drowned, I stood on the rocks in the water at the foot of the cliff. Several young partisan soldiers scaled down the cliff, lifted me out of the water, untangled the chute from the rocks, and swam out to collect the debris I had left behind in the water (flying boots, leather helmet, gloves, etc.). They were very solicitous, giving me a cigarette, having me strip off my wet clothes and dressing me in an ill-fitting partisan uniform from their own backs. Soon a launch arrived and took us back to the quay and town of Vis, and an American ranger led us up to partisan headquarters where I was reunited with other members of the crew.

We stayed on the island for three days before I arranged with the British naval commandant to ferry us back to Bari on an LCI. A couple of us had hiked to the middle of the island where our plane had crashed, exploded, and burned. There wasn't much left of it. I also botanized, fraternized with the Croatian partisans, American rangers, and British commandos operating with the partisans, and observed the military operations going on. Many refugees and German prisoners were brought in from raids on the adjacent islands. We also visited Lt. Torres who had a bad concussion from his landing amongst the rocks. He was evacuated to Bari by LCI, put in a military hospital, and returned to the States.

We, however, were told by the debriefing officer that we would be the first crew returning from MIA in Yugoslavia to be returned to combat. We were not enthusiastic about that decision. Also we were the first crew to bail out over Vis which the locals had thought to be too rocky for paratroop landing. As a result the island was mined and the Air Force later decided to put an airstrip on the island to save many crews and planes that were short of gas or crippled. Presidential candidate McGovern was one of the pilots who landed his bomber on the island.

Thereafter we flew 29 more missions, often with much excitement, usually with enough holes in our plane "65" from flak to upset our ground crew. Once we landed on fire nearly buying the farm in a tight spin in a thunderhead, and bringing back, against airforce orders, five cripples in six missions. On our last rescue the group operations officer was aboard and we became instant heroes, and the pilot, Lt. Cash, was awarded the Silver Star. It was said if a squadron plane was crippled, not to worry, for crew 65 would bring it home. We were grounded July 25, sent to rest camps (mine was in Calabria), given battlefield promotions, and trucked to Naples on August 17 to await transport home to Newport News, VA.

While grounded I helped plan the group's participation in the invasion of southern France and served as group assistant trial judge advocate. At special courts martials I prosecuted and got convictions of several culprits during my very short legal career. Back in the states after a month's leave and a month of R & R at an airforce hotel at Pass-a-grille Florida, near my home town of Gulfport, I graduated from navigation instructor training to Research & Development in Navigation at Ellington Field near Houston, TX. There, except for proficiency flights about the country and extended detached duty in Chicago, I completed my military service as an Examinations Officer. I was released from the Army in September at Tampa in time to begin my Ph.D. work in botany at Cornell University the first of October 1945.

IVAN SCHREIBER - ARMY AIR CORPS
Rachel Schreiber
My husband, Ivan, served as a B-24 bomber pilot in the Army Air Corps in World War II. We entered the Gardens April 1996 and Ivan died two years later. This is our story.

In July 1942, Ivan enlisted as an Aviation Cadet with the understanding that he would be called to active duty upon graduation. He had just completed his junior year at Wittenberg College in Springfield, Ohio. I was a junior 100 miles further south at Miami University. Sweethearts since we met at Springfield High, we wrote daily. Signing up for summer school and adding courses he graduated in January 1943 and was called to active duty. We became engaged just before he left for basic training at Biloxi, Mississippi. I had also completed requirements for graduation, and began work in the personnel department of the Air Service Command at Wright Patterson Field in Dayton, Ohio. Then came the stages of training for pilots: first to Maryville College in Tennessee for classroom courses; then to Maxwell Field in Alabama; to Dorr Field in Arcadia, Florida; back to Alabama to Gunter Field in Montgomery. During that year, his best friend from high school, also a pilot, was killed in a training accident.

Others who started the program together were inevitably separated. Next up at a table to sign one set of transfer orders, Ivan lent his pen to a friend behind him in line. When the friend and several others behind him had signed, they returned the pen. Ivan stepped up to add his name to the roster, but the transfer group was full. He was shipped to one base and his friends to another. Finally, in March 1944, in Columbus, Mississippi, Ivan received his wings and his commission as 2nd Lieutenant.

We were married on New Years Day 1944 in the chapel at Wittenberg College, Ivan in cadet uniform and I in street length purple wool dress. That same day I returned with Ivan by train to Columbus, Mississippi. There for two months, I lived in a room with bath, read books, took walks and went to the weekly luncheon given by the gracious ladies of the town for wives of Cadets. Ivan was not allowed off base except on weekends.

By contrast, the next two months were almost a honeymoon. Ivan was posted to Westover Field at Chicopee Falls, MA, a holding place for pilots awaiting assignment. We made our home in Holyoke in another rented room, but Ivan reported to base only from 8 to 5. Nights and weekends were free. We explored the East, traveling to Boston, New Haven, and New York, where the USO helped us get tickets to many plays as well as with hotel accomodations. I remember seeing Bobby Clark in Mexican Hay Ride, Uta Hagen in Angel Street, and Mary Martin. For two people who hadn't strayed far from Springfield, OH, this was exhilarating.

In May, the Air Corps decided that Ivan would fly the Liberator B-24 bomber. We moved to Charleston, South Carolina. There the crew of 10 was formed, and after a couple of months of training, dispatched to Mitchell Field, Long Island, the jumping off place to the War. On July 20, the crew left Mitchell Field in a new plane bound for the European theater. I returned to Ohio to live with my parents in Springfield.

Of course the route was secret, but I learned later that Ivan's crew flew from Long Island to Gander, Newfoundland. There, awaiting take off, they watched a plane crash. From Gander they flew to the Azores and then to Tunisia before reaching their assignment with the 15th Air Force, 756th Bombardment Squadron, 459th Bombardment Group. The base was outside Cerignola, near Foggia on the Adriatic side of southern Italy. Ivan grew a mustache. The officers lived in a tent in an olive grove. One day the colonel, passing by, complimented them on their snug winterized accommodation. They had scavenged (stolen) lumber and other items to make the tent more comfortable and engineered a can into a stove, which burned 100 octane gas.

In August the terrible yellow telegram arrived. "Lt. Otis Ivan Schreiber is missing in action." Several weeks later the Springfield News and Sun reported that Lt. Schreiber had been liberated from a Romanian prison camp. I wanted to believe, but I had no official word, no telegram. A few days later his telegram did arrive: "I am safe and as well as can be expected."

The newspaper was right. Ivan was back in Italy. But the story was wrong. This is what really happened on August 24, 1944. It was the crew's third mission. Over Kurim, Czechoslovakia they received flak that disabled the plane. Though steadily losing altitude, they managed to fly south as far as northern Yugoslavia, where all 10 of the crew bailed out.

They jumped together, but naturally, each landed alone in the mountains. Following the training drill, Ivan buried his parachute and gear before moving cautiously about. Soon a Yugoslav Partisan appeared. Before doing anything else, the Partisan wanted to find the valuable chute. They did.

Guided by one or another of the Partisans, Ivan hiked through the mountains, hiding in small villages, barns and camps. Villagers shared food but it was meager. A bowl of curdled milk was offered; he was hungry and drank it. To avoid German troops, travel was often at night. Bit by bit, the Yugoslavs brought the members of the B-24 crew together. One night all were taken to a field with the promise of a rescue plane. Fires were lit to guide the plane to an improvised landing strip. The mission succeeded. All 10 of the crew were delivered back to their base in Italy without injury. (Partisans were paid a bounty for each rescued airman.)

After de-briefing and a week of R&R in Rome, the crew was back in the air. Ivan flew his fourth mission, this time to Munich, on September 22. He completed his tour of 35 missions and had 260 combat hours. Much later, he described his flying experience for a niece's high school research project.

On a typical bombing mission-for example, up the Adriatic and over the Alps to Germany- we would be airborne for nearly nine hours in fairly close formation with the 39 other B-24's of our group. We usually dropped the bombs from an altitude of about 30,000 feet, but even at that height we always met massive barrages of flak from artillery below. (Vienna was said to have 1200 anti-aircraft guns.) It was dangerous. Some planes went down. But we had been long prepared for the highly disciplined job and to accept with little hesitancy or fear what we were required to do. Aerial battle is, of course, a far more detached affair than ground combat, especially in the last stages of the war when the Germans seldom dared any longer to attack us with their outnumbered fighters. Even so, all of us kept close count of how many of our 35 missions remained until we would be shipped home. I chalked bombs on the canvas tent above my cot-one for each mission.

My husband returned by ship to the U.S. in March 1945, eager to get acquainted with two-month old Nancy, who had been born on schedule in January at the Wright Patterson Field hospital. (Bill-$15.00) We had a second honeymoon in April, on R&R, at Miami Beach where we suntanned and got re-acquainted. F.D.R.'s death was announced while we were attending a show in Miami.

In the states, Ivan was assigned to the Air Transport Command in Memphis, Tennessee, pending redeployment to the Pacific. Then, at last, we three settled into our first apartment. We were still there on V-J Day.

Ivan was discharged as a 1st lieutenant on September 29, 1945. He was awarded the Air Medal with three Oak Leaf Clusters. Making the most of the GI Bill, he enrolled immediately in the graduate program at Ohio State University, starting on the path to his life-long vocation as a professor of English.

AIR CORPS DUTY IN SOUTH AMERICA
Fred Blair

I went into the Air Force while I was still 17 and my father went with me to make it legal for me to enlist. I was sent to Ft. MacArthur for processing and was then sent to Sheppard Field in Witchita Falls, Texas for basic training. Two railroad cars went, totaling 64 of whom 63 were draftees. Before we went we were issued all wool OD uniforms. The temperature in the Los Angeles area was about a hundred and several passed out from the heat.

On the way by rail, one fellow developed a rash and the whole group was quarantined. On arrival, we were placed in some unused barracks next to the sewage plant. We spent about 3 weeks there, with drills and other training. There was an old army staff sergeant who had us whipped into shape, except for 6 Chinese who didn't speak English. They were put to do all the work in cleaning the barracks.

When the quarantine passed, we were sent to regular barracks and finished basic training. They said we were all to be shipped out but I only went across the field to aviation mechanics school. After graduation from the school, everyone except me was shipped out but I stayed as an instructor. After two months, I was called in and asked if I would like to apply for officer training. I did so and was sent to basic cadet training at the Boca Raton Club. From there I went to Yale to train as an aviation engineering officer. There was an accelerated course for those who had completed the enlisted mechanics school so I was commissioned in 8 weeks at Yale.

I was then assigned to Peyote, Texas to a training base for B17 pilots. I was in charge of maintenance of the B 17's. After a time I was transferred to the airfield at Alexandria, Louisiana. I had a car by this time and three of us drove, stopping for a wild day in New Orleans. I had been told this was a permanent assignment, so I tried to get my girl friend in South Pasadena to marry me. I was sent to camouflage school at March Field and we were married before we left to return to Alexandria. I had loaned the car to a friend while I was at March and his girl friend picked us up at the train. She gave me a big hug and kiss that rather shocked my new wife. We had trouble finding a place to stay but finally moved in with a family, sharing the bath. This didn't work well but after only two days back at work they told me I was to be transferred to Colorado Springs. We drove and when I reported in, I was told I would be at another field near Denver.

Here we found a single room in an old mansion that had 22 GI families living in it. We lucked into the best room, one with a private bath. I found my outfit at Buckley Field was the base for an outfit being setup to do photo mapping in South America. I was at Buckley for two months getting our B25 planes ready. I drove my wife back to South Pasadena without leave and caught a military flight back from March. We cleaned up the planes and then went to San Antonio for 10 days. From there we made several legs, heading for British Guyana. The B25's weren't adequate for the job as they would only operate to a maximum of 20,000 feet and that was our photo height. It took them three hours to get up to altitude and by then it might be clouded in.

After a few months of unsatisfactory results, we were sent back to Denver to exchange the B25's for B17's. My wife came up to Denver and I bought a second hand Packard convertible. It was supposed to have had an engine overhaul but they had just quieted it and it fell apart in 10 days. We had to transition our pilots to four engine aircraft. The 12 planes were war weary, back from Europe. They had been converted for photo use and had three photo ports in a reconfigured nose, making it look like an odd three eyed bug. This time we were in Recife, Brazil. We had our own photo lab but the pictures were not interpreted in the field. They were sent to Lowery Air Base near Denver for evaluation. Work was slow as even the B17's took 1 to 1 ½ hours to climb to 20,000 feet and clouds often came up during that time and we didn't get pictures.

The planes took a lot of maintenance. They were divided into three flights of four and I was engineering officer for one flight. We moved around South America and various crews had unusual adventures. I flew a lot but not everyday. For some months my flight was operating out of the Navy Base at Bahia, Brazil. I was in Recife for carnival that year.

The unit that preceded us had used a smaller B34 plane and had had planes shot down flying over Argentina. Argentina was strongly pro-Axis and we never flew over it. One plane stopped overnight in Asuncion, Paraguay and the crew was invited to a diplomatic affair. After they were there, a group of German military arrived and our crew walked out, causing quite a furor.

One of our flights was in Chile, also pro-Axis, for a time and the crew had to bus to the airfield. Even in civilian clothes they were jeered and spat on by the children. Many stores in South America carried German goods. Once a crew tried to buy a particular German camera. They were told it was out of stock but would be available in 10 days. They found out that the Germans were shipping high profit small items into South America by submarine.

I wanted a more war related job and put in for a transfer. Finally after about 8 months in South America, I was ordered back to Denver and then to Manchester, New Hampshire. I drove back and arrived on VE day (victory in Europe) to find everything closed down. The next day I reported in and was told that I would be going to Tacoma. They gave me orders for two tires and gas coupons and I went back west. Reporting into Tacoma, I found us a place to live and then found the unit was a weather recon unit. This was part of the 311 Recon wing which had also controlled the mapping units. We were attached to Air Corps headquarters rather than to an area command.

This unit flew even more tired B17's. They flew out 1000 miles over the ocean at 50 feet and then returned at 10,000. The pilots were a crazy group. They would breathe pure oxygen to try to sober up enough to get the plane off. Then they would put it on autopilot, put the crew chief in charge, and go to sleep. Each plane had a mechanic and I had them sit by the autopilot cable with bolt cutters in case the gyros gave out and the plane started down. I didn't fly with this group. We worked really hard and managed to go four months without a mechanical cancellation for a flight. One day the inspector general arrived without warning and inspected the base. I had known him at a previous assignment and he gave me a copy of his report. Our group was cited as particularly outstanding.

Some time after VJ day, the head of operations flew in and wanted a 100 hour check and repair on his plane. We had three of our four B17's down and I said we couldn't do it. He was furious and said he would get my job, even though I offered to take it to the group repair depot for him. Within three days I was ordered back to Manchester to our squadron headquarters. I explained the pressing need for the unit planes but he persisted in berating me and saying I was incompetent. I showed him the inspector general's report and he suggested I just get out of the Air Corps and save everybody from a problem. He put me in for terminal leave and I was sent to the Air separation depot at Santa Ana. I spent 2 months there and was finally sent back to Fort MacArthur and was finally separated in April of 1946.

After the war, I learned that the first copy of all maps of Guyana and Venezuela were sent to Nelson Rockefeller, the good-will ambassador for South America. They were used by Rockefeller oil geologists and provided the information that was the base of the Rockefeller oil exploration effort. This was apparently the real reason for all the mapping and the particular type of maps we were required to produce.

B-24 LEAD NAVIGATOR
Don Stoll

I was working in Los Angeles in September 1942 and received a notice on Friday to report to the draft board on Monday. I went that afternoon to the enlistment office and asked to enlist as an aviation cadet. The lieutenant said that the test would be given the next Thursday. I told him that I would then have been drafted and he ordered the sergeant to give me the test then. He asked the sergeant if he had graded the test. "Yes, he made 92."

The lieutenant then said, "I'll swear you in right now." and did so. I asked for something to take to the draft board and was given a letter and told to wait for a call. The draft board was unhappy that I wouldn't count on their quota but there was nothing they could do.

I finally was ordered to San Antonio classification center. This was basic training together with numerous tests and lasted nine weeks. At the end we were called individually before a board of officers. I was told that I qualified for pilot, navigator, bombardier, or weather schools and asked which I preferred. I asked which I made the best score on and was told navigator. I then said I would go to navigator school. The board was all made up of pilots and several were very surprised that I didn't pick pilot school. The primary school in navigation was also at San Antonio and I went to this for nine weeks. (Everything in the air Corps seemed to be on a nine week cycle.)

At the end of this we were told that advance navigation schools were all full and we were sent to Harlingen Texas to aerial gunner school for nine weeks. We learned to handle, shoot, and repair fifty caliber machine guns. We were the first cadets at the school; all previous classes had been enlisted men only. At the end of this, I was sent to celestial navigation school at Hondo, Texas, near Houston. I received commission and my wings as a navigator in December 1943.

I was sent to Caspar, Wyoming for phase training. On arrival, I was told that there was no opening in the class and was given officer of the guard duty for New Year's eve and day. I had no idea what I was supposed to do but fortunately the sergeant guided me. After a few days of this I was taken over and introduced to the crew of a B-24. Their navigator had been sent to the hospital with appendicitis and I was to replace him. The crew was almost through with phase three training so all the training I received was a few night flights. On one of these we 'bombed' Columbus Ohio.

We received a new B-24 of a new model, the first with a nose gunner, so we had to break in a new gunner to the crew. We then were sent to Palm Beach for 3 days. We were given orders to take off, go south for an hour, and then open our sealed orders. We found that we were going to Trinidad. We reported a couple questionable things on the plane so had an extra day there. Then to Receife, Brazil overnight and then on to West Africa. There were eight or ten planes in the group and two didn't arrive. We were sent out over our course to look for them with no result. However, this was an official mission so we were awarded the ribbon for combat in the American theatre.

Next we flew to Marrakech where we waited seven days for favorable winds to Europe. We flew out to sea to avoid Nazi oriented Spain and up to Wales, a 14 hour flight. Our plane was taken and we were sent over to an English airfield in a C-47. (the military version of the DC-3.) There the crew was split and mixed in with an experienced crew. We made the first US air raid on Berlin and lost 30% of our planes.

Our pilot was an eager beaver and volunteered as a lead plane without telling the rest of us. We were sent for some special training and then became a lead. All the planes were equipped with bombsights and had navigators but they flew in formation and only the lead navigator did any navigation. The other planes also followed the lead plane in bombing and didn't sight their own bombs. The lead planes only flew every four days.

Jimmy Stewart was a lead pilot in our group and I did several missions with him. He was a good command pilot and took responsibility for his flight. Many of the command pilots were generals who wanted to get in their time for flight pay or promotion and didn't really take the responsibility. Once Jimmy saw another B-24 at the same altitude and flying alone. He ordered the fighters to shoot it down and it turned out to be a captured B-24 trying to join and mislead the formation.

One bridge across the Rhine was between high hills with antiaircraft guns on the hills. The B-25's and B-26's hadn't been able to hit it so they turned to the larger B-24. Jimmy led a 16 plane formation and came up the river between the hills. His bombardier was excellent and the bomb landed in the middle of the bridge, followed by those of the other planes.

After 25 missions one was taken off combat duty but later this was changed to 30 and then to 35. Jimmy completed 30 missions and then became executive officer of the unit.

As lead navigator, I led larger and larger missions. Near the end of my time, I was leading the entire formation from the eighth Air Force, including both B-17 and B-24 planes.

One time over Germany, we lost an engine. The B-17 could fly on two engines but the B-24 was difficult without all four. We fell behind the formation so we crossed France at treetop level to avoid giving warning to the antiaircraft batteries. As we came across, we saw a train running parallel to us. The pilot moved over and all the guns on that side opened up. The locomotive blew up and made a loop in the air. The whole train crashed. Another time we barely made it across the channel to Dover and landed at the first airport. It was a Spitfire base and the runway was too short for a B-24. We went over the end and the nose gear finally collapsed. They flew us back to base in a C-47. We didn't expect to see the plane again but it was repaired and flown back to our base.

When missions had to be aborted, the bombs had to be dropped before landing. Some dropped them in the channel but we tried to skip bomb them into the submarine pens at the coastal ports. These were concrete, too thick to hurt by direct bombing. Dropping the bombs in front of them while we were speeding by sometimes bounced them into the pen and would damage the subs.

After 30 missions, I returned to the states in September 1944. I had thirty days leave at the Del Mar beach club. I was now a captain and they asked what I would like to do. I suggested being an instructor. I was then sent to Boca Raton to a school for radar navigation instructors. They were now training for a joint position of navigator, bombardier, and radar operator. They were starting a new school for this in Bakersfield. A major had been ordered to set up the school and asked me to be his deputy.

Bakersfield had been a two-engine bomber base and the general liked it this way. He managed to get our four-engine school transferred to Yuma, Arizona. After some time there I had received orders to Barksdale Air Corps Base in Louisiana to transition to the black widow, the new P-61. We were flying a practice mission from Yuma and had just 'bombed" Catalina when we heard about the atomic bomb on the radio. The commander of the base at Yuma closed it down so we couldn't go back. There wasn't a B-24 base in Southern California so we declared an emergency and landed at the Navy base in San Diego. The Navy had single tail B-24's (by another number) and could handle our plane. The next day we flew back to Yuma.

I had a friend in personnel and asked what to do about my orders. He suggested sitting on them for 10 days. By then they had been cancelled. My points still counted and I was eligible for immediate discharge. I was sent to Fort MacArthur in San Pedro where I transferred to the reserve. They were just changing the Army Air Corps to the independent Air Force and I became Air Force reserve.

I was promoted to Major in the reserve and was called back for the Korean War but failed the physical because I had just had an ulcer attack. They then transferred me to the honorary reserve.

FLYING IN THE CHINA, BURMA, INDIA THEATER.
Paul Smart

I enlisted in the Army as an aviation cadet in 1942 in Kansas. I was told to wait until I was called but no time was given. Finally, in January 1943 I received orders to preflight training in Santa Ana, California. This was basic military training and no flying was involved. I was then sent to Visalia, Chico, and Yuma for flight training, gradually using more advanced trainers. Finally I went to Stockton where I received my commission and wings as a pilot in February 1944.

I was then sent to Mather Air Base near Sacramento for transition to the B-25. Further training and flight experience took me to Kentucky and South Carolina. For a time I flew the A-20 but they decided they didn't need more of them so returned me to the B-25.

Finally I had a permanent crew and airplane. We flew to Gander, Newfoundland and then across the Atlantic to North Africa. In Marrakech we stopped at a new airfield, built for American use. The young crewmen debated what the use of a bidet was. After crossing Africa to Cairo, we stopped in Iraq. Here we were at a big American air base at the base of the Red Sea. Nearby was a huge oil refinery owned by a Dutch company. We were there for several days, waiting for the final base to be ready to accept the planes. It was very hot here and no flying was done between 10 AM and 4 PM because of the heat. (The air is thinner with heat and take off and climb are much slower.)

American fighters were shipped over to this base by ship, partially disassembled. They were put together by American mechanics and test flown by American pilots. Then they were turned over to the Russians under lend-lease and the Russian pilots flew them. The Russians liked to do aerobatics and really gave the planes a work out. However, two Russian pilots landed with their wheels up in spite of radio calls and warning flares. The Russian colonel refused to sign acceptance for the group of planes because two were missing. (The ones that his men had crashed.)

Next we went to Karachi (then India, now Pakistan) and Delhi. Our final stop on this trek was the town of Imphal in northeast India. There was a range of hills above the town and the Japanese had reached these hills and lobbed shells down on the airfield. India was the end of the supply line and supplies were difficult to get. A family friend from Lawrence, Kansas had been commissioned a brigadier general and given the job of controlling supplies on the Indian railways. The gauges of the roads were all different and supplies had to be reloaded three times between the port and Imphal. It took about six weeks for them to arrive.

President Roosevelt wanted Chiang Kai-shek to tie up large numbers of Japanese troops so he gave him almost anything he wanted. Chiang was demanding and getting large quantities of supplies, so that the troops often were short. Chiang rarely put his troops in contact with the Japanese. He was more interested in preventing the communists under Mao from taking over territory. He was able to influence the choice of bombing sites and it seemed that many of the missions had no relation to the war with Japan. Chiang often gave or sold the supplies he received to the local warlords in return for their support.

General Stillwell could be unpleasant and difficult but he felt that Chiang wasn't conducting the war properly and tried to get our government to quit being so supportive. He wasn't very successful, but in the end turned out to be right.

The Americans in the theatre mostly felt that their higher officers were second rate. They were assigned there to dump those who they didn't want in Europe. We weren't doing a lot and really had no specific goals. With all this there was not a great deal enthusiasm for the fight and American troops were bored and frustrated.

They had arranged for the British to give us fighter cover rather than send American fighters. The Spitfires were designed for maximum protection for Britain and had very short range. They would only be able to cover for a few minutes before returning to base for fuel. As a result we lost many bombers to Zeros.

We had both B-25 and C-47 planes at our field. Volunteers were requested for the C-47's to fly evacuation missions with injured troops. As we weren't very busy, I found this very rewarding. It was a pleasure to feel useful and to be helping someone. There were times that we couldn't make it in because of weather or enemy action and wounded men died who could have been saved. I ended up flying both types of planes interchangeably. Our commanding officer was very sharp and arranged the schedule to keep us busy and to get the work done. General Slim's British Army was moving up Burma and we flew support for it. We flew many C-47 missions into jungle fields, often at night

We moved the base 4 times in the 11 months I was in the area. For six weeks we were in Chungking and bombed in China. We bombed the city of Kweilin several times. We also flew in special supplies that were urgently needed and flew out American casualties.

After I had completed my required missions, I was flown to Calcutta and then home. I had leave and we went from Kansas to the family ranch in Colorado. On the way home we heard on the radio about the atom bomb. Instead of returning to duty, I was sent to Fort Leavenworth and was discharged.

DUTY IN TWO SERVICES
Robert Bills

I was in graduate school in bacteriology at Ohio State University in 1940 and one of my duties was as proctor in a dorm. All the fellows were going down to Wright-Patterson airbase and taking the exams for pilot. Almost all failed and they kept telling me I should try. Finally I went down and took the exam. I was reading down the chart and couldn't see the next line so I told the doctor, "I might as well go home now." He told me that it was the 20/10 line I couldn't read and I had passed and was accepted. They sent me back to school to await a call.

I was tired of waiting, so I enlisted in the Air Corps. They sent me to Kelly Field where I worked with Link trainers (the simulator of that day.) Then my acceptance in the flying program came up and I was made a flying cadet. I was sent to one of the two civilian contract schools that did some of the training; Cal Aero in Ontario. We called it Major Moses School for Boys.

A class ahead of me was made up of West Point graduates so they made it more military. My roommate was rather wild but one day I came in and he was very quiet. After a bit he told me his story. He had flown his Stearman over to Mt. Baldy and gone up a canyon. He was getting closer to the ground even with full power and the canyon was narrowing. Finally he pushed the nose down for speed and made a very steep turn, just missing the canyon wall but getting out. He was cut out to be a fighter pilot.

The Air Corps sent in regular military pilots to do our check rides. They weren't used to flying as slow as the Stearmans and had a hard time. I was sent to Stockton for advanced training in the AT6. About this time I developed vertigo. The military doctors tried everything to get rid of it, including pulling my wisdom teeth, but nothing worked. Finally I was grounded just as I was getting my orders to go to school for B-17's. They didn't have anything for me to do so I asked to go to the Sanitary Corps and work as a bacteriologist. No one knew how to arrange a transfer between Corps so they discharged me.

A year later I was visiting my parents in Altadena and ran into the man who had been my navigation teacher in flight school. He was now in the Navy and wanted to know why I was a civilian. He arranged for me to have Navy testing and I was accepted and sent to OCS at Columbia. I had never been in a big city and this was downtown in New York. Our dorm looked over to Harlem on one side and the Hudson river on the other. A New York family I met sort of adopted me and I saw a lot of New York while I was there.

My first assignment was to an old four stack destroyer, the USS Ellis. We started off in the North Atlantic. I was assistant gunnery officer but one of my duties was decoding messages in the rolling ship. Once I managed to get a footprint on the overhead of the office. When the ship was painted, the footprint was preserved. We spent a lot of time in the Mediterranean. Once a German JU88 bomber tried to sink us. We weaved around at top speed until finally he had to give up for fuel. We stopped in the Azores and I still remember the people painting their houses, using their hands rather than a brush.

At a port in Libya I ran into a school-mate who was in the Army. He borrowed a jeep and we went out into the desert. This was shortly after the Rommel-Montgomery battles and we found much burned out equipment still there. We went to a British officers club and tried to get some wine. They let us have wine and said, "Drink what you want but be sure we get the bottles back."

I often had the job of going ashore and bailing come of the crew out of the local jails. Among other places we spent a few hours in Casablanca but didn't see much of it. At one port a kid was selling coins. He said they were very old. "See. They even say BC on the coins."

After more than a year on the Ellis, I was reassigned to a new construction destroyer. My first assignment was to the Douglas Fox but before I reported this was changed to the Hugh Purvis. I later learned that the Fox was hit by a kamikaze off Okinawa. The control bridge where I would have been working was destroyed and everyone on it killed.

The Purvis was being built at Brooklyn Navy Yard but before going to it, I went to the Naval Gun Factory in Washington for training. The Ellis's guns we just sighted in but the Purvis had new range finding and gun control mechanisms. It was hard to find a living place in Washington and another officer and I finally found a room in a basement. A WAVE officer from the Gun Factory had the best room in the house. We were married while I was there and she always says I would do anything to get out of that basement.

The executive officer was in charge of the ship and several of us reported early. We spent our time trying to get the ship built with changes representing the exec's experience in combat. The crew gradually reported in and the ship was commissioned.

The commanding officer reported only at the last minute and we went on a shakedown cruise. At first we were very disappointed in him. He merely sat on the bridge and watched, saying nothing. After a few days he suddenly took the ship over. He had learned all about the ship and crew and was very well organized. The ship ran like a clock. The cruise was so successful that we were assigned as a training ship on the East coast rather than going to the Pacific. We trained the crews of other new ships before their ships were launched so that they would be ready to take over. We went from Maine to Guantanamo Bay. We stayed as a training ship until the end of the war.

Once we were coming into Norfolk. The CO usually took over from the officer of the deck on port arrivals. This time I was OD and I kept waiting for him to take over. He was sitting on the bridge. I did what needed to be done and finally realized he wasn't going to take over. I maneuvered the ship into dock and made it all safely. Then the CO said a few complimentary words and walked off the bridge.

At the end of the war I was a lieutenant and had been in longer than most of the officers so I was discharged early. Both my wife and I were discharged from a station near Virginia Beach at the same time.

I think I learned more that has been useful to me from the military than at any other time of my life. Our first skipper on the Ellis was well qualified but wasn't organized and had trouble communicating. The comparison with the skipper of the Fox was valuable. I was also lucky as most of the pilots from my class didn't live through the war.

After getting out I managed to get hold of a car and we drove out to California and visited my parents in Altadena. I didn't know what I was going to do but over Christmas we were driving the Pasadena Freeway and my wife suggested I check with University of Southern California Dental School. I went in during the vacation and dropped off my records with the janitor. They called and said they were starting an accelerated course in January and I was accepted so I went to dental school on the GI bill.

LEARNING TO FLY
Lee McDonald

I entered the University of Oregon in the fall of 1942 on a scholarship and signed up for ROTC. At this time the country was having scrap metal drives and the fraternities competed as well as other groups in town. One night at 2 AM one of our members came in, woke everyone and announced he had found an abandoned car. It was pouring rain but we all went out in pajamas and raincoats. The field had mud up to our ankles but we lifted the car and put it on a truck, sure that it would win the scrap drive for us. However, we came in second.

At Christmas vacation the first year, I went to the recruiting offices in my hometown after a pep talk to us by the former president of the fraternity. The Marines had an officer candidate program and I signed up for it. I was sent for physical and then turned down on the basis of an enlarged heart, though my family doctor said this was a dubious finding.

Back at school, I enlisted in the army reserve corps as part of ROTC. This corps was called in April of 1943 before I finished the first year and went to Ft. Lewis, Washington. My father had gone to Ft. Lewis in World War I and then to Texas and the Air Corps and I followed the same pattern. Going to Texas, we passed a dust storm on the train.

The Army didn't know what they were going to do with the students from the enlisted reserve corps and for a time we didn't do anything, though we developed a championship volley ball team. Then they decided to make radio operators of us and we were shipped to Camp Walters in Texas. Here we went through basic training. An officer started teaching us drill. He said he would explain left face and knew we wouldn't understand the first time. Everyone did it correctly the first time and we covered the days program in a few minutes. The officer didn't know what to do but finally took the initiative and started us on the next day program.

We rotated as guards at the stockade. We had been issued M1 rifles without ammunition but were given old Springfields for guard duty, with ammo. We didn't know how to use them and fortunately never had to.

The Colonel was from Salem, Oregon and he invited three of us from Salem to dinner. It was embarrassing: I didn't know what to say to a Colonel and then the other soldiers wondered how we were special.

I went to Texas, passing a dust storm in the train. There was a notice on the bulletin board that they needed pilots and I applied. My first sergeant had to sign it. He was an old Army man and looked at me as a traitor. He was so furious he almost tore the paper signing it. I was sent to Love Field in Houston for physical exam and passed. I was then ordered to Sheppard Field in Witchita Falls, Texas. Before I went, our group took the final test of our training, with live fire. The first sergeant wouldn't let me participate and I was disappointed.

I had a week leave before reporting and went home. I had a marksman medal on my uniform but then saw a captain with many ribbons and a badly burned face. This first brought the realities of the war home to me.

I arrived at Sheppard Field in August 1943. It was a huge base of 30,000 men, with new draftees, pre-cadets, and men back from combat. Training for pre-cadets was run by a big, dominant tech sergeant. We rarely saw an officer. We drilled most of the day and the sergeant ran it with an iron hand. Once one guy came to formation with dirty fatigues. The sergeant made him take off his pants, wash them before the formation, and then put them back on wet. At the end of drill we had 10 minutes drilling with gas masks on. In that heat, the mask would fill with sweat so that by the end of 10 minutes we were about ready to drown inside the mask.

The next stage was cadet and I went to Kansas State. The teaching was low level for a college but I ended up getting credit for the courses later. I was assigned to a frat house as a dorm. The one we had was for those with "M" initial and all the cadets there had names starting with M. One weekend two of us made up our beds in the shape of a man and took off for Kansas City, AWOL. A lieutenant made bed check and didn't notice our dummies in bed. We had two or three flights in a Piper Cub at the Manhattan Airport. These were demonstrations and we didn't get to fly at all.

In November of '43 I went to Santa Ana Army Air Base for preflight. We had ground courses in aeronautics, weather, and similar material. On time off, I went up to Pomona College to see an old girl friend and met my wife who lived across the hall from the friend. During my time at Santa Ana, we saw Bob Hope and Bing Crosby who came to entertain the troops. The base started a band and I volunteered, playing the baritone horn which I had played in high school. Because of my work in the band, I had the chance to pick my flight school and chose Tulare as the closest to Claremont. At Santa Ana I was again faced with the real war when the brother of a bunkmate was killed flying a P-47 in Europe.

The Tex Rankin Flight School in Tulare had been taken over by the Army. We flew Stearman PT-13's with civilian instructors. Mine was caustic and gruff. We had to solo in 13 hours or be washed out of training and go back to the infantry. At 12 hours, 20 minutes the instructor said, "I'm not going to let you kill me. I'm getting out. Go ahead and fly." I made one of my best landings ever and he motioned me to go around again. The next time I bounced badly but he had gone into the building.

One day one of our group didn't come back. We went to bed worried. At midnight he walked into the barracks carrying his parachute. He had gone out of the area and above the clouds, both against the rules, and became lost. He ran out of gas and landed at a farm. He called the base and they picked him up and got the airplane the next day. Fortunately the farm was just within the legal area so he wasn't washed out.

We had check rides and my first was with a young hot-shot who gave me a low grade because I entered the pattern at 47 degrees instead of 45. On a second with an older pilot he asked me to do a loop. I did one so tight that he blacked out but he gave me a good grade. There were quite a few accidents in the various phases of training. Tex Rankin was still around, though he no longer ran the flight school. One day he showed up and put on an amazing aerobatic show for us.

After basic I moved up to Merced for intermediate training. Here we flew the BT-13 Vultee "Vibrator". On an early flight I took off and the instructor said to do a slow roll. I had left the canopy open and my earphones were sucked off in the roll. I received a bad mark and had to pay for new earphones. Once doing night landings with an instructor the radio failed. We circled until the other planes had landed and the tower gave us a green light. Suddenly the instructor grabbed the controls and dived. We just missed another plane that we didn't know was there. We were also learning formation flying. On week-ends I would hitch hike down to Claremont.

On D-day all the cadets were lined up along the runway. A P-38 fighter went over, doing a slow roll over the runway and then landed. It was Major Richard Bong, our leading ace. He gave a talk to the cadets; he told us to be good to our ground crews but we didn't have ground crews at this point. At Merced we also had Spike Jones for a troop entertainment concert.

It was time for advanced training and the groups split up. A few went to fighters but at this time more were needed in multiengine for bombers. I was sent to Pecos Texas for multiengine training. Those who didn't do well were made warrant officers rather than second lieutenants and went to glider school. We all had cards made for graduation, just saying pilot as we weren't sure until the last minute who would make lieutenant.

The advanced trainer had two big engines but fabric wings. We flew to various towns around. Our low level practice scared the cattle, of which there were many in this area. February 1945 I had leave and my future wife and her family came to meet me at Burbank. There was fog and we landed at Long Beach. Finally we got together.

After this, I went to Las Vegas as a co-pilot in B-24s. We flew some of them in target practice. The B-24 was big and very slow in response. A B-17 visited the base and I was able to fly co-pilot in it for one flight. It handled much better than the B-24. Our cadet commander at Santa Ana, a very popular man, flew co-pilot one Monday with a pilot not well liked. He had been drunk Saturday night. They lost one engine and made a bad approach. The pilot tried to go around and crashed. Only the tail gunner lived. The co-pilot and his wife were expecting a baby. We were all upset by this crash.

I expected to go to the Pacific and was disappointed when the war ended. I was ashamed of this but I felt the training was wasted. After the war, we flew B-24's to Oklahoma. It was spectacular at the base - rows and rows of surplus B-24's. At this time the first jet fighters came to Las Vegas.

We didn't have much to do. I was assigned to be in charge of a school that taught 50 caliber machine guns. It was run by older sergeants who knew much more than I. I merely signed the papers they needed to make things run. I was discharged in November 1945 and stayed in the reserve. I applied to Pomona College. On the application for reason picking Pomona I put, "My wife goes to Pomona." Southern Cal had some off-season accelerated courses starting in January and I went there. We were married in the summer and I started Pomona in the fall.

CHAPTER 8

SUPPORT SERVICES

There were many services that the military needed but some of these it preferred not to supply with uniformed personnel while others could be better supplied from a civilian background. Some of these, such as the WASPs were closely related to the military. Others were able to provide a touch of home and were better run as civilian projects. Often it is difficult to understand why some projects used uniformed military personnel and others, equally closely related, maintained a civilian workforce. Still others were necessary to the government and the war effort but weren't really related to the military, such as the FBI.

The residents of Mt. San Antonio Gardens include a wide variety of people who were utilized during the war. Some of these activities are little known, while others, such as the WASP pilots, were widely publicized. However, they weren't recognized by the military as having participated in the risks of piloting and weren't allowed pensions or health coverage, as were military personnel, even those who were never in harm's way. Similarly, the risks of the merchant marine were often greater than those of the Navy but merchant sailors did not receive either the publicity or the health coverage.

Peg Calhoun flew for the WASPs, delivering a number of types of planes. Besides all the gear, she had to carry extra pillows so she could see out the windshield.

Carlotta Welles was in charge of occupational therapy for areas of the western US, which increased as the war progressed. Why this group was retained as civilians when other, similar occupations were commissioned is unknown.

Louise Hall left her work as a laboratory technician to work with the Red Cross on military bases. She served in Okinawa after it was taken.

Dorothy Christiansen was employed by the FBI. Although not an agent, she was in contact with a considerable segment of the department's work.

Mary Winslow worked in special services with the Army. Being near Los Angeles, she was helped by MGM movie studios in her development of programs for the troops.

Don Gibson served in the merchant marine, both on freighters and on Army hospital ships.

Emily Da Silviera and her husband Ed were both in intelligence, she with the FBI and he with the Army.

Jack Crawford joined the merchant marine and spent 14 months in the Pacific working in the engine room of a liberty ship. On his return to San Francisco he went to the Maritime Academy and became an engineering officer. He returned to the Pacific conflict as a third engineer on larger cargo ships.

WASP's

Peg Calhoun

I don't consider my flying a major part of my life like most of the girls did. It was something I did with and for my husband Cal. In 1940 he was in a terrible auto accident with his lumbar back crushed and one foot torn off, hanging only by the arteries. We were in Palo Alto where he was being cared for at Stanford when the Civilian Pilot Training program started. He talked me into doing that while he convalesced. The program was mostly men, 25 or so in a program and only a few had a woman in the group. He was in a cast from neck to knees but he came to the airport to see me solo and was there when I got my pilot's license. We built airplane models together, even had working parts on the control surfaces. He took the ground school with me and it was all a joint endeavor.

In 1943, all licensed women pilots received a telegram from Jacqueline Cochrane, saying that women would be acceptable to the Air Corps and asking them to apply so they could do the domestic ferrying. Cal said, "Of course you can do it." I had to go to Sweetwater, Texas that had been a RAF training base for Canadian pilots. It was out in the middle of the Texas plain. Between his operations, Cal would come to Sweetwater and spend the time during my eight months or so of training there. When we arrived, there were still men cadets training there and it was coed for three months until that class finished. We stayed at the Blue Bonnet hotel and were close to the Canadians. We were told no fraternization, not even speaking in chow line. In spite of this there were a lot of dates. When I hear stories of this time, they don't follow my impressions but I was older and happily married. The windows were low and we had to be very careful when undressing for bed.

After the Canadian class left, we took over the whole base. A group who had started training in Dallas then flew up and joined us. There was quite a bit of resentment from some of the male pilots. They felt we were taking their jobs and they didn't really look forward to going to combat. The plan had been to make us part of the Air Corps but the reaction prevented that and we were civilian employees. We earned $250 per month and had no benefits such as military medical coverage or insurance.

During training they brought combat pilots in to be our instructors as a rest break for them. Each instructor had four trainees. We had one that was very difficult. He put me under the hood for instrument flying and then took me hedgehopping with many maneuvers close to the ground. It was dangerous and not helpful in learning. Later he was doing night flights and asked who had the least time. One of the girls in my group had minutes less than I in her log book so she went with him. They found the wreck with both dead the next day. I felt bad for her but felt that the ten minutes had saved my life.

After graduation, there were four places we could go: Dallas, Michigan, Wilmington, Delaware, and Long Beach. I was lucky to be assigned to the Air Transport Command at Long Beach airport. We were based right next door to the Douglas aircraft plant. We would pick up planes at the factory and deliver them to training facilities, modification plants, or ports of embarkation. Some of the planes were already obsolete when they came off the line, so went to modification, or they may have been modified for such specialties as photo. We did a lot of basic trainers up to twin engine bombers. They would drop in the engine and we would take off, testing the operational functions en route. The delivery flight would be the test flight.

Some of the girls were flying worn out B26 or B25 aircraft and towing targets, both for ground firing and for fighters. Some of the gunners were poor and the planes returned home full of holes.

The Air Transport Command group was started by Nancy Love, whose husband was a pilot in the Command. She recruited pilots with 500 hours or more and they went to England to train with the British women pilots. This was the WAAF (womens' auxiliary air ferrying). Cochrane came a year later and recruited any woman with a pilot's license. The WAAF was pulled into the Cochrane group and it became the WASP (women air service pilots). However, it was divided into two camps. Those in the ATC felt loyalty to Love and felt that Cochrane was pushy and publicity hunting. The Long Beach group were ATC and Love supporters, though the publicity was now all Cochrane and WASP.

Cal was still the most important thing for me and I flew while he was convalescing. I had to be at the airport at official dawn and I had a motor scooter to go the seven miles from where we lived at the beach. I was always anxious to make my delivery and to get home again. Cal often said, "I regret that I have but one wife to give to my country." We had double B priority on the airlines. This meant we could bump most important travelers. Many times high officers or government officials couldn't understand why this lady was allowed to bump them but we were to get back for the next delivery. I also rode back many times in Army transports, sitting on a pile of mail sacks.

We flew mostly east, as we didn't go out of the United States. I flew a lot of Vultee trainers, basic and advanced, as well as Douglas planes. I often flew as copilot when they had one military pilot for large planes like the B17. I was approved as first pilot for the C47 (Military version of the Douglas DC3) but more often flew copilot. Because of the fogs in Long Beach we often couldn't take off until later in the day. It was common to pick up a plane late, fly to Palm Springs for overnight and then get an early start so that the delivery could be complete by dark.

Though Cal couldn't walk without crutches, he could hike without difficulty and often came out to see me take off. Once when I went to Palm Springs he decided to ride to Palm Springs. He knew the hotel I usually stayed in but arrived and it was full and I had gone elsewhere. He called hotels until he found me. When he got to the hotel, in shorts with no luggage, they wouldn't believe that he was connected to us. My roommate saw him in the lobby and brought him up. The next day he rode to Idlewild for overnight and then back home.

We had to carry a B4 government bag with clothes, maps, and equipment and our parachute. In addition, I carried four pillows so that I could put them behind me and reach the controls. I sat on the parachute. It was sometimes difficult to carry all this. Once I made a delivery east and was then routed to Wichita to pick up a Beech trainer to take to California. The plane couldn't go higher than 12000 feet and the passes in the Rockies were 11,000. After sneaking through one pass, it started to snow and I had to land at Geiger Field in Wyoming, a United Airlines emergency field. A B17 with a full crew had also been forced in there. We had to stay five weeks before the weather cleared enough to let us out. There was only one motel and we all stayed there. I had a good time with the bomber crew while we waited.

Toward the end of the war I was an engineering test pilot as that kept me at the home field. I would fly planes that had been repaired and see if everything was working before they were sent back to duty. I never had an engine failure, though there were a few that failed due to sabotage - someone put sugar in the fuel. I had about 1000 hours total flight time but have lost my log book which had the exact records. I never felt my flying was an important thing. It was a cooperative venture with Cal participating vicariously and enjoying it. It was something I did as the contribution to the war effort for both of us.

2500 women applied, 1800 were accepted for training and 1097 women completed the training. 38 were killed in flying. In 1944 Congress was asked to make us part of the air corps and to give us benefits of all the men pilots. This was turned down and in December, 1944 we were disbanded. We were given no warning, no thank you, just: "That's all. Go home." Other bases did have farewell parties and took the women home in military planes. I was ready to leave but a few were kept on to ferry planes to storage. Many of them made flying their lives and followed it in different ways. After the war, Cal soloed but that got it out of his system and we never flew again except many commercial miles.

I didn't see any of the others until a reunion ten years later. Cal was always anxious to go to the reunions. They all knew him and he was active in the reunions. Now we have a week reunion each December at Palm Desert and about 50 still come to this.

ARMY MEDICAL SPECIALIST CORPS
Carlotta Welles

I was trained in occupational therapy at the Boston School of Occupational Therapy that later became a part of Tufts University. It was one of five original schools in the profession, at a time when none was yet affiliated with a university. I stayed in the New England area for my first employment, initially at the Hartford Hospital and later, also in Hartford, for the Foundation for Infantile Paralysis where I worked with patients in their homes helping to arrange/assure their access to the care they needed. That was during the beginning of polio epidemics in the U. S. Then along came World War II.

In 1942, when the Army began requesting occupation therapists for military hospital duty, I volunteered in what was initially to be a civilian role, even though serving in military facilities. Later we were made part of a group, then known as Women's Medical Specialist Corps, along with physical therapists and dieticians. Anticipating duty on the West Coast, I drove from the Boston area to Pasadena to await orders. When I arrived, my orders had arrived also, to Birmingham Army Hospital in Van Nuys, CA. After the war, it became Birmingham High School, still in existence.

Two local therapists had applied to be Chief of the program but the hospital director had decided that I was to be Chief and to organize the program. I employed the two applicant therapists as well as 12 other therapists and 40 volunteers whose activities I would supervise while serving the 1200 bed hospital population.

Then the patients started coming, with a wide range of injuries, illnesses, and treatment needs. They came by the trainload. The staff soon grew to 21 therapists. At this time the Army initiated OT War Emergency Training Courses in universities and colleges around the country, to meet growing personnel needs. Soon dozens of new therapists were ready for clinical internships. USC was one of such emergency training sites, so we at Birmingham soon added 10 student interns. We had all types of patients, with many different needs for recovery and rehabilitation. It was at this time that the term rehabilitation emerged due to a program of conditioning and retraining developed by Dr. Howard Rusk in New York. Soon "rehab" was the focus of treatment in all military settings.

Our patients were treated on the wards for those still bedridden or in our clinic where ambulatory and wheel chair patients could engage in a wide range of activities, crafts, and prevocational skills. I remember one man who had brought back a bag of Australian coins and wanted to make jewelry of them. He found the right hammer in our clinic and was soon working on his coins, using the tracks of a nearby rail spur as his anvil.

Our volunteers, most from the nearby movie community, also added much to our patients' needs, bringing all kinds of skills and activities to the program. Mary Astor was one of most loyal and best; she came regularly and was willing to do anything to help the staff. One thing I had her doing was cleaning and keeping order in our cupboards - often untidy with so many staff members using them. Charles Laughton came often to the hospital to read the Bible and Shakespeare to patients. Walter Wanger was also among the regulars. These people forgot who they were and filled in anywhere they were needed.

The program continued to grow and change as the war progressed. The Corps was gradually integrated into the military. Some dieticians and physical therapists were sent overseas but occupational therapists were not. All were still civilian employees. Army hospitals were well run and efficient. Equipment came on time and was what was needed. Orders were correct; everything went very smoothly despite staff working long hours and most living in hospital quarters and eating military food. Usual program needs could be handled through military channels. However, the head of OT in Washington and I were good friends and a couple times I phoned directly to her when we had problems. I could get away with this because I was a civilian.

The accelerated training programs were turning out larger numbers of students who required eight months of internship after six months of class work (all were college graduates). In time, there was a total of 800 occupational therapists in 40 Army hospitals at the peak of need. They were divided into areas; the West Coast had 10 hospitals and 160 therapists. I was transferred to Fort Douglas in Salt Lake City and made supervisor of the entire West Coast group. I had a staff of 16. We took interns from all the schools and thus were able to hire the cream for staff as we needed to add. I traveled a lot in those days.

After the war some of the occupational therapists stayed on and the Army changed their status to military and commissioned them. The name was changed to Army Medical Specialist Corps. The program at the University of Southern California was integrated into the regular academic curriculum in 1944 since rehabilitation services were being established in many more hospitals and staff was needed. When the war ended, I was offered the position of head of occupational therapy at Los Angeles County Hospital. As County Hospital was associated with USC for internships and other college programs, I was designated a clinical professor at USC.

RED CROSS EXPERIENCES

Louise Hall

I was working in the laboratories of Columbia Physicians and Surgeons Medical School in New York when the country entered the war, doing studies on the cytology of the pituitary gland. The doctor with whom I was working was transferred to administration as people were taken for the military and research gradually faded out. I worked for Ciba Pharmaceuticals in New Jersey for a time but felt I wanted to do more for the war effort.

In early 1944 I volunteered to work with the Red Cross. After acceptance, I went to Washington, DC where a number of new workers spent several weeks being trained in the duties of their new job. I was taught a lot about recreation for the troops but told almost nothing about the changes in life and the adjustments needed for working in other countries and living in different conditions. The new workers were asked if they would rather have a hot or cold climate. I had heard of the heat and humidity of some of the Pacific Islands and requested cold.

I was given orders to Seattle and took a train across the country. I had never been west at all and really enjoyed the beauty and grandeur of the Rocky Mountains. At Ft. Lewis, Washington, I spent a few days and was then ordered on a troop ship. A large group of Red Cross workers was accumulating at a convent outside Honolulu. They were gradually divided up and I was sent to Lanakai, a nice residential area across Oahu from Honolulu. There was a military rest camp here. Duties were working with the soldiers, working with the soldiers' clubs and setting up programs for the soldiers. I still have my pass, signed by the chief of Police of Honolulu that allowed me to be out during the night curfew.

Several months later, I was moved to the big island in the ranch land near Mauna Kea, the volcano. The Marines had a large camp here, training new marines for the invasion of Japan. This was a very active, lively group and many of the Red Cross people were doing projects with them. I was here when the atom bomb was dropped and the surrender signed. This was the most unusual experience of my Red Cross time. The troops didn't celebrate when the end of the war was announced. They couldn't believe it. It took days for them to believe it was real. They had become so used to the idea of the invasion with such a strong mind-set that took time to adjust to a new way of thinking. Their attitude was so remarkable.

I was ordered to an air field for a new assignment but was kept there several days. I wondered why but then it was explained that there had been a severe typhoon in the Pacific and all transit had stopped. Interestingly, the typhoon was named Louise. When the weather finally cleared, I was flown to Okinawa. The island showed a great deal of battle damage and many rats were forced out of their living places. At first the Red Cross girls lived in a wood hut with a tent roof. Rats would walk along the edge at night and if they could reach hanging clothing, chew on it. Girls would get up and put on their pants only to find large holes. Later we moved to Quonset huts. The showers had only cold water and soon it was November and getting cold. The girls lived in a small compound, fenced in, with 10 Quonsets and about 80 Red Cross workers. This adjoined the Army compound within a guarded perimeter. Mess halls and recreation were within the perimeter. If the girls went out of the Army perimeter, they had to be accompanied by two armed guards.

The compound was on the south part of Okinawa where the landings had been made. The soil here was a very heavy, sticky red clay. This stuck to everything and made even basic walking difficult. The roads had been coated with crushed coral so that vehicles could move around.

The Red Cross girls went out at times to other bases such as Kadena Air Field to set up activities for the troops. If the girls dated, it had to be double dates. The date had to sign them out at the military government control office and was responsible for their being back within the compound. Some of the officers' quarters had hot water and one way for the officers to get dates was to offer a hot shower or the use of hot water for shampoo. One of the most enjoyable things was to watch the sunsets over the China Sea. They were remarkable, much more picturesque than in most places. Sometimes we Red Cross girls were able to make a trip up to the north part of the island to the more mountainous part, where we could see native dances and programs.

Life was rather primitive in many ways and took a lot of adjustment. Some of the girls adjusted better than others. One Christmas morning I woke to screams. One of the girls in the group had committed suicide during the night. There was really no explanation in the group as to why she had done it but they felt that she just couldn't cope anymore. One of the problems for the girls was the attitude of the troops. In Hawaii, they had been lively and spirited, enjoyed whatever could be done. In Okinawa, they were bored and dispirited. They didn't cooperate well with programs and mostly just wanted to watch movies or drink.

A friend and I often went to a nearby Navy Seabee outfit. I felt that the Navy, particularly the officers, lived well. They taught me to make pousse-café. At the Seabee base, I met Harold Hall, an engineering lieutenant in the Navy. We became engaged and when we married, went to Manila and were married in a military chapel there. The military government rules on marriage were so complicated on Okinawa that it was easier to go to the Philippines. Harold was sent to the states and later I returned. I was again in Manila on the way home, waiting a few days. It was some time before Christmas but the people were singing Christmas carols and then having Chinese style fireworks.

I was very pleased by the Red Cross people I worked with. The leaders and the people in Washington had had important jobs and were well educated and good leaders. The Red Cross girls were mostly a joy to work with and I kept up with several for many years. We shared the unusual experience of Okinawa and most of my friends just couldn't picture what it had been like. I still have pictures from my war time experiences. One of Hawaii was painted by a Marine who was trying to develop an artistic career. Besides photos, there are pictures painted by Okinawans. One is dated 1949 but was painted in 1946 - the Okinawans couldn't understand why 6's and 9's had a different meaning and alternated them indiscriminately.

My time in the Red Cross was a defining event in my career. I was more interested in people and helping. Instead of returning to the lab, I went back to school and became a medical social worker.

THE FBI IN WARTIME
Dorothy Christiansen

I attended the Conservatory of Music at Morningside College. Upon graduation, I obtained a position in Randolph, Nebraska, where I taught music in grades one through twelve. To make a good impression on the people in Randolph, I played in the City Band. If you could find me, I was in the back row with a Susaphone wrapped around me! That job didn't last too long. It was during my second year at Randolph (1942) that it came to my attention the FBI was hiring clerical employees to work in Washington, D.C. The thought of working for the FBI really intrigued me, and I decided to make application. It didn't take very long before I was called to the FBI Field Office in Omaha for an interview. A few weeks passed, and I found myself making arrangements to leave my teaching position and moving to Washington, D.C. I had a friend in Virginia at that time who helped me find a room.

It was so interesting living in that area at that time. Every day on my way to work in D.C., I could watch the Pentagon being built. Negroes were still required to sit in the rear of the bus. After a thorough orientation, including a very strict dress code on our part, we become familiar with our surroundings and employee activities. No pants for ladies, no smoking except in designated areas. Men wore suits and ties and hats at proper times.

And now about the work I would be doing. I was assigned to Division III, which is the Administrative Division. It was here that I briefed investigations. Briefly put, when someone made application to work for the FBI, an agent was assigned to check every known thing about the applicant. They talked to neighbors, relatives, just everyone the applicant ever knew and recorded it. My job was to brief their findings into one paragraph.

About this time, the Lindbergh trial was about to take place. I was in the area where it was to take place, so was moved to another area on the 3rd floor. Shortly before the end of the war I was assigned to the Payroll office. During this time (the dates I can't remember), I was asked to be assigned to the Director's office when their mail clerk was away. This was fun. We called ourselves "Glorified Messengers". Our work consisted of carrying mail from our little cubicle to Miss Gandy's office. She was THE SECRETARY for Mr. Hoover for many years. The Director had two personal aides. They did everything for him and were known as Worthy and Sam, the only two black men in the entire FBI and were wonderful people.

I left out one important part of my life and maybe you can guess what it was. In April 1943 I married the science and math teacher from Randolph, Nebraska. He was almost immediately shipped overseas and into the North African Campaign. He was about to be shipped to Japan when the war ended in Europe, and he returned home in 1945.

I worked for the FBI for six years. It was an enjoyable, rewarding, and interesting experience.

HOLLYWOOD AT CAMP ROBERTS
Mary Scott Winslow

During World War II, I was asked to join special services for the U. S. Army artillery. I was stationed at Camp Roberts, a training camp in California, for two and a half years. My job was to help produce shows and entertain the trainees who were usually there for a twelve week training program. I had no idea how we were going to manage the entertainment but with the help of MGM and the trainees, we came up with a show called "Girl Crazy". Red Skelton was just beginning his training. We placed him in some of the smaller shows, doing his wonderful routines. When I worked with him in our big stage productions, like Girl Crazy, it was a challenge! We would let him go "off script". He was so great. But what a challenge to get him back on.

I helped "hire" soldiers for bit parts in musicals and in the orchestra, even though they were in training. Besides being co-producer for several shows, I worked with make-up, costumes and arranging for transportation. I was busy seven days and nights a week. Jack Cathcart was stationed at Roberts. We asked him if he could help conduct some of our shows. He said, "Yes, if he could bring along his wife Sue". She was a dancer who was also Judy Garland's sister. I had worked with Judy at one time so it was now becoming old home week. We now had a conductor and a dancer. We found a soldier who had worked with sets, another with lighting, and others with sound in stage productions. I even helped some soldiers paint scenery, something none of us had done before.

When we found a tenor soldier trainee, Brian Sullivan who with his great voice went on to the Met after the war, we decided to try some opera. I ended up singing with him in Pagliacci. I incidentally met my future husband who sang opposite me in the Harlequin scene, Act 2. Brian also did Don Jose in "Carmen" with us. I played Michiela and a very sexy lady, Lucille Norman from MGM, sang Carmen. The boys really did like this opera. We took out all of the recitatives and replaced them with dialogue, another big challenge.

Jan Clayton, a starlet at MGM at that time, did many shows with us. Also Janice Page who went on to Broadway shows in New York. Marion Bell sang in our production of "New Moon". She went on to do "Brigadoon" on Broadway. I was privileged to sing the leads in "The Merry Widow" and "Pinafore". We were most grateful to MGM for loaning us some big stars for shows, as well as the lesser "starlets".

There were holiday productions in churches as well as in the theatre. There were shows given weekly in the non-commissioned officers' club as well as the officer's club.

What an experience and what a wonderful audience we always had! Just to hear the boys laugh and for some of them to participate was the best part of my time at Camp Roberts. They were having fun in a not so much fun place. I am most grateful for having had this great learning and loving experience.

FROM POMONA TO THE MERCHANT MARINE
Don Gibson
Right after December 7, 1941 we had blackouts and air raid sirens. It was strange to hear a car coming down the street but without lights on. We had to keep our window shades pulled down so no light could show to Japanese planes. I worked in a store in Pomona that sold window shades and we were very busy cutting new shades to the various window sizes. Everyone wanted dark green shades as they kept out (or in) more light. We couldn't keep up with the demand.

Later I worked for Kaiser Steel in Fontana. We made ship plate steel to use on Victory ships. Mr. Kaiser and his wife, Bess, would come up to the furnaces in their big black "limo" and ask us what the men were doing! And it was his steel mill. He was smart - he hired experienced workers from the East, built new houses for them, and shipped the men and their families out to California.

In May 1945 I joined the Merchant Marine. I was sent to Catalina Island for the basic training. We had classes and practice sessions. I remember getting up early, putting on a life preserver, and having to jump in the ocean. Among the classes was one on swimming away from an oil fire. One has to push the water away from him to carry off the burning oil. We had a demonstration and then some of the students had to try it. I just had to watch this time. At the conclusion of the training I received my papers certifying me as an able seaman.

I went to San Francisco on the cadre of the Army Transport Service that assigned ships to the seamen. My first ship was the Etoain, a World War I vintage troop transport that would only make about 8 knots. I was signed on as a storekeeper. We took about 3000 replacement troops to Okinawa. There had been a very severe hurricane in the Pacific and it was too rough to go into the harbor. We had to unload the troops by having them climb down rope nets into landing craft. We then returned with troops who had been there long enough to return to the United States and went back into Seattle. There were so many troops on these trips that only two meals a day were served. The mess crew worked long hours and served continuously from 7 AM to 7 or 8 PM. The ship's crew had our own mess and had the regular three meals. It was so much better that soldiers would volunteer to do our dirty work to get to eat at our mess.

Our contracts required that we be returned to our original point so the Army paid my train fare to return to Los Angeles. From here I was assigned to an Army hospital ship, the Charles Stafford. We went through the Panama Canal and then over to Bremerhaven, Germany. Going over, the Army medical unit was aboard but we didn't have any patients. I remember that in spite of the cold and snow, the captain conducted a life boat drill. In Germany, we picked up a full load of ill and injured, including many mental cases. The ship's crew had no relation to the hospital and we saw almost nothing of either the hospital staff or the patient passengers.

After my return, I took the Admiral C. F. Hughes, a new Navy transport that had been turned over to the Army, out of San Francisco to Manila. Again, we had three groups on board: the merchant marine crew who sailed the ship, the Army crew who planned and administered the handling of passengers, and the passengers. On this trip we had wives and families and civilian employees as well as military personnel as passengers. This was a very nice ship. I had worked up to be chief storekeeper on the hospital ship and I was purser on the Admiral Hughes, in charge of all the storekeepers and the ship's finances. We furnished perishable foods for the passengers' mess but the staples were provided by the Army and the cooking and planning were done by the Army. I enjoyed the chance to travel and see the world but my wife wanted me home so I left the merchant marine at the end of this cruise.

INTELLIGENCE SERVICES
Emily da Silveira

Ed and I met as graduate students and teaching fellows in the Romanic Languages Department of the University of Washington in Seattle, a few months before Pearl Harbor. A professor who left the university that year to work in the Pentagon recommended Ed for a job with Army intelligence as a Spanish/Portuguese specialist, so in June 1942 Ed left Seattle to work in Washington, D. C. Suddenly it seemed very important that I go there also to help the war effort. My cousin Howell Webb, then an FBI agent, told me that the Bureau was hiring people with language skills and said I should go to the nearest FBI field office and take their French and Spanish exams. That fall I was offered a job in the Bureau as a "cryptographic code clerk" and followed Ed to Washington. Washington was an exciting place to be during the war. Almost everybody of any importance passed through and if one couldn't see them at least we heard who was around.

The FBI agents were trained at Quantico but they were completely separate from those of us who worked in various Washington offices. Some important work was done in the FBI's cryptographic lab, including cracking a Japanese cipher. The cryptographic lab had about 60 people. Much of the material on which we worked was from intercepted cable traffic and a great deal from the censorship of the mails. We had to study the material for encrypted messages but also often had to translate it from foreign languages. For this reason, the FBI encouraged all of its people in the study of foreign languages and courses were offered on one's own time. I studied Portugese in one of these classes and it became very valuable when I later lived in Brazil.

In late 1943 Ed was drafted into the Army. After basic training at Ft. Sill, Oklahoma, he was transferred to an Army Intelligence unit at Camp Ritchie, Maryland. We were married in Baltimore in May 1944, just before he was shipped out to Recife, Brazil, the headquarters of the U S South Atlantic command. He served here until the war's end, putting his Portuguese to good use. An Army Signal Corps photo shows him, a gravely handsome corporal in suntans, pointing out the progress of the war on a big wall map to a United States general, a Brazilian general, and other lesser brass.

When the war ended, Ed was assigned to the joint Brazil-U S Military Commission in Rio and I was finally allowed to join him.

MERCHANT MARINER IN THE PACIFIC
Jack Crawford

I had polio at age 10 and knew I couldn't pass the military physical. In early 1943 I saw a cousin who was a second engineer in the Merchant Marine. He was sure he could get me on the engine crew of a ship if I went to Fort Mason. Sure enough, I was made a wiper on the Liberty ship Andrew D. White. By the time we left port I had been promoted to fireman.

We took a supply cargo to Brisbane, Australia. After unloading, we remained in the area, going back and forth to New Guinea, mostly Port Moresby. When we stopped in Cairns, I developed an appendix attack and was taken to the First Army General Hospital which was at Gordonsville, 16 miles west. This fine hospital, organized in Boston, was placed here because there were three divisions of paratroopers assigned there. The nurses all spoke with a Boston accent. My appendix was surgically removed. While convalescing, I found that the paratroopers had taken over the small town, buying houses and cars. The battle of the Coral Sea occurred while I was in the hospital and Navy casualties were brought to the hospital. One was in the next bed to me.

I was sent back to Cairns but the ship was gone. There was no naval office and no one to do anything for me so I took a troop train to Brisbane. Here the Naval office radioed the ship and found they were in Port Moresby, scheduled to go to Melbourne. They gave me a train ticket to Melbourne and quite a sum of money. I stopped a time in Sydney for sightseeing as the ship wasn't due in. I relaxed and enjoyed Melbourne. Artie Shaw was in the Army and was assigned to playing for troops at a club in Melbourne. Only American men were allowed in the club but they could bring Australian girls. Girls would be lined up around the area trying to find someone to take them to see Artie Shaw.

Then one day I met the ship's captain on the street. He said they had been in a week but no one told me. I reported back to the ship. The nucleus of the 1st Marine Division went to Melbourne after being taken from Guadalcanal. They had been there for nine months, reconstituting the division with replacements and training. Our ship took some of them to Bougainville. There was trouble rounding up all the Marines as some had become part of the local community.

Milne Bay on the north coast of New Guinea was a huge port, able to take about 70 ships with supplies for MacArthur's army. Here we unloaded directly into trucks rather than onto the pier. They were planning an officer's club and we took a load of liquor for it. We unloaded it but it was never seen again. Investigations showed nothing. Once we tied up along a C-3 transport at Finschhafen. We asked what their cargo was. "Ten thousand tons of beer and Baby Ruth candy bars." We managed to obtain quite a bit of this before we left.

We took part of the Aussie 4th division to Finschhafen, New Guinea. I was now a water tender. At Finschhafen, they announced that the ship would go home, having been away for 14 months. When we reached San Francisco, I applied for the Maritime Academy. I didn't expect to pass the officer's physical but I did and was sent to Oakland for officer's course. There were two courses and I was in engineering. We spent six months in the school and had to take tests in other areas before graduating, including rowing a small boat. I didn't do well in this but the instructor passed me, saying, "If your ship is torpedoed you aren't going to be able to get out of the engine room anyway so you don't need to row." The class was divided alphabetically and all the six students in my room had last names starting with "C".

I was licensed as a third engineer and sailed on several ships, mostly the new C-class which were faster and larger than the liberties being 14,000 or more tons and having steam turbine engines.   These ships were rarely out over three of four months at a time. We visited many of the islands of the Pacific: Guam, Saipan, Noumea, and Kwajalein among others. One time as we arrived at Kwajalein the third fleet was coming out. We had to wait several hours for them all to exit before we could go into the harbor. There was carrier after carrier, battleships, and many cruisers and destroyers. It was most impressive. Once we stopped at Goodenough Island to supply the PT boat squadron there.

We never saw a Japanese sub in the Pacific and I didn't know any ships that were torpedoed. There were no convoys of ships such as the Atlantic had. Once, going from Pago Pago, Samoa to Noumea we were given a sub alarm but nothing happened. Each ship had a Naval gun crew. They didn't have much to do and spent much time eating. We got along well with them. The only ones to give me any problem were a few old merchant sailors who resented a young officer.

One evening in Pearl Harbor on the way to take supplies for the invasion of Japan, now a second engineer, I had the watch and heard explosions. I rushed up to see if we were being bombed but a sailor yelled, "The war is over." We went home instead of Japan and I was mustered out of the merchant marine. I had a great time, saw a lot of the world, and didn't have to work too hard. Except when entering or leaving harbor I merely had to make sure the temperature and pressure gauges stayed in normal range.

CHAPTER 9

MILITARY MEDICINE

Young, healthy men don't need a lot of medical care. Medicine in wartime involves a great deal of waiting and busy work. Doctors and nurses treat colds and venereal disease with an occasional accidental injury. But then during the time of battle, the work may be overwhelming, with hundreds of severely injured men arriving in a few hours. Triage, identifying those who have the best chance of recovery with the available treatment, and emergency first aid are the first steps. The surgery suite at a field hospital may work for days without pause.

Patients are evacuated through a series of increasingly complex medical facilities. From the first aid station, the injured soldier may go to a mobile field hospital such as a MASH unit. When he is stabilized, he can be transferred to a general hospital further from the combat area for more definitive treatment. Often in ocean warfare, the general hospital may be a hospital ship. Even the Army had hospital ships, specially designed ships carrying all the personnel of an Army hospital but sailed by Merchant Marine crews. Finally, if the injury is severe enough, the patient will be evacuated to the home country for final care and rehabilitation.

Most of the doctors and nurses were not initially trained for military work but had to expand on their civilian experience to handle the problems of front-line care. Much of the work in the field, and also the less technical work in hospitals, is done by medical technicians or hospital corpsmen. To disrupt the attacking forces, enemy sharpshooters targeted the officers and the medical personnel. The incidence of casualties and also of awards for heroism were extremely high in medical personnel involved in the battlefield.

During the war there was extensive research in the medical handling of burns and certain types of wounds. Diseases of the Pacific Islands and the African desert only became known to American medicine through the stationing of troops in these places. The development of penicillin and its uses were considerably increased by the military needs for it.

The record of military medicine during World War II was remarkable; it has continued to improve with the use of helicopter evacuation that allows by-passing of some of the layers of treatment previously used in handling the wounded. New generations of antibiotics, anesthetics, and blood replacement techniques have built on the foundation of the developments from World War II.

John Gius participate in the Iwo Jima invasion and his descriptions of the action are taken from letters to his wife, Martha.

Donn Stewart was administrative officer on the Army hospital ship, SS Marigold. Lucille was assigned to the ship as a nurse and they met on the ship. The ship was used for evacuation of casualties and the two of them saw service in both the Atlantic and Pacific theatres. They later married.

John Ritchie went into the Army at the completion of his medical internship. He served with a field hospital in the New Guinea campaign.

Dorothy Jenkins was a young Army nurse who was assigned to the hospital at a camp for German POWs, only to find that the prisoners were given more privileges at the officers' club than were the African-American nurse officers.

John Hazlett was a Navy dentist who was in the Pacific, assigned to an aircraft carrier. Following this he worked in Navy dental clinics.

IWO JIMA

Dr. John A. Gius was a Navy medical corps officer in the Pacific. His grandson published his letters to his wife as "Letters to Martha". This is an exerpt from that, detailing his time on Iwo Jima. Dr. Gius, a resident of Mt. San Antonio Gardens, died in 1999 and this is published with the permission of his wife, Martha Gius.

February 28, 1945

We came ashore yesterday with the Medical Battalion on D plus 9. This place is a beehive of activity with more military gear of all types than anyone can imagine. I've done a great deal of "bird dogging" and collected a few souvenirs and saw many things.

It is now 6:30. The sun is setting, and soon taps will be sounded. Everyone will have to extinguish fires and lights and crawl into his foxhole until daylight. I am writing this while sitting on a packing box overlooking the ocean. Innumerable ships of all types are in front of me, and the sky is filled with aircraft. Behind me is a cliff and above that is Mt. Suribachi, still inhabited by a few enemy snipers. A buddy and I climbed to the top of the mountain and got a birds eye view of the island, surrounding ocean, crater of the quiescent volcano, and our front lines, which are about three or four miles distant. We could easily see our men going forward cautiously against the entrenched enemy. The view from the top of the mountain was excellent, and I only regret that I didn't have my camera along.

On the way up, we passed numerous mounds covering bodies of Japanese who have recently gone to their ancestors. Also, there were many concrete gun emplacements and pillboxes that have been knocked out. These fortifications are extremely well built, and it took much pounding to destroy them. From each comes the stench of decomposition. In some caves are hundreds of dead Japanese soldiers. At one point, we rested on a rock, and suddenly a hand and forearm appeared through the loose sand. Then a head appeared, and it was soon apparent that a Marine was coming to the surface. Both of us covered him with our carbines and fortunately for him, we held our fire. He told us that he had been exploring for souvenirs but found only dead enemy soldiers in the tunnel.

My foxhole is partly under a large boulder, where I joined up with Dr. P., a neurosurgeon. I believe the foxhole was originally dug by the Japanese. It's quite a cozy spot, but I'll admit it was tough sleeping in it last night. Not only was the ground bumpy and hard, but the air was cold, it rained, and the beach was under fire. Shrapnel landed on the beach throughout the night. Also we had both an air and gas alert, which really threw the fear of God into us. Fortunately, no planes came over. The gas alarm was false too, but I had my gas mask on for about 20 minutes before the secure was called over the loudspeaker on the beach. Outside of that, foxhole dwelling wasn't too bad.

Thus far, I haven't minded the rigors of camping out. I haven't shaved in three days. Water is scarce and has to be conserved. I look pretty tough-I don't think you would want me to kiss you in this condition. I did take a bath in the surf tonight, and it was cold but invigorating. It was the first time I used salt-water soap. The food has been okay. There is a tent set up nearby where we can get hot coffee from a large G.I. can, similar to a garbage can. Tonight they also had hot vegetable soup. In addition, we have been eating K rations and C rations. Can't say I mind them at all, but they would get tiresome in time.

It's getting quite dark and windy. It's about time to get in the hole. After dark, the snipers get busy. God bless us all and keep us safe....

March 2, 1945

Certainly seems I'm getting mail with an undue amount of hometown publicity. After all, "I was there" but I didn't do any shooting on the front lines. I'm referring to the Red Cross quotation and the Medical Society Bulletin. After witnessing the assault troops in action, I think my contribution was insignificant. If I saw the newsreel of the invasion, I might be able to tell you which ship I was on, but there were hundreds, and I doubt if ours even got into the picture.

March 3,1945

This island is rapidly being cleaned up, so far as enemy soldiers are concerned. I mean dead ones. Any live ones are confined to the caves, most of which have been sealed up, and, from the odors they emit, it isn't difficult to conclude what has happened. I believe Iwo may be secured soon.

I am writing to you while sitting on a rock close to my foxhole, and just now there was a big explosion, throwing some sand and gravel on to me. The explosion was either to seal up a cave or to get rid of a dud shell or a bomb that did not explode earlier. No one believes it was from the enemy. The breeze from the ocean is pretty brisk, and the sun is shining brightly. It is a beautiful, cool day, but the island is one mass of dust. The amphibious tanks, caterpillars, jeeps, etc, make the damnedest clouds of dust. Now the action is confined to the very northernmost tip of the island, about three miles away, and we can't see what is going on. However, the artillery is emplaced all around the plain, and firing goes on all day and all night. Company B Hospital was set up yesterday and is receiving some casualties. We (Company C) will probably set up tomorrow.

Just in front of me about 200 feet away is a seaplane, which washed ashore when it broke its moorings night before last. The aircraft is being pounded to pieces by the surf. There goes $200,000 to $300,000 in war bonds for no good purpose.

This rugged life seems to be agreeing with me. I even shaved this morning, so I feel like a new man. I would give a lot for a good shower, but that's impossible 'till we get our hospital in shape. Then we will have plenty of hot water. The beach where I bathed a couple of days ago is now covered with trash and oil from the wrecked plane, so it's no longer suitable. I could take a sponge bath out of my helmet as many do, but I don't smell that bad yet.

The first night ashore in the foxhole I slept on a shelter-half and one blanket. The ground was uneven, and the excitement between the air and gas alert was pretty intense. Since then, I have used my bedding roll with a pillow and mattress spread on the ground, so I was in the sack for 12 hours. I tried to read the newspaper by flashlight for awhile, but soon the Marines ordered the beach darkened, so I had to give up.

I have just finished censoring mail written by the enlisted men. They all received stacks yesterday and are pouring out letters in answer. The censorship restrictions are relaxed now until we have another operation. I don't know when or where that will be, but now that we have the enemy on the run, you can look for things to happen. Before we go out again, however, we will have a rest period and replenish our supplies.

March 4, 1945

It rained heavily this morning, and the only good thing about it is that the dust has settled and the air is cool. I stayed in my foxhole reading TIME for February 13, the one with Himmler on the cover, and got a lot out of it.

I went over to the new area where Company B is already set up and my Company C is getting set up. We expect to be in operation tomorrow. I hope we do enough to make the work of setting up worth while. Company B is fairly busy and probably will have a lot to do tonight. They have asked me to stand by in case they need help. This isn't an ideal place to do surgery, and the cases aren't exactly ideal either, but then war is war and we do the best we can. The cases are nearly all serious ones-multiple wounds of the head, chest, abdomen, and extremities. Very dirty, very tired and many badly shocked. Favorable aspects are the youth of the Marines and the relatively short time between injury and reception at the hospital. The Marines are now fighting at the extreme northern tip of the island, about two miles from here, and the word is that it should be secured in a day or so. But that's what they said a couple of days ago, so it may take longer.

It's dark now, and I'm writing by flashlight in a tent with six or eight cots in which Medical Officers of Company C live. This will be much more comfortable than the previous foxhole, but I didn't mind too much until today when it started to rain. Now I will have to look around for another foxhole nearby, in case we have an air raid.

Just now there were several load blasts from the artillery behind us. The explosions about knocked my head off. Each blast is followed by a "woosh" as the shell passes overhead. This is really war. I don't believe the nearness of the artillery will do our patients any good, but we won't be able to do anything about it. Many patients are now being evacuated by air to Guam or Saipan or other places. Today also, a crippled B-29 Superfortress landed on Airfield #1, which considering the circumstances, is in pretty good shape. It is a historic landing that I will long remember.

Yesterday I walked where the original landings were made and looked over the countless wrecked tanks, amtracks, ducks, jeeps, landing boats, tractors, etc. There are millions of dollars worth of inoperable equipment just rusting on the beach. But there is still plenty of functioning equipment in action here. I'll bet more gasoline is burned here every day than in the city of Portland, and this island has an area of only eight square miles.

The most impressive part of my jaunt was the cemetery of the 3rd Marine Division. There I witnessed the mass interment of Marines who had given their lives for their country. This was a large cemetery, part of which was already filled. But in an unoccupied area, a trench had been dug, into which the bodies were placed side by side. Each had been marked for identification and wrapped in a waterproof covering. Then after a short religious ceremony over each body, a bulldozer replaced the sand that had been removed when the trench was dug earlier.

While I stood there and reflected on what was happening before me, I wondered why life had been cut-off in its prime and how the grievous loss had affected the hero's family and friends. Also, it became clear to me that war is so unnecessary and unfair. These are such large issues that it is not likely a simple doctor like myself can have any impact on them.

MARIGOLD
Donn and Lucille Stewart

Donn: I was drafted in the prewar draft for one year in the spring of 1941. I was assigned to the cavalry. The 113rd cavalry regiment had three troops of horse cavalry and 3 troops of mechanized and I was placed in the horse cavalry. We actually learned to ride and maneuver horses in combat situation. When Pearl Harbor came I had been looking forward to my release but then realized I was in for the duration. The Army sent me to Ft. Beaumont in Texas for training as a medical technician and then I returned to the cavalry in the medical group.

After two years in the cavalry, I was sent to OCS. This was a special OCS course for medical administrative officers. It was a very intensive course and only about 1/3 of the students were commissioned. At the conclusion of the training, when I was commissioned, I was assigned to the 212th hospital ship complement and sent to Seattle. We spent about 6 months working to set up the unit, train and be ready for the MARIGOLD to be finished in the shipyard in Tacoma.

MARIGOLD: This ship had been built in 1920 in New Jersey at 11,342 tons. It was called the Old North State and went between England and France and the Mediterranean. It was then sent to the Dollar ship line and became the SS President Van Buren and made around the world cruises. The Dollar line went broke and the ship was at anchor for four years in San Francisco Bay. It was then renamed the President Fillmore and again did cruises around the world. At the beginning of the war, it was taken as a troop transport and took troops between the West Coast and Alaska. In December 1943 it was sent to Seattle for conversion to a hospital ship and renamed Marigold. As a hospital ship, it had about 800 beds. There was an operating room and almost the complete facilities of a stationary hospital.

Lucille: I completed nurses training in San Francisco and then went to Washington State University where I worked as a nurse in the dispensary and completed my BS degree. At the end of 1942, I went in the Army nurse corps. I was sent to Oregon for basic military training and then to Ft. Lawton general hospital in Seattle. While working there, there was a request for volunteers but we were not told for what. Two of us decided we would like something different and volunteered. We were sent to the hospital unit but were only there about a month before the ship was completed. The unit then transferred to the Marigold and then left for the Panama Canal, Charleston SC and then Naples.

Donn: The Naples Harbor was bombed shortly after we arrived and we realized that we were now in the war. We went to the French Riviera and loaded wounded from the assault on Southern France. The landing craft were still taking men into the landing and they brought wounded out as they came back. Each litter had to be carried from the landing craft over a pitching gangplank and then up the stairs in the hospital to the wards. We loaded the ship in one day. We were asked to leave hastily as German planes were coming and we were still loading patients as the ship pulled out of the harbor. We took these patients to the general hospital in Naples. We returned to France, to St. Tropez, for another load of wounded and then back to Naples. After this we were ordered to the Pacific.

MARIGOLD: Again the ship stopped in Charleston, SC and then went through the Panama Canal, enroute to New Guinea.

Lucille: The merchant marine crew made a big thing of crossing the Equator. They had a ceremony and several of the nurses were placed in handcuffs. Donn was put in the brig and left overnight. Though the crew were civilians, they were very cooperative and worked hard to do their best, particularly after we began having wounded patients. This really brought the war to all of us.

Donn: I was the senior administrative officer and was promoted to 1st lieutenant. I had two other administrative officers. The colonel was a surgeon and worked hard both at seeing patients and supervising medical care so he left almost all the administration of the hospital unit to me. I was promoted to Captain during my time on the ship but Lucille was never promoted. The Army wasn't good about promoting nurses and she ended the war still a 2nd lieutenant. Neither of us was ever seasick, though some of the staff were. We had a very severe storm in the Pacific, with 40 foot waves which swept across the decks. The lower decks had to be kept clear of people or they would have been taken over the side.

In New Guinea we operated out of Hollandia which had a big general hospital, though it was mostly still in tents. We picked up patients in Milne Bay and Biak to go to Hollandia. We didn't get much time ashore, though we did get to see some of the natives at the places we stopped. We then went to the Philippines for Mac Arthur's invasion. Again we were off the beaches as the troops went in. First from Tacloban in the South and then from Manila, we made six trips from the Philippines to Hollandia.

Lucille: At first I worked on the general wards of the hospital but then I went into the psychiatric ward. We had several locked, padded rooms as well as a controlled psychiatric ward where we had breakdowns and "shell shock" patients. In the Philippines we received some prisoners of war as well as wounded. We had one group of nurses who had been prisoners of war. In spite of all the privations and infections, the first thing they wanted was make-up.

Donn: The ship needed a number of repairs and we had found things that could be improved so after the Philippine campaign, we returned to San Pedro for overhaul. Everyone was given leave except me. Someone had to be responsible for the ship during this time and since my home was in Southern California, the colonel decided I could be there and still get time at home. We were in overhaul for about six weeks and then returned to the Pacific. We stopped at Leyte and then Manila and Okinawa. We were in Manila in August 1945 and were immediately ordered to Japan on the surrender. We were the first American ship in Yokohama harbor.

Paratroops were in the POW camps in Japan and we were to work with them. Our first night we were concerned if there were still Japanese who wanted to fight. The paratroop regiment sent two soldiers down to guard our dock that night. It seemed too few but there were no problems. The next day we started loading POW's. We filled the ship with POW's.

Lucille: The biggest problem we had was preventing the POW's from overeating until their systems were reaccustomed to food. They were skinny, bloated, and had sores and infections. They seemed very stoic when they first came aboard but then they began to wake up and realize that they were free. As soon as their condition was good enough, they were flown back to the United States and we would get more. We stayed some time in Japan, rehabilitating the POW's. Most of us had enough points to fly home and be discharged but we decided to stay and return with the ship and finish our job. We brought back a full load of patients from Japan.

Donn: On our arrival in San Pedro, I received a call from an agent in Hollywood. They were anxious to have a program for the wounded troops. That was fine, but the weather was bad and the Colonel refused to have the patients out on the open decks. The group came and included Doris Day, Jimmy Durante, Danny Kaye, and Gary Moore. When I told them we couldn't get the patients all together, they spent several hours doing short programs on each of our 12 wards. They had brought a small piano for the performance and our largest men moved the piano from ward to ward around the ship.

The next day the patients were unloaded and taken to general hospitals in the area. The hospital personnel were then rapidly discharged. Only I remained as someone had to close out the books and the administrative work as the ship was inactivated. Finally I was able to be separated from the service and went home. Lucille and I were married and we still remember how the MARIGOLD brought us together.

PACIFIC TRAVELS

John Ritchie

I graduated from medical school at the University of Oregon in June of 1942. This was the last class before the accelerated schedule that all the schools adopted. I then interned at Emmanuel Hospital in Portland. Near the end of internship, Marian came out to a teacher's meeting. I had known her since I was 12 and she stopped to see me and we became engaged. We went home to Idaho after my internship and I had orders to report to the Army on July 4 to the barracks at Vancouver Washington. I was there for 6 weeks in basic training. We had drill, Army indoctrination, and other training. Previous classes had live fire training with machine guns. One of the guns had broken and pointed down, killing a trainee so they decided not to give us this training. I was then sent to the Army hospital at Ft. Lewis, Washington and given a ward in the hospital to care for.

I reported into the hospital as the only one in civilian clothes. My brother had given me $300 dollars to buy uniforms but I had spent it on a diamond ring for Marian. The executive officer was unhappy with me but had them advance me a month's pay and sent me to get uniforms in Portland. On my return, still in civies, I was walking along the perimeter fence to the gate and I saw a soldier trying to climb the fence as he was late back from leave. He said, "Can you boost up my leg, buddy?" and I helped him get over the fence. Later I wondered what he would have done if he had known I was an officer on the post.

After I had been there a month, I applied for a two week leave to get married. Surprisingly, it was granted. We spent our honeymoon at a ski resort near Mt. Rainier and I skied for the first time. Marian wanted a picture but said I never was upright long enough to get one. When I reported back to Ft. Lewis, all of my group had been sent to Europe. They were opening a new general hospital at Ft. Lewis, so kept me there for three months. I was put in charge of a ward of soldiers with sulfa resistant gonorrhea. I had to get a positive smear and culture and prostate sample before they could be put on penicillin. It took longer to do this than to cure them and get them back to duty.

During this time we rented a small house on Tillicum Lake, across the highway from Ft. Lewis. It had a wood burning cook stove and I had to cut wood for the day each morning. I had had a knee injury in high school and it bothered me with running. I was sent to a consulting hospital for evaluation and they said surgery was an option but not really necessary. I didn't want surgery so they placed me on limited duty status and sent me back to work.

Then I was ordered to San Francisco for staging and sent to New Caledonia on the SS General Howes, a troop transport. It took us three weeks and the officers slept on the deck as there was no air conditioning. The men had to stay below where it was very hot and uncomfortable. We had a big ceremony when we crossed the equator. We had to climb a ladder and jump into a tank of water. I caught my finger in the ladder and tore the ligament in my left ring finger. My finger is still deformed. This was my first war injury.

When we docked in New Caledonia, there were many natives on the dock. They were very dark with lots of fuzzy hair. However, the hair was orange on top. We had quite a number of black troops on board and I remember one saying to another, "Look at that two tone Negro."

I was assigned to the 8th station hospital which was a field hospital getting troops and supplies for the New Guinea campaign. This hospital had been in the Pacific for some time, having moved to New Caledonia from Bora-Bora. There were many cases of filariasis on Bora Bora. Some had swollen legs and swollen scrotums so large that they need to carry them in a barrow.

There wasn't a lot for us to do on New Caledonia, so a couple of us were sent over to a troop training unit. We had to do the marches with them and lectured to them on first aid and other medical topics.

After six or eight weeks on New Caledonia our unit was ordered back to Hawaii since they had been in the Pacific so long. Even though I was new, I went with the unit. The doctors were to fly and we left in a two engine flying boat. We lost an engine and a lot of altitude but made the island that was our next stop. Instead of merely refueling, we were there three days while they worked on the engine. Taking off again, the engine failed a half hour out and we returned for another week. They then put us on a larger, four engine seaplane and we finally reached Pearl.

Our group was assigned to Maui and we went over by ship with all our gear and equipment. We made a hospital out of a school we took over and took care of the fourth Marine division that was recently back from Saipan. The casualties had mostly been cared for so we did day to day care. I was sent to a small building where there were 75 Marines with hepatitis. There were also a couple Navy doctors but I was the commanding officer. I had had hepatitis in high school with some jaundice so didn't get infected again. When the jaundice cases went back to duty, I returned to the main hospital and was then sent with two other doctors to examine recruits.

My father died in Idaho about this time. He had surgery for colon cancer and died of a massive stroke two days postoperative. I received a month leave and flew to San Francisco and then trained to Idaho. Marian was teaching women's physical education at the College of Idaho and we were able to spend time together. I was then sent back. By this time I had been promoted to Captain.

Six months later my stepmother was terminal with colon cancer and I had another leave. My leave started the day the war ended and I was in Pearl Harbor with all the whistles and rocket going off in Honolulu. I left the next day. Again, I had a month and when it was nearly over I tried to get a post in the US until my discharge but was refused and sent back to Hawaii. I was sent back on the USS Bunker Hill, an aircraft carrier that was transporting replacement troops to the Pacific. We left Seattle and went to San Francisco. As we pulled in there were rockets, bands, and whistles. They thought the ship was bringing back veterans from the Pacific. On the way to Hawaii, we played games on the flight deck.

Playing volleyball, I ran into another player and cracked the head of the radius. It was not displaced but was painful and I wore a sling for several weeks. My second military injury.

There wasn't much to do in Hawaii but they said families could come out if one signed up for six more months. I had been applying for residencies and didn't want to extend so Marian decided to come on her own and had a cabin on the S.S.Lurline. I received orders back and called her just before she was to leave so she didn't get to Hawaii. My first acceptance for training was in Baltimore but they wanted me immediately and I couldn't get back. Later I was accepted at Ball Hospital in Muncie, Indiana. I got home just in time to pack for Muncie. Getting settled there, we were looking for a house. An agent asked if I wanted a modern house but I didn't care. When he showed us houses, it seems that a modern house was one with an inside bathroom rather than an outhouse.

AN ARMY NURSE IN POW CAMPS
Dorothy M. Jenkins

When I graduated as an RN from Prairie View College in Texas, I was excited about volunteering in the armed forces. I had just turned 21, the youngest age for entry into the services as a nurse. My application to the Navy was rejected with the polite reply, "We regret that we are not accepting Negro nurses in the Navy." In October 1944, I was accepted by the Army, commissioned as a 2nd Lieutenant, and sent to Camp McCoy near La Crosse, Wisconsin for basic training. This was the most beautiful country that I had ever seen. There were eleven other Negro nurses, and the people there were especially kind to us. We had courses in ward and clinic management, control of respiratory and intestinal diseases, and chemical warfare as well as drill and physical training. The Army sent a news item and photo of us to the newspaper in my hometown in Oklahoma. Mine was returned with the suggestion to seek publication in a Negro newspaper. I did.

Following basic training our group was sent to a Negro army base at Fort Huachuca near Phoenix, Arizona. After a short time our group was enlarged and transferred to the Camp San Luis Obispo Station Hospital where Japanese and Italian prisoners of war were being held. Nursing was routine with very few acute or serious conditions. Prisoners were fed nutritious food and appeared contented.

The nurses were invited to a weekly dinner by the friendly Italians. They served Italian cuisine and entertained us with music and song. This was the highlight of our very limited social life. One day, being curious about the Officers' Club, I went to check it out. A courteous Warrant Officer showed me around, but I was soon aware that the other officers were glaring at me and passing very close to me. The very next day the head nurse, a Negro, called the nurses in and told us that we were not to go to the Club. Someone had notified the Commander of the camp of my visit; thereupon he got the word to the Supervising Nurse. "You make the white officers and their wives uncomfortable."

Soon after I was transferred to Papago Park, south of Phoenix, a hot and very desolate place. This POW camp for Germans was staffed by white physicians and a few enlisted men. It was very clear that there was more acceptance of the German prisoners of war than of the Negro nurses. A number of the German prisoners were professionals and were working in the hospital along with us. We observed social and friendly relationships between the whites and the POWs, but were keenly aware of the subtle hostility to the Negroes. Of course we served all patients: giving injections, working on the general and surgical wards, delivering white babies, and assisting in the operating room.

I had a very frightening encounter at a football game in Phoenix. My civilian friends and I soon became aware that a group of white enlisted men sitting below kept turning around and looking up at us. Then one of them said, "I'm going to snatch those damn bars off her shoulders." As he made the move to do so he was wrestled back by the others. I stayed in place for the whole game.

My two and a half years of service as an Army nurse did not leave me with good memories. I was promoted to 1st Lieutenant in November 1945. After discharge in January 1947, I took advantage of the GI Bill to enroll at UC Berkeley and continue my education to become a Public Health nurse.

AIRCRAFT CARRIER DENTIST
John Hazlett

I started dental school in 1939. I was out of school one year with amebic dysentery, acquired in Chicago when I went to the world's fair. The outbreak was traced to defective piping in the Congress Hotel, where a sewer pipe leaked into the water supply. I also had undulant fever at the same time.

When the Navy started the V-12 program in the summer of 1943 I was taken into the Navy as an apprentice seaman. Because they had to work with people, the V12(S) students, medical, dental, and chaplain, were given midshipman type uniforms instead of the usual Navy enlisted uniforms. No one knew exactly what we were. When I graduated, I was commissioned as a reserve lieutenant, junior grade, and sent to work in the dental clinic at Great Lakes Naval Station near Chicago. I liked the Navy so applied for a regular commission and some months later was accepted. They then sent me to Bethesda Naval Hospital for Navy training for three months. This included a week at Quantico Marine Base where we were familiarized and qualified with weapons.

At Bethesda we rotated through different specialties. When I was working the periodontal chair, an older man came in with a filthy mouth and teeth. I told him to go back and brush his teeth, then return. He did so and I later found out this was Admiral Byrd, the polar explorer. He was in the hospital for mononucleosis and it affected his mouth.

After the course, I was ordered to the USS Cabot, a CVL or light aircraft carrier. These were small carriers, built on cruiser hulls when the demand for carriers was great. The Cabot was at Hunter's Point Naval Shipyard in San Francisco for overhaul. I spent two months working at the shipyard dental clinic, providing care to the crew of the Cabot. When overhaul was completed, we sailed to Hawaii and then on to Enewetak in company with the battleship USS Pennsylvania which had come out of overhaul at the same time. The Pennsylvania used her big guns and our planes strafed the Japanese held Wake Island as we went by. Later it was known that only a few people, mostly civilians, were left so we didn't do much at Wake toward winning the war.

The Cabot had a reputation for the best radar in the fleet and in their previous engagements had been very successful in directing the downing of enemy planes. Those in the crew who worked with radar felt that the new radar installed at the overhaul wasn't as good as the one they had previously used. We anchored at Einewetak where the fleet was to gather for the invasion of Japan. We were there about 10 days and the atom bombs were dropped and the war was over.

The Cabot was scheduled to come into Tokyo Bay for the surrender but one of the other carriers, assigned to provide air cover outside Tokyo, was withdrawn and we were ordered to replace them. However the admirals didn't think there were enough planes as the Cabot only had 34 and we were sent up to the China Sea, along the Korean coast. This area was supplied by the British and we were loaded up with Australian mutton.

The story of the other carrier's withdrawal was told by the medical personnel. One oiler kept coming to sick bay complaining of gaining weight. He didn't seem heavier on the scales but felt he was having increasing difficulty passing a narrow place between the engines. Finally somebody checked the area and found that the weight of the planes was warping the ship and the area was getting narrower. The ship was sent to Guam for repairs and reinforcement.

After VJ day there were two severe hurricanes in the Pacific. In one of them the officers had calculated that the ship could stand a 39 degree roll. When it reached 37 degrees, the captain left the ordered course and went to one that seemed to be less taxing on the ship. When we returned to Okinawa later, the only damage was about $10 worth to a steel door. Two other larger carriers who had changed course to pick up our survivors had severe damage to flight decks, up in the millions of dollar range.

During the typhoon, a signalman was sent out on the bridge to check the signal flags in case the ship was in danger. While he was opening the signals bag the ship took a severe roll and he and the flag bag fell overboard. He couldn't swim but was able to keep afloat with his life vest and the signal bag. He released the emergency marker dye in his life vest and he was picked up by one of the following destroyers.

The Cabot had been designed with only room for one dental office. However more people were aboard than had been expected and two dentists were assigned. We worked from 6:30 AM to 8:30 PM, alternating work. Thus I had periods of freedom and was able to watch flight operations. Once they put me in an F6F fighter and showed me all the instruments and controls. Then the air officer announced that I was trained and could now take off. I course, I wasn't able to fly and didn't try. The Cabot had no heavier planes; dive or torpedo bombers but had two types of fighters: the F6F Grumman Hellcat and the F4U Vought Corsair. The heavier Corsairs were able to carry some bombs if needed.

The plank owner Captain of the Cabot had been very well liked and had run an outstanding ship. He was promoted to Admiral at the time of the overhaul. The new Captain was opinionated and changed things just to be different. The crew didn't like the new Captain much. His executive officer was a very good leader and partly made up for the Captain. When the war was over, he had been at sea for seven years.

As the junior dental officer, I was given the additional duty of being treasurer of the officers' mess. I was supposed to collect the charges each month. In practice, I just noted to the supply officer who deducted it from the officers' pay. Enlisted men are provided food by the Navy. Officers are not and must buy their own. The Navy provides cooks and messmen. At sea we merely bought what the supply officer had but ashore we could get other things. A Committee decided what they would like and I was supposed to get it. Actually, I had an excellent chief petty officer and he did most of the shopping and supervision. The Captain doesn't eat at the officers' mess in the wardroom but has his own mess and cook.

I was responsible for the cleaning of the wardroom and officers' quarters. The messmen also had the additional duty of cleaning the officers' area and quarters. Once the Captain had them call, "Junior dental officer to the bridge." On arrival, he wanted me to have someone clean up the cigarette butts around the door of his cabin. Some of the crew lived very close to the dental office. The bunks were 4 high. In junior officers quarters, we had three to a room.

The hanger deck was an exclusive area. This was where the planes were stored and serviced when they weren't flying. No one went there, unless he had duties in that area.

After the end of the war we were sent home to Philadelphia from the China Sea via Hawaii, San Diego, and the Panama Canal. I was on the party designated to mothball the ship. One of our engineers did much of the designing of mothballing and I did the medical spaces. He wrote a manual on mothballing and I contributed a few pages about the medical areas on the ship.

When the ship was mothballed, I was ordered to Notre Dame University. They had a V-5 Naval pilot training program. We thought it was to be a few weeks but they decided to complete the present class and it was kept open for six months. I provided dental care for the students and staff. One of the students there was Henry Ford II. His father Edsel had died and he was discharged to take charge of the Ford Motor Company. I examined his mouth as part of his discharge examination. He had several gold foil fillings, an expensive and time consuming technique that most dentists don't have time for.

I was kept there partly because our second son was due and I didn't want to go back to sea before he arrived. Then I was ordered to Hawaii, which then counted as overseas duty. I was at Megrew Point. This was a small point aimed at Ford Island. It was named after a merchant captain who had his home there. He had interested the Navy in having a base at Pearl Harbor many years before.

The Navy had built a hospital on the Point, mostly Quonset huts, planned for the casualties of Iwo Jima. However, the hospital ships at Iwo were able to handle the problems and the hospital had never been used. Parts of it were being used as an outpatient service and I worked here for two years. I then decided to resign from the regular Navy and was sent back to Great Lakes Navy Station for separation.

CHAPTER 10

THE HOME GUARD

Of the nearly ten million people who served in the US military during World War II, only between 15 and 20% were actually engaged in combat. There were many soldiers and sailors who never left the United States. Some may have appreciated this, but others were very unhappy not to be able actually to use their training against an enemy. Some felt their time was wasted while others did extremely important jobs and could provide greater service than those in overseas positions.

Some of those remaining in the country had been exempted because of their civilian work and were later drafted and then sent back to their previous jobs, now as military personnel. Others were commissioned because it made administration or security easier. Ranks were extremely variable, with enlisted PhDs working for "ninety day wonder" officers or holding extremely important positions that they had previously held as civilians.

Some of those staying in the country were involved in training of others, while some were in training themselves and didn't finish in time to participate in a more active way.

Although inducted into the Army as a private, Dean Bowman worked for the OSS (the Office of Strategic Services, which later became the CIA) and ended the war in command of an OSS field training office with a dozen trainers, many academic professors, and ninety Naval officers in training.

Bob Pay wanted to come to California, so he shopped the services until he found a placement there. He then developed his own niche in the local unit publication, so that he had interesting work throughout the war.

Henry Meyer was an historian who was recruited as an analyst for the OSS. Later he was commissioned as an Ensign in the Navy but continued in essentially the same job.

Sam Atkins worked with the group that broke the Japanese naval code and thus warned of the Midway attack, leading to the American victory at the battle of Midway. He gives an introduction to the techniques that were used to get access to the information of the codes.

Jack Keyser was an aircraft engineer but was offered a Signal Corps commission. He was trained in radar and had expected to be involved in maintenance. However, he was assigned to a group that was to write manuals, both for use and maintenance of the radar. This job lasted through the war as by the time the work was complete, new and improved radars became available and the manuals had to be updated.

Newell Johnson was first assigned to the Army Chemical Corps but then transferred to the Sanitary Corps where he was able to use his microbiological experience in working with bacteriological warfare. He contracted and was cured of anthrax during that time.

Cleve Turner was a Marine who was given officer training. He completed it just in time for VJ day.

WORLD WAR II IN THE OSS
Dean O. Bowman
In 1937 and '38, like most people, I had few thoughts of war. I was beginning my career as a teaching fellow at the University of Michigan, spending the '39-'40 year as a Fellow at the Brookings Institution in Washington, D.C, followed by a year of teaching economics at Purdue. In April of 1941 the University of Michigan awarded me a Ph.D. and an offer to join their economics department. Then, as everywhere, the Pearl Harbor attack on December 7th created a huge emergency.

Almost immediately the University's President (in a meeting during which he disclosed the huge losses the nation had suffered) offered leave of absence status to those faculty members going into war work or the military. I requested leave and applied for a job as an economist in the war effort.

Early in 1942 I was assigned by the Office of Price Administration (OPA) to its Chicago Metropolitan Office, but this was quickly changed to the OPA's Regional Office. This office supervised price administration for Illinois, Minnesota, Wisconsin, North and South Dakota, Iowa, and Nebraska.

In late 1943 I was drafted and sent to the Quartermaster Corps at Fort Lee, Virginia, for basic training. There were many shocks in basic training. One in particular was my great surprise at receiving only 43 cents at the end of my first month. This was my pay after deductions for insurance, bonds, and the amounts sent home to my wife and my parents.

One morning as I laboriously practiced typing, an officer came in and said, "You're being sent to Washington. Go to your barracks, pack your gear, and you'll leave on the train tomorrow."

I said, "Where do I report in Washington?"

He replied, "You'll get your orders tomorrow." I did, and they said, "Report to the OSS in Washington." (OSS meant Office of Strategic Services. It later became the CIA.) The OSS dealt with intelligence and espionage. I was assigned to the Research and Analysis Section of its Far East Division.

My first assignment was to read intercepts which concerned cargoes from all over East Asia destined for Japan. Another assignment, much more important, was to figure out Japan's production of aircraft based on the amount of bauxite being imported. (Bauxite yields alumina, which yields aluminum.) By then I had received a field promotion to officer status, which greatly facilitated my interviews with experts.

In late '44 a Joint Target Group was formed. There were about thirty-five members: eight of us from OSS, eight from the Office of Naval Intelligence, eight from Air Force Intelligence, and eight from G2, which was Army Intelligence, plus support personnel. This group was formed to select bombing targets in Japan, with the objective of destroying their economy. I was assigned to work on oil and chemicals, which by that time were in desperately short supply. B-29 bombers were now rolling off the assembly lines and they were bombing sites such as Japanese rail yards, fuel storage areas, and engine factories. Knowing from my previous assignment what havoc submarine warfare had already caused on Japanese imports, I thought the bombing of oil and chemical facilities was probably not a high priority and so reported.

In early 1945 my boss said, "Pack for California!" I was sent to command the 'Outpost' located at the Presidio of Monterey. (Outpost was the name applied to an OSS working office.) At the Presidio preparations were being made for the invasion of Japan. There were twelve OSS people on my staff, many of them former professors. There were historians, geographers, and political science people. There were also ninety Navy officers assigned to OSS who would be participating in the invasion, and my staff was to provide information to them. We had no knowledge then of the atomic bomb, and it was assumed an invasion would be necessary. The invasion was scheduled for November 1st and would go ashore on the southernmost island of Kyushu. Official estimates at the time said there would be 125,000 casualties in the first month.

The atom bomb was dropped, and that changed everything. On August 14th Japan surrendered. On that day my secretary and I were en route to San Francisco. Stopping for gas, we heard the news. The attendant said, "Go back! You can't get to San Francisco. The streets are filled with people! "

Within a month I flew back to Washington, D.C., and was processed out of the OSS and out of the Army and immediately became the price executive for the regional OPA office in Chicago. About a year later I had a call from my former OSS boss. He was now with the State Department, working to help Japan's economy recover. I found his job offer interesting. After helping to pick bombing targets in Japan, I would now at State help to formulate policies to get Japan's economy back on track!

In reflecting on what kinds of lessons the war years provided, four emerged that command attention.

A. Direct price controls are sometimes necessary, and they can and do work. From 1942 to 1947 the Consumer Price Index moved about six points, which meant that prices moved up hardly at all. This in turn signaled tremendous savings for the citizens of the country. More importantly it meant indirectly that the military got the materials they needed to fight the war.

B. The aluminum example cited above demonstrates how intelligence information can be used successfully. The best post-war estimate was that we were about 90% correct on our aluminum/aircraft production figures. Current developments in technology with respect to information will enhance the intelligence work of the future,

C. In retrospect it seems to be increasingly clear that the all-out bombing of Japan was probably not needed. Apart from the atom bomb, the Japanese economy was on its knees by reason of the US submarine warfare. At the time, however, we were so bent upon destroying that economy that we spared nothing.

D. The resurgence of the Japanese, Russian, and German economies all attest to the resiliency of social institutions and their great capacity to recover from disasters. Although the war enabled tremendous technical progress, war is a terrible waste.

HOW I MADE MY MILITARY CAREER
Robert Pay
Children often learn by listening to or watching their fathers. I did that somewhat in reverse. As I was growing up I often heard my father complain of the cold weather we endured in wintertime in Kentucky. Every year he made plans to move the family to the warmer climes of Florida, and every year he found reasons to postpone the journey. The result: my father spent his entire life fantasizing life in Florida and I developed a determination to leave the cold of Kentucky as soon as I was old enough and not to put off making the move as my father had done so often.

As I grew older my goal was to go west to California instead of south to Florida. My only problem was a lack of money. The December 7, 1941, attack on Pearl Harbor by the Japanese changed that. Uncle Sam was prompt in requesting my services via the draft and I reasoned that selective volunteering would probably result in my being sent to California for basic training in some branch of the service.

My first stop was at a Naval recruiting station in Louisville, Ky. The recruiter there welcomed me with open arms and promised rapid advancement following basic training at the Great Lakes Naval Training Station in Evanston, Illinois. Now Evanston, Illinois, is even colder than Kentucky so I promptly declined and sought out the Marine recruiter. Again I was promised rapid advancement in rank following training at Camp LeJeune, South Carolina. But South Carolina was even farther away from California than Kentucky and held no attraction whatsoever. Once again I declined to enhance the Marine Corps by my presence and I set out to continue my search for some type of military future in California.

Determined to keep my feet on the ground, I avoided the Air Force altogether. I thought that if I volunteered in the Army instead of waiting to be drafted I might have a better chance of getting a desired assignment. The Army was happy to see me as a potential volunteer and promised great military advancement through the ranks. But first I would have to leave the civilian habits behind me with a little bit of Army training. Where? At Fort Knox, Kentucky, of course. Having already been to Fort Knox and having no desire to return, I thanked them and quickly departed.

It began to appear as though I had exhausted my options without any success when a Coast Guard Recruiting station appeared on the horizon. Following my usual pattern of inquiring about enlisting, I was told that despite my college degree and eagerness to destroy the wicked Jap, no officer candidate positions were waiting to be filled and only apprentice seamen were being accepted. Almost totally deflated, but curious as to training locations, I asked where these hapless enlistees were sent for six weeks of boot camp. The answer to my question determined my future for the next three years of my life.

Coast Guard inductees from the Louisville, Ky. recruiting station were sent either to Baton Rouge, Louisiana, or Alameda, California. The magic word "California" held sway over my visit to that Coast Guard desk and I did not leave until I learned all the details and tricks of enlistment which could guarantee my inclusion in the next California contingent.

Departure date soon arrived and I together with about thirty other civilians boarded the train bound for San Francisco where we would be met by Coast Guard personnel for the short journey to Government Island in Alameda, California.

Six weeks at Boot Camp is a disaster regardless of location, even on the French Riviera, but spending six weeks on Government Island is like a year's exile in Hell. After my time was up, I was ready for anything, even an enlistment in the Foreign Legion. A few days passed and I discovered a line of hopeful escapees in front of one of the cells (or buildings). Thinking this meant a possible assignment elsewhere, I joined the group. Upon inquiry I learned that those of us in the line were volunteering for assignment to a horse patrol which was being formed to ride up and down the California coast looking for Japanese submarines. My eagerness to escape the confines of Government Island coupled with my Kentucky Bluegrass and Kentucky Derby background turned out to be sufficient to qualify me for the job. I was loaded onto a waiting truck for transportation to a Receiving Station located on North Beach near Fisherman's Wharf in San Francisco.

Fortune soon smiled on me because a note posted on the bulletin board led me to a young man who had started a publication for the unit only. He found out that the job called for more expertise than he was able to offer. My background in civilian and college life enabled me to save a project for its originator and at the same time create a position for myself. Assignment to Headquarters Company soon followed and the horse patrol never knew what it missed.

Beginning with the second edition, I became the Assistant Editor of the Barracks Watch, the official publication of the Coast Guard's Captain of the Port Battalion. The horse patrol, now a distant memory, was replaced by a typewriter and a telephone, and I began creating a job for myself within the Coast Guard structure. The job grew in areas of responsibility as the Coast Guard unit grew. I soon became a sort of Athletic Director, the correspondent for four daily newspapers of San Francisco, captain and general manager of the Coast Guard tennis team, and a general recruiter for the baseball and football teams. Our office also served as a liaison between the men of the battalion and the Chaplain's office as well as that of the Commanding Officer.

As I settled in to the myriad duties of the position that I had created for myself, I took advantage of free gangway, allowing me to come and go as I needed. My work day began at 8:00 a.m. and ended at 4:00 p.m., with weekends off. This schedule enabled me to resume civilian activities of coaching junior baseball and basketball and serving as gym instructor for the San Francisco Boys Club.

This work and play schedule which I have described lasted until the war was over and on October 20, 1945, I was discharged from the service. In the three years I served I got no commission as I had been promised by the Army, the Navy, and Marines, but I made it to California courtesy of the U.S. Government and wound up in a job I was good at and one which I thoroughly enjoyed.

HENRY CORD MEYER, OSS ANALYST

Dr. Henry Meyer was writing his story for this volume when he developed an acute lymphoid tumor and expired within a few weeks. His wife, Helen, summarized his notes with an apology for not being able to fill in the extra stories that he would have told.

In the late summer of 1941 Henry received a call from a professor at Yale, now on leave to the newly formed Research and Analysis Branch of the Coordinator of Information (COI) established on July 11th by President Roosevelt and headed by Col. "Big" Bill Donovan. By October Henry and 100 other scholars from Harvard, Yale, Princeton, Duke, Michigan etc. were at work in Washington. Initially there were three topics; intentions of Japan, the situation in Iberia and in North Africa, and the problem of our exposed right rear in South America. After Pearl Harbor, the pace increased and there was a constant demand for research and analysis reports on additional areas.

By August of 1942 Henry wrote a friend, "I can tell you now that since early summer our office has been taking part in the preparations for the North African campaign. Of course, we did not know the exact date for its beginning, but I can say that I have been following events there with a real degree of intimacy! Stories are now appearing in the newspapers that passed through my hands half a year ago. You would be amazed to know of the scope and intensity of our activities in Africa."

In June of 1942, the COI was reorganized and became the OSS - Office of Strategic Services - under the Joint Chiefs of Staff. The plans for the invasion of Sicily, Sardinia, and at Salerno on the mainland of Italy were next worked on by the Mediterranean Division that Henry was assigned to. By 1943, most civilians had been given commissions or army ratings and many had received the standard 6 weeks of training as did Henry, an Ensign in the Navy with basic training at

Princeton. His only ship experience was on a dry-docked ship in Baltimore. However he learned the flag signals, Morse code, celestial navigation, and survival techniques. By then many documents needed for research and analysis had been classified and military rank was needed to use them.

In June of 1944 Henry was transferred to San Francisco, given gas coupons to drive because train travel was needed for troop transport, and charged with interviewing European refugees along the coast in search of useful information. He visited military bases including the one on Catalina Island and made contact with professors at Berkeley and Stanford who had subcontracted with the OSS for special projects.

In 1945 he returned to Washington and after V-J day was demobilized, having decided not to make a career with the OSS.

BREAKING THE JAPANESE CODE
Sam Atkins

This is taken from a talk that Sam Atkins gave at the Gardens. He is deceased and use of the material from his talk is courtesy of his wife Jeannette.

How come the rags and tatters of the American Pacific fleet managed to pull off the victory at Midway within 6 months after having been practically obliterated? There were miscalculations and mistakes made by the Japanese, American luck, and skill and bravery in the American fleet but there is another part. This is little known and understood and seldom mentioned: the Navy's radio-intelligence establishment. At the start of the war, this consisted of 700 officers and men. Two thirds were engaged in radio intercept and direction finding at various stations. Some were in the US, at Cheltenham, MD and Bainbridge Island, WA, while others were found in such places as Guam and Corregidor.

The intercept operators were trained in Japanese Morse code. Direction finding allows one to fix the location of a ship and by repeated fixes, to trace its course. Such findings form the base of "traffic analysis", a valuable technique of intelligence gathering. This deduces the lines of command of military or naval forces by determining which radios talk to which. Since military operations are usually accompanied by an increase in communications, traffic analysis by watching the volume of traffic can make pretty accurate guesses as to how soon an operation is going to start and how big and where it will be.

The other one third of the radio intelligence personnel were engaged in cryptanalysis and translation. Even before Pearl Harbor, the Navy was beginning an expansion in this whole area, making a particular effort to draft individuals from university faculties. I was recruited in the summer of 1941 and began taking a correspondence course in elementary cryptanalysis. Three months after Pearl Harbor I was called to active duty as a lieutenant (jg). Without any orientation course, I was put to work immediately in the main Navy building on Constitution Ave. in Washington. In the course of the next year and a half a lot of academics appeared on the scene. Among those I worked with were two psychologists from Temple University, 3 English professors and one in philosophy from the Univ. of Virginia, a classicist and a modern language specialist from Princeton, classicists from Bryn Mawr and Brown. Also represented were Harvard, Chicago, and Georgetown. Many bright fresh graduates from Wellsley, Smith, Mt. Holyoke, Radcliff, Vassar, and similar schools were recruited.

Charles Scribner, Jr., later the president of Scribners, was in the group. He and I played a lot of chess. Mine never amounted to anything but the discipline helped the current work and also my bridge. We also had with us for a short time the bridge and poker expert Oswald Jacoby. He soon went to the Honolulu communications unit where he spent most of his time playing cards with admirals and captains, to his considerable profit.

Although our group was heavily academic and a bunch of amateurs, there were other professional types. I remember a navy chief petty officer. He had never finished high school and smoked five packs of cigarettes a day. He was far brighter than any of the rest and made many important discoveries. Another was Lt (jg) Francis Raven who worked on the reconstruction of the famous purple machine before December 7. This allowed us to read the Japanese diplomatic code before and all through the war.

However, our concern was JN-25 Baker, the code and superenciphering system used by the main Japanese fleet. We learned after the war that the Japanese called it Naval Code D. This was first placed in use on December 1, 1940. On December 4, 1941 they changed the superenciphering system but not the code. Up to that time, with a very small crew, the Navy had been able to recover some of the Baker code and read some parts of a few messages but it was a hit or miss business. With our own fleet now more than half destroyed, it became imperative for us to learn everything we could about their strategy and tactics; the principal source of such information was obviously JN-25 Baker.

Let me show you the problem our unit faced. JN-25 was a five digit code, i.e., each code group was made up of five numbers. Of the 100,000 possible groups, only those divisible by three (one third of the total) were assigned Japanese meanings. There was an encode volume where the arrangement is according to the Japanese semantic units; ideograms, katakana characters, phrases, numbers, punctuation marks and even English letters are included. The decode volume had the same information with the code groups arranged in numerical order. Every ship and station had both volumes.

The 33,000 were not enough so they added 12,000 more by setting aside several numbers which meant "begin auxiliary table" and others "end auxiliary table". The numbers divisible by three between 00003 and 36000 were given second meanings. If these numbers were preceded by a "begin" number and followed by an "end" number, they had meaning two. This increased the number of usable meanings to 45,000 groups. An example, using English meanings is:

00624   23199   18723   64113   00624   23199   18723   79026
destroyer dead   ahead   begin at   depart   port   0600   end at

The purpose of divisibility by three was to make it easy for the receiver to identify a garbled group immediately, if there was an error by the encoding clerk or the sending or receiving radio operator. The stages of message preparation:

1.   Write out message.

BMH carrier 5 destroyers proceeding south from beginat A T T U endat stop change course and intercept

2.   Rewrite to conceal true beginning of message.

course and intercept BMH carrier 5 destroyers proceeding south from beginat A T T U endat stop change

3.   Look up the 5-digit groups in the encode book and write under the text.

course   and   intercept   BMH   carrier   5   destroyers proceeding
48201 35106 74220   92448   88800   21609   00624   63621
south from   beginat   A   T   T   U   endat stop   change
22293 06312 55770   00069 21213   21213 15630 67221 98151 65712

4.   Now the message is encoded but the next step is to conceal the code. Every station and ship also had a 1000 page volume containing 100,000 5-digit groups, a hundred to a page. The encoder picked a page (example 001) and a starting point (row 6, column 3) and then wrote the sequence of groups under the above code groups. These numbers were called additives. Then the two numbers were added, without carrying when above nine. The bottom line is the superenciphered, encoded message, then sent by radio to the addressee. At the beginning the starting point was set down twice and enciphered by two additives from a special list held by all stations.

course   and   intercept BMH   carrier   5   destroyers
00163 00163 48201   35106 74220   92448   88800   21609 00624
77251 36428 11047   55250 45486   24740   44296   81678 63093
77314 36581 59248   80356 19606   16188   22096   38198 63617

proceeding south from   beginat   A   T   T   U   endat
63621   22293 06312 55770 00069 21213 21213 15630 67221
59419   27844 75724 13371 88731 31068 38311 49964 68693
12030   49037 71036 68041 88790 52271 59524 54564 25814

stop   change
98151   65712
71466   07791
69517   62403

This system is designed to prevent the code groups themselves from ever being seen by anyone not having a copy of the additive volume. If you can't see a code group there should be no way to even guess its meaning. Actually there are ways of getting hold of code groups. Humans make errors, particularly under wartime pressure. Occasionally a code clerk would send out the wrong line, not the enciphered line but either the line of code groups or the line of additives. A line of additives would not be recognizable but a sequence of code groups would be recognizable because they would all be divisible by three. As soon as 15 or more code groups were available we were on our way to eventually breaking the system.

Try to visualize the wartime scene! Hundreds and hundreds of ships and stations were communicating with each other constantly. In some weeks, thousands of messages were sent, all using the same 1000 page additive book. A station in Japan might have sent a 100 group message to a destroyer in the Solomons, using additives beginning on page 054, row 8, column 7 and going to page 055, row 7, column 6. Two days later, a cruiser might have sent a 70 group message to a troop ship, starting at Page 055, row 3, column 0 and going to row 9, column 9. Parts of both messages would have used the same additives. As time passed, parts of several other messages would use the same additives. In a couple months, most of the 100,000 additives would have been used more than once, often six or more times. By making a difference table of the known code groups and applying it to the mathematically handled groups, eventually the additive could be obtained.

By May 1941, 80 to 90 % of the 100,000 additives had been recovered, the translators were recovering the meanings of the code groups and we were reading in toto more than 90% of the messages. The result was that we knew of the Japanese Midway attack plan, the diversionary attack in the Aleutians, the locations of various fleet units, and the date in June, 1942 of the assault. This was crucial to the favorable result at Midway.

After Midway, there was a large expansion of communications intelligence. In Washington, the Navy bought the Mt. Vernon School for Girls and added new buildings and a high chain fence. For the rest of the war, work went on here 24 hours every day, with Marine guard protection.

Shortly after Midway, the Japanese changed JN-25 Baker to JN-25 Charlie and in August changed the additive book. There was a long period of not reading the code, during the time of the Guadalcanal operation. A code book was captured on Guadalcanal and recovery of additives quickened so that by late October we were back in business. Throughout the war, the Japanese changed codes and additive books but always made stupid mistakes so that we could break in. We provided information that assisted the invasions of Tarawa, Kwajalein, Eniwetak, and Saipan. It was also important in the battle of the Philippine Sea and the battle of Leyte Gulf, where the Japanese Navy was shattered, never to be effective again.

One episode illustrates the firepower of the communications unit. In early April, 1943 we read a message giving the schedule of a trip to be made on April 18 from Rabaul to Bougainville by Admiral Yamamoto. On that day P-38 fighters from Henderson Field on Guadalcanal shot down his plane over Bougainville. On May 21 the Japanese radio announced his death and he was given a state funeral in Tokyo.

The U. S. Navy read 75 Naval codes, including JN-25 versions and JN-10, the merchant shipping code. The information given to our submarines was so accurate that by the end of the war they had almost completely destroyed the Japanese merchant marine.

In spite of the results, some admirals and others mistrusted communications intelligence. However, the authorities felt otherwise and in March, 1946 all personnel in this intelligence were awarded the Navy Unit Commendation, the first time for any land based unit.

RADAR MANUALS
Jack Keyser

My experience with the Army really began the summer after I graduated from Cal Tech in 1940. I had my degree in Electrical Engineering and a job, but the Air Corps was seeking people willing to join the Air Corps and take a course in weather forecasting from the country's foremost scientific weatherman, Professor Krick, at Caltech. The attraction was that this would lead to an MS degree paid for by the Army. Also, we all pretty much knew that war was coming and this could be getting in on the ground floor with a commission.

A friend and classmate, Bill Stone, was going to take the course anyway, and he was applying to the Air Corps to have it paid for. He didn't really expect to be accepted since he was near sighted and literally had a hole in his head behind his ear from a childhood mastoid operation. Why not since he was taking the course anyway? I decided if he could do it, so could I.

We both flunked the army physical although Caltech accepted me. I flunked my physical because I was near sighted and the Air Corps didn't accept anybody at that time that couldn't qualify as a pilot, no matter what their job was to be. Bill also flunked the physical, but he went ahead to get his master degree, expecting to pay for it himself. I dropped the whole idea, but after classes started in the fall, the Air Corps suddenly realized that Bill was somebody they couldn't afford not to have since he was already taking the course and they needed him in spite of his physical shortcomings. He was an excellent choice. After he went on active duty he found himself in the Manhattan Project and ended the War as a Brigadier General.

I eventually became an Engineer at Vega Aircraft and among other things was involved with the production of B-17 bombers at their Burbank plant. December 7, 1941, Pearl Harbor, brought the war effort at Vega to a fever pitch, but in January 1942 I met Leta Frances Weaver. We managed to find time to see each other, became engaged on Valentine day, and were married May 16, 1942.

We lived happily in a duplex on Dixon Street in Glendale and I was resigned to having my war efforts restricted to being an aircraft engineer at Vega, but in early January of 1943, I received a surprise offer of a commission in the Signal Corps. Apparently my earlier application was screened again and the Signal Corps decided that nearsightedness was no drawback for them. Leta was a bit miffed that I had not told her about my application to the Air Corps, but I had completely forgotten about it. I don't think she really believed me. In any event, I accepted and was commissioned as a 2nd lieutenant in the Signal Corps on January 10, 1943.

I reported for active duty at Fort Monmouth, NJ on January 20 and was given two and a half months of officer's training. Basic officer's training was similar to regular basic training, except not as long or as rigorous. We did learn to be officers. At the end of that training period, Leta came back to New Jersey to be with me and we were together for most of the rest of my army duty. On April 3rd, 1943 I was assigned to study radar at Harvard and MIT. This course consisted of 2 ½ months of study at Harvard followed by the same amount of time at MIT. Radar was a very new technology and the military needed experts in a hurry. Selected personnel from the Signal Corps, the Air Corps and the Navy attended the courses. During this time, Leta and I became acquainted with the Boston-Cambridge area and took time to study its history. Leta's direct Adams ancestors were at Lexington when the revolution started.

In late August of 1943, I was transferred to the Signal Corps Radar Training School at Camp Murphy, Florida, a few miles north of Palm Beach. We bought a car and traveled down the East coast and did a little sightseeing on our way. At Camp Murphy, training on specific army radar equipment was given prior to permanent assignment. I was picked to study the SCR 584 air tracking Radar and therefore expected to be assigned to 2nd and 3rd level maintenance of them.

Three incidents in Florida were memorable. When we first arrived at Palm Beach, Leta had a bad cold, so I took her to the army infirmary, which was the Breakers Hotel on the beach. The army, expecting large numbers of casualties from the invasion of Africa, had taken over the hotel for use as an Army hospital. They had virtually no patients! They could hardly wait to get her into a hospital bed in the finest room in the hotel overlooking the beach. It took a lot of effort to get them to let her go home when she was better. She enjoyed the deluxe room, but hated the lack of company.

While Leta was in the hospital, I was living in a rather ratty apartment in town. We took what we could get. I was awakened in the middle of the night by a knock on the door. I answered and a couple of GI's looked and said, "Sorry, I guess the girls don't live here any more."

While at Camp Murphy, we were subjected to basic army training. One exercise was a night exercise in which we were placed in the boondocks and expected to find our way back in the dark. As it happened just a day before the exercise a U-boat torpedoed a tanker just off the coast. The crew of the tanker managed to beach it on fire just off the coast at Camp Murphy. We had very little trouble finding our way that night with that huge fire on the beach to the east.

Just before the end of training at Camp Murphy we were asked if anyone would like to write technical manuals at Fort Monmouth. In time honored Army tradition we all declined to volunteer. On January 27, 1944, I reported to the Fort Monmouth Signal Corps Publications Agency. The Signal Corps Publication Agency had the task of preparing Technical Manuals and Technical Bulletins or seeing to it that the companies supplying electronic equipment prepared them. At that time they had received a special task to prepare basic textbooks on radar for use in the field. Equipment was being built and shipped overseas without proper instructions on its use and maintenance. In fact, the users often didn't even know what radar was, let alone how to operate it. There was not only a dire need for maintenance manuals, but also for understandable basic radar texts. Both the Army and the Navy had the same need and in an unusual arrangement for that time agreed to do the job once instead of having two different books covering the same material. The publications agency was chosen to prepare the manuscripts although each branch published them within its own manual system.

I was assigned to this special project. There were four of us. The Navy supplied two officers, a Junior Lieutenant and a Senior Lieutenant whose surname was also Senior. I was the Army representative along with Charlie Devore, a Civil Service employee of the Signal Corps. Between January and June of 1944 the job was done. TM 11- 466 Radar Electronics Fundamentals was published June 29, 1944 and its confidential follow-on manual, TM 11-467 Radar System Fundamentals, was published April 28, 1944. The Publications Agency later received a Meritorious Service Unit Plaque for work done during this period. Those of us who worked on these basic manuals received the Army Commendation Ribbon on January 15, 1946 for TM 11-466 and TM 11-467. Both of these manuals were published for many years with many reprints. After the war similar manuals were published on the commercial market. Many of them simply lifted much of the material we produced. I have often thought that the royalties from these manuals would have been appreciable if we, the authors, had the copyright instead of the Army and Navy.

July 18, 1944, I was promoted to 1st Lieutenant. Following the completion of the basic radar manuals, I was assigned to the job of determining which maintenance manuals were to be prepared for new radar equipment and working with the contracting officer to get them included as a deliverable with the equipment. In some cases, we spent considerable time with the contractor helping him write these essential manuals. I even spent several weeks in Los Angeles on temporary duty with Gilfillan while actually living at home in Glendale. This kind of work continued for me with the Signal Corps through January 1945 and with the Air Corps until October 1945. In January 1945, the Air Corps took over responsibility for the radar equipment used solely by them. At that time, the personnel of the Publication Agency were split between the Air Corps and the Signal Corps. I was transferred to the Air Corps at that time and worked at Watson Labs in Eatontown, NJ, near Fort Monmouth.

Our first child, Jacklynne Ruth was born August 17,1944 at the Fort Monmouth Army Hospital. She cost us all of $15 for a blood transfusion! It seemed that all the junior officers and their wives at Fort Monmouth were living in our row of duplexes in Long Branch and they were all having their first child at the same time. This meant that women and children had plenty of company in the neighborhood.

On May 8, 1945 Germany surrendered. On August 6, the Atom Bomb was dropped on Hiroshima followed by another on Nagasaki on August 9th. I was in St Louis when Japan surrendered August 15th. The commanding officer at Watson Labs had a dire need for more engineers. The Civil Service had been unsuccessful in finding them, not surprising at the end of a war when engineers fully were employed. He thought, however, that sending out officers under his control might somehow produce better results. I was in St Louis on such a search for engineers when VJ day came. The place was a bedlam. For the whole day I found myself standing in line at the only open restaurant available to me, the one in the hotel. When you finished a meal, you almost had to get in line immediately so you could be seated in time for your next meal.

The War was over. Next step, get discharged and get on with life. Wrong! On October 8, 1945 I received orders to report to the Overseas Replacement Depot at

Keams, Utah near Salt Lake City on orders that were basic to the invasion of Japan! Leta and Jacklynne went home to Glendale, CA. These orders started a massive movement of troops and equipment west toward Japan. Such a massive operation once under way does not stop or reverse easily. I had progressed all the way to Camp Stoneman in Pittsburgh, California at the end of November. Because the war was over, practical men in the Army realized that these orders were bound to be changed and dragged their feet at every step of the way. Normally I would have been in the Far East within a few days or weeks, but foot dragging stretched out the trip to over two months. My shipment was split into two parts. The first part actually shipped out late in October. The second part was scheduled to leave late in November and I was on my way to board the ship the next day when the points changed. I did not have to go. Leta broke down and cried when I called her that evening. Being shipped overseas was fine when there was a war. After the war it was senseless and unacceptable.

There was more waiting while the Army decided what to do with me. They finally ordered me back to Watson Labs where I remained for a few days until I was discharged. I chose to be discharged in California from the Santa Ana AAF Separation Base. February 19, 1946 I was promoted to Captain. My Honorable Discharge is dated March 28, 1946.

BIOLOGICAL WARFARE
Newell Johnson

I was attending Connecticut State, now the University of Connecticut, and majoring in chemistry. I had a job with the state laboratories monitoring cattle for tuberculosis and Brucellosis. I found this so interesting that I changed my major to bacteriology and received my degree in this. As I graduated mid year, my teaching fellowship at the University of Massachusetts didn't start until fall, so I worked as a lab technician with cattle in New Hampshire for the interval. Here we were working with the use of the new drug penicillin for mastitis in cows. It hadn't yet been approved for human use. I received a draft notice and decided I would rather be in the Navy. They turned me down for color blindness and I waited for the draft.

I was processed at Fort Devon, Massachusetts and sent to Edgewood Arsenal, Maryland where basic training was given to those assigned to the Chemical Corps. Part way through training, they took out eight of us with college degrees and assigned us to working with a training film on decontamination. At the conclusion of this job, I was offered a chance to go to OCS.

After my ninety days, I was commissioned a second lieutenant in the Chemical Corps and assigned to teach chemistry at Edgewood Arsenal. I remember going home to Connecticut on leave after commissioning and returning on a very aged train car with wooden benches. I was coming down with an infection and had a temperature of 104 and it was a very miserable trip. The teaching job was followed by assignment as officer in charge of a platoon of cadets. This wasn't using my training, so I requested transfer to the Sanitary Corps. I was accepted as a microbiologist and transferred to the group at Edgewood Arsenal planning bacteriologic warfare. Most of the planning was done by the heads of departments from several large universities and I was merely a helper.

The department was given a hangar at the airport at Frederick, Maryland and they asked if anyone had experience with engineering drawing. As I had, I had the job of helping in the planning of the conversion of the hangar to labs and offices. I was then assigned to Frederick with two lieutenant colonels to work with engineers to plan the unit before the building was done. There really wasn't anything for me to do so I applied for transfer to the infantry but was turned down.

When the unit was running, we were working both on offensive warfare and on defensive protection against the enemy attacks. My next job was rigging a satisfactory autoclave with inadequate materials. It finally worked and I was working with animal experiments but turned out to be very allergic to guinea pigs. I then went to work on anthrax and later developed a cutaneous anthrax lesion on my elbow. It was cured with the new drug penicillin and I didn't find out until later that such lesions had a 25% mortality.

A tube of botulinum toxin broke up in the centrifuge and all in the lab were given shots of horse-serum based antitoxin. I had a severe allergic reaction to this and was in the hospital for a time. Later I was sent to Dugway Proving Grounds in Utah for some experiments where sheep and goats were treated with organisms, particularly Serratia marcescens. This organism had some characteristics of anthrax and was supposed to show means of spread without the danger of anthrax spores.

When I returned to Maryland, now a Captain, I was placed in charge of the company to which all the lab techs at Fort Detrich were assigned. I had some enlisted PhD's under me. At Detrich I worked with a number of microbiologists, including one assigned from England, David Henderson , who had worked with Lord Stamp. Dr. Dack, a specialist in food caused illness, suggested that I should go to medical school. As the war was drawing to the end, I went down to Hopkins University and took the medical college aptitude tests and applied to several schools.

I was married while at Fort Detrich and soon after was transferred to Washington to the office of the head of bacteriologic warfare where I was a liason with the rest of the Army. As my wife was training in Maryland, we lived in Baltimore and I commuted to Washington by train each day for several months. I received an acceptance at the University of Chicago Medical School, provisionally on taking embryology and comparative anatomy. I didn't learn until two years later that Dr. Dack was a member of the admissions committee at Chicago. At the end of the war, I was released from the Army and started medical school.

MY WORLD WAR II DAYS AS A U.S. MARINE
Cleve Turner
The battle for Guadalcanal was a major focus in our efforts to overcome the Japanese in 1942-43. I was a 17 year old high school senior in the California bay area city of San Leandro at this time working part time and continuing school towards graduation. However, the fever of war got to many of us, and the Marine

Corps seemed to be at the center of action at this time so my buddies and I decided to join up.

We drove to the Marine Recruiting Headquarters in San Francisco in January of '43 to enlist. It turned out that to enlist at that age required parental permission. However, the Marine Corps had just started a program to train boys of our age who were taking college preparatory coursework to eventually become officers. It was the now well known V-12 program that required us to meet the minimum of two years of college in sixteen months to become eligible to enter into officer's training. We were excited about the opportunity this presented, but disappointed that we could not directly "go to war". Our parents were not disappointed!

Two of us were sent to Southwestern University in Georgetown, Texas. This was an interesting experience - we wore uniforms, undertook military training (Marine Corps style) and completed standard coursework for an eventual degree. However, the war was progressing and we were not in it.

Our "college days" soon came to an abrupt halt with several months in Marine Corps Boot Camp at Parris Island, S.C. and additional infantry training at Camp Lejune, N.C. Then came four months of officer training at Quantico, VA. Then off to war!

Hardly - The Marine Corps gave us two weeks "off" after receiving our commissions. I reported back to Quantico on what turned out to be VJ day - The war was over!

I spent my final active duty days at Cherry Point Marine Airbase N.C. with the 9th Marine Air Wing as a materiel officer and captain of a company of marines awaiting discharge. This was not a fun time. Remember, I was a 20 year old shavetail lieutenant with my first command being a company of the toughest, roughest bunch of veterans you can imagine, all of whom were awaiting discharge on points. Many couldn't wait - being AWOL was their prime recreation! Unfortunately, Navy Regulations requires that the commander of a military unit periodically hold a kind of judicial court called Captain's Mast to "impose discipline" on such miscreants. I was now one of those "commanders".

I was not alone in this miserable assignment. Six of us "newbies" were suffering similar assignments. We tried to drown our miseries in beer at the local "O" club. One of this gang (a future lawyer no doubt) announced one night that he had found a "nugget" in that same navy bible called Navy Regs. It was a full page outlining how, in peacetime, an officer could copy an enclosed form letter respectfully requesting discharge from the navy.

In our freshman ignorance, enhanced by alcohol, we thought this was a wonderful discovery and soon sent six such letters to the Secretary of the Navy. Of course in the light of day we fully recognized the absurdity of such an action; especially since we hadn't bothered to send our letters through the customary chain of command.

As you suspect by now, we were amazed and elated when several weeks later we received orders to report to our base of enlistment for discharge from the Marine Corps. Someone up there had a sense of humor or perhaps went by the book - after all we really were "in peacetime".

CHAPTER 11

OUT OF THE COUNTRY

At Mt. San Antonio Gardens, there are two other types of people who were out of the country during the war. There are several who are not natives of the United States and came to this country after the war. Some came as war brides, others because of friends or relatives in this country.

There is also a group of Americans who were out of the country during the war, either working, with family, or for some other reason.

Mary Westlake was in an American high school in Chile when the war started. She had both English and German classmates.

Jackie Garcia was a teenager in France during the War. She moved around with different family members and was in contact with German soldiers as well as helping with identity papers for Jewish friends.

Jean Lemm was a British army teletype operator in the underground war rooms in London for three years. There was much more to this bomb safe haven than is seen in the present day tours of Churchill's rooms. Jean never ran into Churchill.

Lois Schery spent two years in Brazil with her botanist husband who was procuring natural rubber for the US war effort.

Marguerite MacIntosh was also a French teenager who traveled over much of France with her family to avoid the Germans. She finally returned to school in Paris and was a courier for the underground.

MY EARLY WORLD WAR II EXPERIENCE
Mary Westlake

I was living in Santiago Chile, when war broke out on September 3, 1939. I recall that Europe, where Hitler's forces had marched into Poland, seemed very far away.

Chile was a neutral country and so was the United States. At our American school the war was never referred to. The student body included girls representing both sides of the conflict. While I saw, little by little, the pool of possible boyfriends dwindle as they went off to fight in England, my German classmate likewise saw her friends off to Germany. There were enough left over for parties, where we did the Lambeth Walk.

When we went to the movies, because of official neutrality, both English and German supported newsreels, loaded with propaganda, were shown. The statistics given for downed enemy planes were always favorable to the side producing the newsreel. The audience indicated its preference by clapping either for the Allies or the Axis.

Otherwise life continued very much as before, but there was a dark undercurrent. We lived in a neighborhood whose population was largely European; British and Germans lived in uneasy proximity. I observed military marching practice at the nearby German Sportsverein. My father was part of a secret telephone network organized by the British Embassy to alert the community in the event of an uprising by local German residents.

I left to go to the States to college on a Chilean ship. This was after Pearl Harbor. Chile was still officially neutral, and a large brightly-lit Chilean flag was painted on the side of the boat. Towards the end of the trip we passed through the Panama Canal to the Caribbean on our way to New Orleans. In Havana harbor I saw an American ship that had been damaged. I later learned that the height of submarine activity in the Caribbean had taken place in August 1942, the very time I was there.

WARTIME IN FRANCE
Jacqueline Garcia
My father was a colonel in the French Army. The neighbors always watched him to find out what was going on during the times of stress with Germany. When a car came for him one time in the middle of the night, the neighbors all felt, correctly, that the war had started. He was called to the front and left my mother and me in Nice. He told us that if the Italians entered the war, we were to go across the bridge over the Var River and stay with an aunt on the other side as bombing the bridge would cut off all the food to Nice. When Italy entered the war, we did this and stayed in the aunt's villa.

Once when on the balcony overlooking the Mediterranean, we saw a plane smoking. My mother said it was making smoke to cover maneuvers but then I saw flames in the tail. It seemed to be coming directly toward us and we saw the people bail out with parachutes. I ran out in the street to see what happened. Then the men in the parachutes opened fire on the people on the ground. A French soldier pushed me back against a wall; I felt the heat of the plane as it passed to crash close by. The soldier then sent me into a house to hide. One of the crew, a young Italian boy landed in the tree in our yard.

The bridge was left intact, so we returned to Nice and our apartment. We received a telegram from the Red Cross that my father was missing in action. We were terribly worried but then heard that he was a prisoner of the Germans and had been sent to a camp in Silesia. This was a very cold area. Later, we heard that the enlisted soldiers were sent out to work on farms and received a little extra food from the farmers but the officers were kept in camp for interrogation. Their nutrition was very bad. My father developed tuberculosis with complications. The Germans did an operation and then sent him home to keep the disease from spreading. We met him at the train in Nice. He was very thin and worn down and had no shoes. His feet were wrapped in cloth. He was sent to a French Army sanitarium in middle France.

My mother's sister lived in Normandy, where her husband had a pharmacy. I had visited them before and my mother sent me to stay with them for a time. I was on a trip to Paris with my aunt when the German Army entered and marched through the Arc de Triomphe. All the French turned the other way as they walked by. In Normandy, I helped my uncle in the pharmacy. The hotel next door had been taken over as a German troop billet. One soldier fell for me and would wait outside the pharmacy to see me. I only spoke to him once to say, "Thank you." when he picked up some tennis balls I had dropped. Once he came into the pharmacy looking for me and the nurse had me give him some chocolate. It actually was the French version of "ex lax" and he never came around again.

The pharmacy was equivalent to an emergency room for the area. A nurse was on duty there and injuries were brought in for the nurse to bandage and to decide if they went to the hospital. Most of the medicine was given by the pharmacist, and also on doctors' prescriptions. I had a nice bedroom in the building behind the pharmacy but the Germans requisitioned it for a German officer and I had to be less comfortable.

My aunt was quite a heroine. When the Allies invaded, she went out and met the first tank. She and my mother had gone to school in England during World War I, so she spoke English well. She welcomed the Americans and showed them where the Germans were. She received two awards from America.

As the Germans took over northern France, my mother told me to come home to Nice. I took the train back by myself - I was about 14. In Nice there was a nice social group which included many Jews who had moved south away from the German occupation. I had several good Jewish friends. When the Axis countries occupied all of France, they went into hiding in various places. The Italians were no problem; they didn't like to fight and didn't bother anybody. The Germans, however, were very strict and domineering.

A number of Jewish families gave my mother their family records to keep. This would show we helped Jews and was punished by death if the Germans found them. Jewish families split up so that if the parents were captured all wouldn't be caught. I took communications between various members of the families we knew and also tried to take them food. The bridge had been destroyed and food was hard to get in Nice, even with a ration card. My mother wouldn't use the black market on principle, saying if no one used it, it would stop operating. We were almost always hungry.

We lived in a fifth floor apartment and had to go down to the basement almost every night for a long time because of air raids. Nice was bombed by German planes at various times. Most of the damage was done by the Germans. I learned to tell who was flying by the sound. The British came in lower than the Americans and their engines had a different sound.

One of my Jewish friends sent me to the Belgian consul for false ID papers. My mother didn't know I did this or she would have forbidden it. Once I was given a group of cards and two guns to take to my Jewish friends. I took the tram and stood on the platform as I liked the breeze. Two German soldiers joined me and I was terrified that they would ask for my papers as I had several forged papers in my pocket book with them and also the two guns in a straw basket. They finally exited the tram and I watched carefully until the next stop to see that they weren't following.

Once taking something to one of the Jewish hideouts, I saw a Gestapo car pull up in front. I waited outside as many people were there. One of my friends came out with Gestapo agents. Five minutes earlier and I would have been with him. I saw instances of Jews throwing themselves out of three or four story apartments rather than be taken by the Gestapo. Of the group I knew, only this one family was caught. The rest came through the war safely.

One friend I had made in Normandy had a Jewish father and Aryan mother. I dated him a few times and he told me that he could help if we needed anything. Later I discovered he was a collaborator and had turned in his own father to promote himself. Luckily I hadn't told him anything.

We had a radio and sometimes listened to the BBC to get real news. We always listened in the back of the apartment where no one could hear and kept the radio very low.

I was engaged to a Jewish Frenchman who went into the Army. I never heard from him. Finally he came to see me after the war was over and I had been married. He had been in the underground and could not communicate with me.

I met American soldiers after the Germans had been driven out of southern France. At nineteen, I married one who was stationed in Nice for a long time as manager of the PX. He remained a time after the war and when he returned to the United States, I was pregnant and not supposed to travel. I had my first child in France (he has dual citizenship) and then went to America to join my husband. My father said that if he had not been in the sanitarium, he would have prevented the marriage. When I went to America, my husband lived on a farm without even sanitation facilities. Many of the war brides returned home but I had two children and didn't feel I could. The marriage didn't last.

The war was an interesting but very stressful time for a teenager. I always felt that I missed a lot as I had just reached the age when my parents started taking me to social affairs and cultural events like opera but the war prevented me from participating in much of the normal life.

SERVICE IN THE LONDON WAR ROOMS
Jean Lemm

I lived in Yorkshire when the war started. I enlisted in the Army and took basic training in York in 1941. I became a soldier there, a uniform, gas mask and all. I had been to business college for two years and it was obvious that they needed competent typists. I was probably the only one at that time with the correct qualifications. I was taken out of the group and sent on the train to London, to report to the War Office. It was after the initial bombing and we sent messages all over England by teletype. We worked three shifts: 8 PM to 8 AM, then back at 2 PM til 8 PM and then 8 AM to 2 PM the next day. Then we had 36 hours off. I would often visit my cousins the Swans in Surrey on these times. (Ed. note: Mr. Swan owned Swan's Hellenic tours.)

We were billeted at the Buckingham Court Hotel near Buckingham Palace, only a few blocks from the War Office. It had been taken over by the Army though at first some of the Hotel functions were still running. It had an Army mess and three or four girls shared one of the large rooms. It was much better than the barracks that many of the women soldiers used and I think the girls assigned to the war office were a little better educated and higher quality than the average. I didn't think about it at the time and realize that I was in a very good billet.

Later some of us were moved to a nearby residence. One day while I was at work a doodle-bug (a V1 or V2 buzz bomb) destroyed the top floor and I was transferred to another residence but the mess was still in the hotel. The army was able to get enough food so we didn't worry about rationing. The mess used the hotel kitchens and I think the war office got a little special attention. We did exercises and calisthenics in the Buckingham Palace Mews where all the horses were. We always walked to work as a group, accompanied by an officer and an orderly, who carried the dinner prepared to eat on shift. We had war office insignia on our uniform sleeves and could go places other people couldn't. They didn't check our ID's when we went to work; just looked at the war office slash.

At first I was in the old war office but it was hit by a bomb. It didn't explode but did a lot of damage and we moved to the new War office, the famed underground war rooms. It was an underground rabbit warren. Churchill worked down there but I never saw him. I worked the teletype about a year and a half, sending and receiving at the same time. All messages were prefaced by WOTER, War Office Terminal.

Then they asked for volunteers to go on the wireless high speed, which was a new development at that time. To do this we had to study Morse code. A group of volunteers was sent to an estate outside London for training. Then we went back to the same billet and the War Office. When we went back, the soldiers who had been doing this weren't too glad to see us. When we were able to take over, it meant they would be sent somewhere else. There were three channels. It was recorded on two tapes. One was a punch tape that could print out on a machine. We had to play the undulating tape back and correct any mistakes on the other tape. We checked the messages against the Morse tapes. We worked in groups of three and there were three or four groups per shift. It was the first high speed wireless station in the country. The equipment was in use all the time and was never updated or replaced during the entire war. The internal communications within England continued to be by the teletype system. This was mostly on supplies, troop movements, etc.

In the wireless room, I first heard about El Alemain. That came through in plain language as a communique to the Prime Minister. Communiques came through faster as they weren't in cypher. This one was a great thrill, probably the greatest of the war. Most of the material was in cypher, five letter groups. We couldn't understand what was being said, which made it harder to check the accuracy because there were no words. I asked to work in cypher but that was a completely different group and they didn't move me there.

The queen came down one time to see our work. (This was the Queen Mother that recently died at 100 years old.) She looked at all the equipment and remarked that the high speed room looked like H. G. Wells picture of things to come. Tickets to plays were easily available free to the military and many times we would go to the office that kept tickets and go to a play that day. Often we went to the final dress rehearsal where we were supposed to participate and make suggestions. There were American, Canadian, New Zealand troops, almost everything in London at that time. There was a good feeling and we felt very safe with the troops.

My uncle on the other side was American; he married my mother's sister. Colonel Goodrich was commanding the eighth Army Air Corps in Britain. I saw him while he was in England and went to visit his command. I later visited him in Florida and that led to my visit to California and meeting my husband.

In those days it was a job and you didn't go into what you were doing, why you were doing it, or how it was done. I wish now I had asked a lot more questions. Many years later in Corona del Mar our landlady in a temporary apartment told me that she knew someone else who had done this work and she got us together. It was a Scottish girl who had been on my shift. Isn't that amazing? She had a sister and they were a little wild. She moved to Arizona and we gradually lost touch again. Her sister had died.

At the end of the war I was so tired of shift work that I couldn't sleep well. When the war ended they transferred me temporarily to administration until I could be demobed (a British shortening for demobilization). Because of my age and time in service, I had a low number and was demobed very soon.

Afterwards I worked for about a year as a civilian driver in Yorkshire, taking various government officials to see government projects in the area. Then I was secretary to a military adjutant before going to the United States.

WHERE WAS I IN WORLD WAR II?
Lois Schery
Salvador, Baia, Brazil, and Rio de Janeiro were my successive homes from Nov. 1943 until Dec. 1945. I had joined my botanist husband Robert where he was sent by the U.S. government's Rubber Development Corporation. I lived in boarding houses, borrowed houses, and a rental apartment while he, as a field technician in charge of procuring natural rubber in the non-Amazon area, was absent a week or

two at a time traveling the interior (encouraging native tappers in the Sertao). One long trip even took him to Paraguay looking for signs of smuggling into pro-Axis Argentina.

Brazil was a non-combatant nation, who nevertheless made available to the U.S. military bases on the Atlantic Ocean, cooperated with our civilian specialists such as rubber and crystal commissions, and did send a small expeditionary force to a war theater. (Their motto: "A cobra esta fumando") In the U.S. the stockpile of natural rubber, necessary as a core for synthetic rubber production, was ominously low due to plantation rubber's having been cut off from Malaysia by the Japanese.

At Baia was the US Navy's major supply base for the south Atlantic fleet. A civilian, in a major city, I did not have PX privileges, but I volunteered at the USO and welcomed sailors to our family. Especially appealing to the GIs were relating to our toddler daughter and listening to Bob's tales of his forays into remote areas. The very young men were frustrated at being in a safe harbor while their brothers were in danger at other stations. Navy personnel were permitted apartments offbase, but Baia was still operating as a feudal community. Girls of white families were cloistered so couldn't socialize. The marvelously garbed African daughters of Santos had status as original settlers with their special dogmas. Only during Carnival time did we all mingle.

In Rio the international community embraced a different open life style. Visiting their Rio families, responsible young Baian women were allowed out without a chaperone. From my apartment in Copacabana I could observe the international society-European royalists and refugees, journalists, airline officials, and hardworking American civil servants with diplomatic status like us. In our own way our little family made a statement to the local people, who always enjoyed us. Only one incident caught me off-guard. I was refused entrance to the bus and was sent to another door at the rear section with the vendors - my diaper bag for the baby disqualified me for first class treatment - two kids and necessities were excess baggage for sure.

President Truman shut down the wartime bureaus immediately after VJ day so by early December we headed home on a big commercial Pan American plane with our Portuguese speaking daughter, our Carioca infant son and fellow passengers, merchants, adventurers, and patriots. This flight was quite a contrast to the one that brought us to Brazil: then we'd been on a small four-engine seaplane (maybe a Martin M-130 or a Sikorsky S-42). This had delivered 40 plus US civil servants and service men to Manaos after daylight puddle-jumping from Miami, Haiti, Trinidad, and Guyana, with overnight stopping and mechanical challenges along the way. This trip continued on another sea plane which en route to Belem was forced to land on the Amazon River in a tropical rain storm and had negotiated the take off in uncharted waters. From Belem to Fortaleza and finally Baia, it had taken many days.

Early December 1945 we returned to Webster Groves for shelter with our parents and for job hunting. Ongoing contacts with GI's and Brazilian friends reassure me that maybe we had been goodwill ambassadors in those scary times.

MOVING AROUND FRANCE IN WARTIME
Marguerite Loyau McIntosh

I was born in Paris, the oldest of five children. My father had been in the infantry in World War I and was a hero with medals from the fight for Verdun. He stayed in the reserve and later was a pilot in the Air Force. Both my parents were sculptors and my father met William Bennett, the chief architect of Chicago. Father received the commission for the sea-horses in the Buckingham fountain in Chicago, at that time the biggest fountain in the world. He also did the main entrance to the colonial exposition in Paris. He was quite successful and we had a large house with 30 rooms. Soon the great depression hit France and Father lost his whole fortune. Then in 1936 he contracted pneumonia and, because he had been gassed during the war, died suddenly. Finding herself alone with five children and not a penny, mother had to accept a teaching position in the south of France and place us all in boarding school or orphanages. France had a special school, the Legion of Honor, for children of those who had won this award. It was very good, very difficult, and had military discipline. I went there after father died and was assured of a good education.

When the false war came in September 1939, my mother spent the winter preparing for war. She bought a house in the country near where my father's family lived, 200 miles from Paris. We made weekend trips to the country and we stored rice, sugar, flour, and other things that kept well.

When the German invasion started, we saw refugees from Belgium and Holland with all their possessions on ox carts. This was a shock to a teenager. Mother had a job teaching art in Clermont-Ferrand. I was at the Legion of Honor and the others were staying at an orphanage. When the Germans arrived, mother came to Paris and picked us up and we moved to the country. We were there two weeks and the Germans arrived. We put our bikes and mattresses on the car, together with a statue of Buddha that my father had bought, as my mother hoped the Buddha would protect us. Also it was from the 14th century and was valuable. It took several months to get to Clermont-Ferrand. Sometimes it took days waiting to get across a bridge. At the crossing of the Loire River, the bridge blew up 3 minutes after we crossed it. The French Army had blown it up to stop the Germans.

We slept that night in the stable of a farm. Here I learned to milk cows. Near La Rochelle mother and all five children stayed in one room. We had a cold water faucet in the courtyard where I had to do the laundry and wash the dishes. After two months the Germans came and we reloaded the car. We had to get fuel from fliers who blackmarketed the gasoline from their planes.

In the town of Niort my mother became very ill and had to go to the hospital. On the way I met a friend from boarding school. Her family took mother for care and found a hotel room for the children. In the town of Aubusson, I had a severe infection where the flesh eroded down to the bone and I had to be in bed for several months. We finally reached Clermont-Ferrand and stayed there six months. My mother's best friend had a son six months older than me who had volunteered for the resistance. He was accidentally killed when another resistance man fired a gun he was cleaning.

The German occupation had stabilized and then we moved back to Paris for school and spent summers in the country. The Legion of Honor was occupied by the Germans and the school was moved to an old monastery by St. Denis basilica. We spent evenings in the cellar to avoid the bombs and I did most of my studying in their cellar. Finally we had a very powerful bombing attack and they moved the school to a renaissance castle north of Paris.

After graduating with my humanities degree, I was governess for a time at a house where the mother was ill and there were five children. I ran the house. The mother had run a relief center in an area of railroad yards between Paris and St. Denis that had been bombed out by American bombers and the father asked me to check on it. Most of the area was bombed flat but the center building still stood. I found the former cook and talked him into coming back. I went to the government offices to see if we could get potatoes to make soup for the inhabitants. On the way I saw a group and went over. A mother was holding the hand of her four year old daughter who had been buried in the rubble with a large stone on her. When I got to the government office, I asked to have a doctor go to the scene. I later learned that he had to give the child a lethal injection as she couldn't be rescued.

I had wanted to be a ballerina but had to stop dancing when I went to the Legion of Honor after my father died. I also studied piano. I started teaching at a private school for wealthy girls. I wanted to teach art and art history but also was assigned to teach general history. I had to study the material in the evenings. Later I also began to teach art in the public schools in Paris. I had been interested in literature but decided to work in art because I could continue my own studies as well as teaching. Art could be done on ones own while literature required daily class attendance. I was a student at the Ecole Normale Superieure de Dessin, which taught how to teach art in the Paris public schools. Meanwhile, I continued my studies at the Ecole Nationale superieure des Beaux-Arts, the National Academy of Fine Arts. Unlike many of the colleges in Paris, here the majority of the students were from the center of the country. They were often older and had less parental supervision then other students. Therefore the Academy became a center of the resistance. Here I started with the underground. I met two men who were leaders and I took their place when they were in danger and had to disappear for a time. They were each 25 and I was 17 so they avoided giving me tasks that were too difficult or dangerous.

German soldiers who became isolated were often killed. Young people who were found out after curfew were kept overnight at the police station and had to polish soldiers' boots. When a soldier was killed, the Germans took 12 young people from the district police station and shot them all.

The political prison was in back of our home and we could hear the screams. In spite of the terrible things the Germans were doing, the Germans were disciplined and were ordered to be very polite. They taught the French to give up seats to ladies in the subway. A German officer visited mother's studio and admired the sculpture. We became friends and I took him to the Rodin museum in Paris. If

I had been seen I could have had my head shaved. He said later that my mother was a spiritual mother to him. He knew I was in the underground but never reported it. He had to stop seeing us because the Gestapo were watching. Much later, after the war when Harrison (my husband) and I were in Germany on a design contract, we met him again in Munich. He was now bald and was a successful sculptor. He visited us in Paris and we visited him several times in Munich and have remained close friends.

We had resistance meetings. Girls who went with German soldiers would have their heads shaved by the resistance. There was one shady character who gave names of resistance members to the Germans. I rode on a train with him and found his address and other things. I reported this and my resistance friends found him and put him in jail.

In Paris, I worked in intelligence, passing letters and information on German activities. I would carry them to trains that were often late. I had to stay around but try not to attract the guards' attention. If I was too late to make it before the curfew, I had to go home along the river. The riverbank was so isolated from the guarded area above that the German soldiers avoided it to prevent being killed.

In the summers when there were no classes we went to the country, staying in the village of my grandparents. The underground was simpler in the country. There I distributed ammunition to underground soldiers. When we went to the country, we would carry eggs and chickens back to Paris. I carried them on a bike, using my father's WW I bike that was too big. When planes came by we would quickly go to the ditch to avoid strafing. I couldn't brake and had to fall off to stop it. Sometimes I would eat raw, broken eggs while in the ditch.

As the Germans pulled back to Paris, the German cavalry stationed at the edge of our village was selling excess horses. These were small Russian horses, captured at the Russian front. Friends dropped me off with a motorcycle and I had to pass the German sentries. I didn't know anything about horses but I looked in a horse's mouth and asked questions. I finally bought a horse for $6. The cavalrymen helped me on and I rode bareback home, holding on the mane

As the Germans pulled out, there was a lot of feuding between the resistance and the collaborators. Once our leader was several hours late as he had been caught in the fire of the collaborators.

As the allies retook France, we were in the country. I saw General Patton come through. My sisters and I put flowers on the jeep hood. He looked very grouchy. We went to the town square when the troops came through and were hoisted up to sit on a tank. We then went back to our big house in Paris. It was close to German headquarters. They had requisitioned most of the houses in the area but didn't take ours out of respect for father as a war hero and famous artist. It had a small grill entrance and was well preserved. The Germans had never bothered it but the British broke the gate. Mother asked to have it fixed. They said they would but never did. When the Americans came they stepped over the wall rather than use the gate. The yard was full of American soldiers making out with French girls.

In retrospect, those terrible years were not as hard for us young people as they must have been for our parents who had known peacetime. Since my early years, life had been a hard experience and I did not know anything else. On the other hand, my generation was nourished by existentialist philosophy. (Sometimes Jean Paul Sartre had lunch with his students at the table next to me at the Deux Magots.) We had a very strong sense of duty and we were fighting Nazism not so much to save our country whose future was uncertain, but to save the value of human liberty.